THE LIVING WORLD OF NATURE

Titles in this series:

The Living World
OF
NATURE

TEXT BY
David Stephen

London   **COLLINS**   *Glasgow*

First printed in this edition 1962
This Impression 1972

ISBN 0 00 100104 3

CONTENTS

CONTENTS

CONTENTS

WHALES
Monsters of the deep

The great whales, now the largest animals in existence, are placid, fish-like mammals inhabiting the great oceans. In modern times, the end for most of them comes about in a welter of blood and foam caused by a harpoon wedged inexorably in their enormous flanks. Modern whalers are the great predators on whales generally.

Mammals are defined as that class of animals with warm blood and a covering of hair, which breathe atmospheric air and suckle their young. In the whales the hair has practically disappeared, and the form has become fish-like, due to their highly specialised aquatic existence. But the whale still has to surface to breathe, has warm blood, and supplies its young with milk from typical mammary glands. The whale is, therefore, a mammal just as much as the horse or the dog.

Just how and when the whale became transformed and so highly specialised in its marine existence, is not precisely known. As a result of its entirely aquatic existence, how-

A fine example of the common whale. The skin of the back is bluish and the iridescent plume which rises from the air-holes may reach a height of 15-16 feet.

ever, its large size is no handicap in modern times, and it has survived the gigantic reptiles which roamed the earth in remote times. Despite its fish-like appearance, the whale is still a quadruped under its skin. The lateral fins are still arms of articulate bone, while in its hind body, deep in the layer of blubber, can still be seen the vestigial hind legs.

The biggest of the whales of the present day reach a length of more than ninety feet and weigh something over a ton

for every foot. The body is thick-set and massive, and the whale is the only mammal which cannot move its head on its neck. In adult whales the skin is smooth, oily and almost completely bare (in young whales, at least a few bristles appear on the snout and chin). Under the skin there is a thick layer of fat surrounding the whole body. This repels cold, maintains the body at uniform temperature in the cold seas, and provides a reserve of nourishment during periods when the whale has to go short of his normal food supply.

The adult whale's body colour is usually blue. Young are much lighter in colour and are white about the throat, eyes and caudal fin. Surfacing only to take in air, the whale is provided with great lungs which enable him to stay submerged for long periods and often at great depths. Each time he surfaces to take in new supplies of air, he blows the used air through his nostrils. These are placed close together on top of his head and are usually referred to as blow-holes. This jet of air, coming into contact with water and the cold atmosphere, forms the beautiful white plume that appears

The whale, like most mammals, is strongly attached to her young. She protects it, guides it, and is ready to face death in its defence. The young whale is known as a calf; it suckles its mother like any other young mammal.

The characteristic teeth of the baleen whale constitute a kind of fringe which filters out the small fish and crustaceans on which this giant mammal lives. This is a case where the largest of the mammals feeds on the smallest of prey.

The whale has a number of enemies other than man and the most savage of these is the orca. Orcas make surprise attacks on the whale and concentrate on the tongue. The giant, placid whale has no defence against the orca.

A school of whales in the Arctic seas.

The first whale hunters were Spaniards who sailed to the Arctic in the fourteenth and fifteenth centuries.

above the animal's head and which can be seen from a great distance. This air jet may reach a height of fifteen feet or more.

THERE SHE BLOWS

The spout of the whale when he blows is a fair guide to the identity of the species blowing. In the blue whale the jet will reach a height of twenty-five feet; in the fin whale, fifteen; in the sei whale about ten feet. The spout of the humpback whale is low and bushy; that of the sperm whale directed forwards; while that of some whales is double. It was once thought that this spout was a real water spout, but it is really breath vapour, combined with some water thrown up where the whale begins to blow before breaking surface.

On the list of the whale's special adaptations to its environment is its ability to stay submerged for long periods without fresh air. When it dives it takes oxygen not only into its lungs but also into the blood stream and muscles—for example, it has been estimated that the fin whale takes down nine per cent. of its oxygen in the lungs, forty-two per cent. in the blood, forty-two per cent. in the muscles and seven per cent. in tissue fluids. Biologists have calculated that the oxygen store in a whale seventy feet long is over 3000 litres. Despite this, whales, when submerged, incur what is termed an oxygen deficit—that is to say, their body functions go short of oxygen for long periods. This deficit is made up when they surface. The spouting or blowing is the manner in which it is made up. The spouting of the whale has been likened to the panting of a runner after a prolonged burst of speed.

It is a magnificent sight to see a school of whales breaking surface to re-stock with oxygen. The water is seen to boil up as though a mountain were rising little by little from the ocean depths. The immense bodies of the whales break surface; then one suddenly hears hoarse whistles accompanied by spouts like so many fountain jets. Presently, the enormous shining bodies of the whales appear fully surfaced. Last to

Modern whalers at sea.

The harpooner directs the cannon-fire.

appear are the lateral caudal fins. The whales exhale and inhale many times, renewing their oxygen supply while the sea froths round them; then they dive once more and are not seen again for a long period. Some species of whale can stay down for half an hour, which is longer than the time they take to take in oxygen at the surface. Oxygen is therefore used at a reduced rate during the dive, but the reduction appears to be confined to the body tissues—the brain receiving its full supply.

TWO MAIN GROUPS

There are two main groups of whales, the *Odontoceti* or toothed whales and the *Mystacoceti* or baleen whales. Though teeth are present in the toothed whales, they are for gripping and holding food and not for chewing it. In the baleen whales, teeth are replaced by two rows of horny plates, which hang down from the roof of the mouth forming a sieve,

Harpooner and crew leaving the parent ship.

Before the time of the modern harpoon gun, the harpoon was thrown by hand at close range.

A modern whaler in action. The cannon has fired the harpoon which is now embedded in the whale's body and the animal dies in a confusion of blood and spray. It does not always die quickly.

to strain out the small crustaceans and fish on which this group feeds. Despite their cavernous mouths, whales take only small food, the gullet being too narrow to permit the passage of large organisms. It is unlikely, therefore, that any whale ever swallowed anybody called Jonah.

Looking at the great, ponderous, yet streamlined mass which is a whale, one might be forgiven for doubting that it had any typical mammalian feelings concerning its young. Yet the whale looks after her calf very well. A single calf is usual, and it is born able to move, suckle, and keep afloat from the beginning. A calf of the large whales may measure sixteen feet in length. The young whale is suckled by the mother for seven or eight months. The young are able to breed before they reach their maximum size.

As soon as the young whale makes its first swimming strokes the mother moves solicitously alongside to assist him with her own great fins and protect him from his enemies, and it is a remarkable sight to observe a great whale floating in the water with her young one against her flank. Whales live mainly in the colder seas where food is more plentiful, and, being sociable animals, are often seen in schools. They tend to come closer inshore towards the autumn. The great blue whales are almost certainly monogamous.

SOURCE OF AMBERGRIS

The male sperm whale reaches only a length of sixty feet, and the female thirty-three feet. The sperm whale is polygamous and in the breeding season a mature bull will be found

The dead whales float motionless. The whalers tow them towards the factory ship where specialist workers prepare to cut them up.

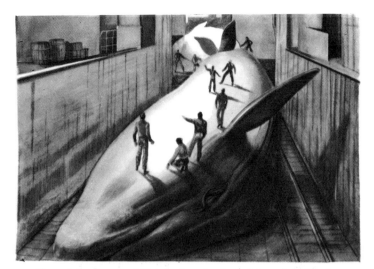

Aboard the factory ship the butchering of the whale begins. Firstly, the skin is stripped off.

Under the skin is found a layer of fat three feet thick. This is stripped for rendering into oil.

swimming with his harem and calves. This species is notable as the source of ambergris, which is so much in demand by perfumiers as a fixative. The ambergris is found in the intestines of the whale, although it may be found floating on the sea.

Modern whaling methods involving the use of power harpoons and factory ships, which follow the hunters, are so efficient that they are now a serious danger to the population of whales of all kinds. At different times there have been international conferences to regulate the killing of whales, but so far there has been more disagreement than agreement. If agreement is not reached in the near future, the great whales may disappear from the oceans, and man will have been responsible for the extermination of another species due to reckless over-exploitation of a resource which, carefully managed, could last for ever.

The humpback whale reaches a length of 50 ft.

The blue whale can eat a ton of plankton.

The Greenland whale is one of the Right-whales.

QUESTIONS AND ANSWERS

What is the blind-worm?

The blind-worm is a legless lizard. It is not a worm, nor is it blind. It is harmless.

Does the woodcock carry its young?

It has now been established beyond all doubt that the woodcock carries its young at certain times.

What is the rain-bird?

The green woodpecker, which is also known as the yaffle, is often called the rain-bird because it is said to be most vocal before rain.

What is the rain-goose?

Shetlanders use this name for the red-throated diver, a handsome bird which is now specially protected by law.

Is a wasp sting dangerous?

It can be highly dangerous. Certain people, sensitised by a first sting, can become dangerously ill or die from a second.

PENGUINS

The Penguin, with his white shirt front and black wings, back and neck, presents an appearance which by human standards is at once comic and formal. He looks like a conventional gentleman dressed for dinner, all very stiff and starchy.

Anyone who looks at a penguin in the flesh for the first time or who sees the birds in a film, immediately gets the impression of a little man formally garbed in full evening dress and, in fact, the similarity is striking. Once he begins to walk, holding himself erect and swaying on his short legs, he becomes almost a comic character. It is indeed difficult to avoid anthropomorphising about the penguin for he looks like a little man. He has a big, hard beak which looks like a nose, and a knowing look, and his whole appearance suggests that of the typical pedant. When confronted with an unusual object he stretches his neck and examines it minutely, first with one eye and then with the other, very carefully, again giving the impression of an acute human observer pondering a problem.

This man-like avian personality belongs to the order of web-footed birds. Though familiar enough in certain zoos, the wild penguin has to be sought in the frozen Antarctic. Colonies of penguins are, in fact, found almost exclusively in the Southern Hemisphere and on the islands of the Antarctic Circle. The penguin is the only bird which can carry its body completely erect when walking on land, an accomplishment which is due to the fact that its strong webbed feet are placed near the tail.

SOCIAL LIFE

Like so many other marine and oceanic birds, the penguin nests in colonies—sometimes very large ones. But its social life has truly special aspects. As the time for nesting draws near (between October and November), small advance parties

A pair of Cape penguins making their nest, which consists simply of a circle of stones.

leave ahead of the main body to explore the area chosen for breeding. A few days later another small group makes its upright advance on the nesting territory, then after a week or so, the main body of breeding birds begins to arrive. When two or three hundred birds are present, nesting begins and with it the long fast, for at this time penguins are too preoccupied to eat.

The male penguins carry stones to their mates, taking some of them from old nests, and these are arranged by the females. The stone is a very important item in the breeding biology of a penguin colony. When the male is courting his mate, arching his neck and emitting soft, guttural noises, he places a stone at her feet.

Once the main flock of breeding birds has arrived, the colony becomes of impressive size. Often a colony may number from five to ten thousand birds, and in such a multitude, where everyone is searching for a nesting site, there is much shouting, stealing, quarrelling and fighting. But, above all, feverish work is the order of the day. It can be said that, in this period of maximum activity, the penguin has two characteristic postures—namely anger—when he ruffles his feathers so that they look like scales and make him appear much bigger than he really is; and the posture following on weariness or defeat—when he droops with tight plumage and appears much smaller than his usual size.

EGG RAIDERS

Once the colony has settled down, and the business of mating and nest-building has been completed, the penguins devote all their time to guarding their eggs. This is not an easy task and involves incessant watchfulness because, in November, rapacious gulls begin to harry the colonies. Fighting is constant and bitter. Struggle is one for simple survival. The predatory gulls, which migrate southwards in summer, at this period feed almost entirely on the eggs and young of the penguin tribes. During such attacks the gulls'

Royal penguins. While the female looks after the chick, the male supplies the female with food.

powerful wings give them an advantage because the penguins, being unable to fly, cannot give chase. If, however, a raiding gull is gripped in the beak of a penguin, it is helpless and the penguin becomes the executioner. It is this ever-present danger of attack by predators that keeps the penguin colony on its toes. The alarm cry from one bird will put the whole tribe on guard immediately.

During this period of more than three weeks, the penguins fast and it is a common thing to see them tortured by thirst, worn out and dirty, standing guard with their beaks open and their tongues hanging out, when just a little distance away is the ice where they could slake their thirst. But everything comes to an end and, presently, when the chicks hatch, the adult penguins find life easier. Then the parents can take it in turns going to the sea—to drink, eat and wash their plumage.

One naturalist, observing penguin behaviour very closely, noted one strange aspect of this trip to the sea. Although each bird was driven by the urge to bathe in the water, each one appeared to be trying to push a companion on ahead to make the first plunge. The reason for this became clear when it was noticed that a shark, hidden under the edge of the ice, was seen to raise its head from the water, pull down a penguin, and devour it on the spot. The second bird, thus saved, jumped ashore, achieving this by his extraordinary ability to run under the water and make a leap of more than three feet into the air.

RETURN TO THE SEA

Once the young penguins are fit to travel the colony returns to the sea with obvious joy, because this means again being able to feed to repletion. The main food of the penguin consists of small crustaceans which are eaten voraciously and apparently unceasingly and, of course, all this time the birds have to supply their families with food as well. Sometimes the penguin stuffs himself so full that he is unable to walk and has to make progress by crawling over the ice on his belly.

The young penguins are fed by regurgitation. By the beginning of the second week of their lives the young penguins have grown visibly and become too voracious to be completely satisfied with the food supplied by their parents from their gullets. At this stage each pair of penguins leads its family to some " shelter ". Here the young birds are herded together in large groups, so that when some parents are foraging, others stand on guard. The young birds are never without adult protection. At the end of a month or a little more, the young penguins lose their down and assume their first plumage. At the same time they make their way slowly to the water's edge to learn to swim, while the adults surround them to assist their progress.

Once the nesting season is over, the exodus from the breeding grounds begins, and the penguins head northwards to avoid the rigours of the terrible Antarctic winter, taking to the open sea where they can find food in abundance.

The best-known penguins are the Adelies of Patagonia. Others are found in the Magellan Straits, the Falkland Islands, and New Zealand. One of the handsomest species is the King Penguin, a thriving colony of which has lived and bred in the Zoological Gardens at Edinburgh since 1919. Other species of penguin have also bred at Edinburgh. Edinburgh has exported king penguins, bred in the zoo, to New York and Washington, and to various zoological gardens in Europe.

King penguins being fed by their keeper at the zoo.

Penguins group together as a defensive measure.

Penguins like standing aboard a drifting ice block.

Around the coasts of Britain we find two species of seal: the Grey and the Common, their distribution being determined by the availability of breeding stations.

One of the famous breeding stations of the grey seal in Scotland is the island of North Rona, where the animals come ashore in the autumn to breed. On Rona the animals are almost completely undisturbed. They will travel some distance from the sea, climbing even to the summit of the island which is 300 feet above sea-level. On Rona, the adults stay ashore for three or four weeks, which is not the habit of this species in other parts of Britain or elsewhere. On the Welsh coast and in Cornwall, certain caves and small islands are used for breeding. On Rona, many of the bulls come ashore and take up their territories before the arrival of the females. In other parts the cows are ashore first. When they come ashore the grey seals are extremely fat, after a summer of rich feeding, but this fat is used up quickly during the short breeding season. The seal pups, which weigh about thirty pounds at birth, grow at a remarkable rate and treble their weight in three weeks, during which time the loss of fat on adult females is noticeable. The cow seals are attentive to their own pups, but are jealous of other cows and pups.

Grey seals are extremely vocal when on their breeding

The nun seal, which is fairly common on the coast of Sardinia, is solitary rather than gregarious.

ground, and this has given rise to such creatures as seal-women and water witches in Gaelic legend. These beliefs are still current in some places. There is some doubt about the food of the grey seal in British waters, but Dr. Fraser Darling says that around Scotland at any rate, the main food is saithe, pollack and mackerel. The food of the common seal, on the other hand, appears to be mostly shellfish and whiting, while from the Highlands have come reports that examination of stomach contents showed large quantities of flat fish. In recent years there have been many complaints in Britain about the destruction of fishing-nets by seals or the depredation by seals of commercial fish. While net damage is undoubted, not enough is known about the food of British seals to say whether their depredation of commercial fish is significant or not.

WHITE WHEN BORN

Seal pups are white at birth, and when the baby coat is lost it is replaced by one of steely blue, with fawn spots which tend to show white when dry. In adults of both species, the colour of the coat appears dark when wet but much lighter when dry. Coat colour is, however, no guide to identity, the real diagnostic feature being the shape and arrangement of the molar teeth which, of course, cannot be

Seals come ashore to stay only during the breeding season. It is at this time that numerous herds can sometimes be seen on the icy beaches where the males fight among themselves to gather harems.

Seal hunting is slaughter on the grand scale and these animals allow themselves to be massacred without any attempt at defence.

seen except in dead or captive specimens. Dr. Fraser Darling has shown that grey seals differ considerably from breeding station to breeding station. For example, the colour of bull seals on one group of islands is olive brown, while those of North Rona are steel grey. There are other differences. For example, the pups of Welsh seals are ashore for only three weeks or so, while at Scottish breeding stations this time is nearly doubled. Welsh pups are weaned a week or so earlier than Scottish pups.

The grey seal is found in the Baltic, Norway, Britain, Greenland and Nova Scotia. The common species is found in New Jersey, Labrador, Newfoundland, Greenland, and from Spain to Arctic Norway; it is also found in the Pacific coast of California up to the Bering Straits and along the Asiatic coast to Japan.

IMMENSE HERDS

The Harp-seal, a small species varying from five to five and a half feet in length and showing great variety in colour, gathers in immense herds to breed on the northern ice of the White Sea, Spitzbergen and Greenland. The young are born (according to locality) in February, March and April. In the Arctic areas and Europe they are hunted by the Norwegians and Russians.

The harp-seal is yellowish-white in colour with the nose, face and ears black, and a black band along each side of the body from which it derives its other name of black-flanked seal. The adult female is bluish-grey above and yellow below, with the black markings shown on scattered patches or absent altogether. The young, after they cast their white coats, are pale grey, dark above and light below with small spots on their backs.

Young harp-seals are about two and a half feet long at birth and are extremely fat. The females desert them when they are about three weeks old.

With the breaking up of the ice the herds disintegrate, being replaced by new groups of moulting animals migrating northwards. The harp-seal does not keep holes open in the ice during the winter. It feeds on crustaceans, gadoids and herrings.

THE NUN-SEAL

In the Mediterranean area there is another seal, still

Hunter preparing to spear a seal as it surfaces to breathe.

The walrus is the biggest member of the Pinnipedia family.

others by having a little ear flap and also in having its strong, rear limbs placed like the limbs of the dolphin. It is found in the North Pacific, especially in the islands of the Bering Straits. But the real giant of the seal family is the Walrus, which lives among the mountains of ice of the Arctic Ocean. In this species the male is over twenty feet long and nearly two tons in weight. His upper tusks are so long that they project far beyond his mouth. The walrus has a yellowish-brown skin, shining because of the fat which impregnates the bristles, and an enormous moustache which becomes longer with age. The hairs of the moustache are big and stiff like reeds. Like the Pinnipedia, the walrus lives in large herds and, when the arctic winter descends, they, too, migrate south to warmer zones.

BOVINE FACES

Now let us look at two curious animals which belong to the family Sirenia (the name in which you will no doubt notice the original of the sirens, the legendary characters who bewitched sailors). These two species are the Dugong

The sea-lion lives mainly on the islands of the Bering Straits. It is considerably bigger than the Greenland seals and has more developed caudal flippers. It has a pronounced mane.

smaller, which lives in small groups or in isolated pairs—especially in the caves of Sardinia. This is the Nun-seal which has a grey hide marked with black, almost white when young. These seals all belong to the family of the Pinnipedia or fin-footed mammals, or true seals (*Phocidæ*), as distinct from the sea-lions (*Otaria*), fur seals and walruses.

The description " fin-footed " refers to the fact that the limbs or flippers are fully webbed and are long and fin-like in shape. The body is streamlined and covered with hair, with a thin layer of blubber beneath the skin. The short tail is non-functional in the true seals, as in the walruses. There are no visible external ear lobes. There are other differences between the groups, although in habits all are similar.

To another branch of the family belongs the Sea-lion. This is a big seal, over twelve feet long, which differs from the

Seals are highly intelligent mammals and have long been familiar to the public as circus performers. Typical of the animal's abilities is the act of balancing a ball on the tip of its nose.

and the Manatee, both of which are furnished with paws in the shape of fins but which, unlike the seals, feed on marine vegetation found in the rocks. They live in warm seas. Both are about nine to twelve feet long, and have a curious bovine face. They are, in fact, near relations to that elusive animal, the sea-cow, which appeared a few times in the course of centuries to astonished explorers and naturalists, and which to-day is probably extinct.

The seals are unfortunate in possessing fine skins as well as the blubber which, for the Eskimo, is a necessity of life. The animals are therefore subjected to hunting which is often ruthless and there is often great slaughter among the herds in their summer quarters. The oil from their fat is used by natives of the north for lamps. The tendons serve for making thread, the bones for fashioning knives, needles and nails. Man makes use of seals in other ways—by taming them for circus performances where their agility and antics are a great joy to children. The seals do not have to be taught to leap or play games, because these are normal aspects of their behaviour in their free wild life.

The dugong (right), is rather rare and lives in Australian waters. The Manatus latirostrus *(left), belongs to the same family. It is found along the coast of South America: it lives on seaweed and often travels far upriver from the sea.*

BEARS

In Britain to-day the bear is either a circus animal or a resident of the Zoo. The old bears of Caledonia have long since disappeared from the stage, although at the beginning of the Christian era they were in great demand by the Romans who caught them and transported them for use in their brutal circuses at Rome. The fate of the British bears befell their relatives in most parts of Europe. There they have been exterminated by man in most places, although they are still found in the Pyrenees, the Alps and Carpathians, in Scandinavia, Finland, the Balkans and the U.S.S.R. The U.S.S.R. has the largest bears.

Apart from the Polar bear, most other species come in some form of brown or black and some of them are simply geographical races of the same species. Thus, the brown bear described as European is found in Europe, Asia and Japan. Depending on locality, individual specimens may

In winter the bear becomes torpid and seeks an underground den, in which he sleeps.

measure six or seven feet in length and range in weight from 450 to 550 pounds.

NORTH AMERICAN BEARS

The brown bears of North America are perhaps best known by reputation because they have been most written about and, to some extent, most closely studied. In addition, there is the black bear of North America which is not always black. It produces brown and cinnamon varieties regularly, and white specimens occasionally.

The biggest of the North American brown bears are the Kodiak bears which will reach a length of nine feet and scale up to 1650 pounds. The Grizzly, scientifically classified as *Ursus Horribilis*, while of uncertain temper, does not deserve the reputation for savagery and unprovoked assault with which it has been credited. Nevertheless, it was a problem to white settlers during the pioneering days in America.

Bears are still found in the Italian Alps.

The Polar bear is the dreaded hunter of the Arctic. It is entirely carnivorous.

19

The black bear from the mountains of India and Ceylon is a vegetarian and the only species that does not hibernate.

The raccoon is a small and graceful animal notable for its habit of washing all its food before eating it.

Grizzlies measure about eight and a half feet in length and weigh up to 880 lb. It will thus be seen that the giant kodiak is twice the size of the average grizzly, yet it is an inoffensive animal, not at all deserving the savage reputation once thrust upon it, and it is now protected by law. All bears are, however, somewhat unpredictable and it is commonly said in North America that the only people ever killed by bears are those who thought they knew all about them.

The Black bear, which is such a favourite in the national parks of North America where it will stop passing motorists to beg for food, is a case in point, and visitors are often discouraged from an over-close association with them. Though the biggest of the land carnivores, most bears are mainly vegetarians, but the black species frequently makes a nuisance of itself by raiding farms, killing livestock, and raiding the caches of foresters and trappers.

While it is true that the North American bears are largely vegetarian, and at certain times mainly so, as for example during the berry harvest in autumn, they take flesh food at any time and are predators on such animals as deer, moose, and snow-shoe rabbits, as well as domestic livestock.

The grizzly is a notable fisherman, and when salmon are ascending the rivers levies his toll during the running period. Predation by grizzlies is not, however, a significant factor in salmon populations. During the autumn the black bears lay on great layers of fat in preparation for hibernation, and their flesh was highly prized by the early settlers at this time of year. In the wild country of the far north the bears are true hibernators, sleeping through the worst of the winter in caves or under the roots of trees.

In spring, they leave their hibernation quarters thin and hungry, having used up their store of fat. It is during this winter sleep that the females give birth to their young, usually twins. When very young, bear cubs are droll and playful little characters, but as they grow older they become as unpredictable as adult bears. A she-bear with cubs can be extremely dangerous if provoked, and a roused bear is dangerous at any time. The animal's tremendous claws are terrible weapons and a forearm stroke from a roused bear is sufficient to shatter a man or break the neck of a moose.

NO SERIOUS ENEMIES

Apart from man, bears have no serious animal enemies, although a senile animal may find himself in a serious

The great bears of North America, like the kodiak and the grizzly, have long been the favourite quarry of hunters. When wounded these bears can be highly dangerous, but they were given a reputation for aggressiveness which they do not deserve.

The man with the dancing bear was once a familiar sight in the streets of Britain. Nowadays we do not allow performing bears in the streets, but they can still be seen in certain eastern countries.

predicament if pursued by a wolf pack in a period of famine. One can visualise the occasional bear being maimed by a heavy stroke from the hoof of a bull moose or having the wind knocked out of him by a buffalo. But, by and large, the modern bullet and the spring trap are the only thing he has to fear. Left to himself the average bear is more concerned about tearing roots apart to find grubs and insects or raiding the honey stores of wild bees than in looking for trouble with human beings.

In South America there is a Spectacled bear, which lives in the mountains of Venezuela and Chile, but little is known about its habits.

The Polar bear is familiar to most people as a zoo animal where, in addition to performing feats of diving and swimming and otherwise entertaining spectators, it will beg unashamedly for food. Considering its long association with zoological gardens, it is surprising how little is known about the polar bear in the wild state, and how much guesswork has been indulged in regarding the habits of the animal.

Polar bears often reach a great size, in the region of nine feet in length and 1600 pounds in weight. Being Arctic dwellers, hunting the snowy wastes and ice-floes, they have hairy-soled feet to give them a grip on slippery surfaces. They are the most carnivorous of all bears, one of their favourite foods being seals, which they can smell a long way off and which they stalk on the ice. As in the case of the other North American species, the cubs are born during the long Arctic nights when the she bear retires to give birth to her cubs and suckle them. This under-cover period does not last throughout the winter and is therefore not true hibernation, and the polar bear is up and about in Arctic weather when other species of bear far to the south are still asleep.

The Eskimos hunted the polar bear as they hunted so many other Arctic animals—for purely economic reasons—the bear providing food, clothing and weapons. Eskimo predation on polar bears, as in other cases where primitive people exploit a species for their own simple needs, was not significant. Modern firearms are, however, another story, and there is a serious danger to the species if present-day hunting is not controlled.

Visitors to America's Yellowstone National Park can always be sure of meeting bears, many of which become friendly. The authorities, however, discourage visitors from becoming too familiar with bears because the animals are unpredictable and can be highly dangerous.

OTTERS

The otter is the sleek weasel of the water, another member of the great family of the Mustelidæ: a night-hunter, rarely seen by day unless put on foot by dogs, and difficult to watch at any time. Anglers, by the very nature of their sport, which is a contemplative and sedentary one, see more of otters than most people—not just otters on the run, but otters going about their proper business of living. To-day, most knowledgeable anglers have no quarrel with the otter. Fishery Boards take him for granted; many river owners accept him as part of the scene, and some believe he is an asset on a river.

The habits and food preferences of otters in this country have recently been investigated by the Otter Committee and their report, prepared by Marie Stephens, has brought to light a lot of new material and in no way justifies routine destruction of otters. This is a very fine report and besides showing what has been discovered, indicates how much work still remains to be done.

Every movement of the otter is beautiful to watch, as his every pose is one of grace. In the water his action is noiseless, sinuous, without press of bone or bulge of muscle; on land his gait is the rump-up, bounding run of the true weasels. Though spending so much of their time in the water, and beautifully adapted for such an existence, otters do a great deal of their playing on land. Everyone has heard of their tobogganing game. In this game the otters slide down wet banks in summer and snowy banks in winter. Such places are usually referred to as otter slides.

MORE THAN A FISHERMAN

Though he is a first-class fisherman, the otter does not, by any means, confine himself to this kind of prey. Moorhens are regularly caught, and some otters occasionally contrive to catch ducks by swimming underwater and surfacing beneath the birds. On ice, the otter will stalk birds after the manner of the stoat, capturing his prey by a final rush. In very hard weather he may raid a poultry house, but if there are rabbits on his range he will take these more readily than anything else when he is ashore.

It is as a fisherman, however, that the otter is in his proper role. Then he preys on eels, frogs, coarse fish, or game fish. There is no doubt that he kills great quantities of eels and likes frogs; there is equally no doubt that he takes salmon and trout. He has done all these things for a very long time —long before men began to record his doings. Naturally his food varies somewhat from place to place. He takes what he can find, and frogs and eels bulk large on his prey list. He also takes carrion, but he has his basic needs, and rivers which cannot support him in the way of fish will seldom attract him, or hold him for long.

Otters are great nomads. The most settled time for them is the breeding season, for the bitch will not move on until her cubs are swimming strongly and catching their own fish. Dog otters usually lie downstream from their mates and will fight with any other dog otter who tries to move past them. Just what part the dog otter takes in the rearing of his family is still a matter of argument. It is unlikely that he sees the cubs until they are in the water. After that he may play with them and catch fish for them but this is one department of otter-behaviour requiring much more study. Some dog otters do form a close association with bitch and cubs.

BIRTH OF CUBS

Otter cubs may be born in any month. This has long been suspected, and many people were sure of it. The investiga-

Otters are easily tamed, respond well to kind treatment, and thrive in zoological gardens.

Although he is a first-class fisherman, the otter does not confine himself to hunting fish.

tions of the Otter Committee support this. There may, however, be some variation between one district and another.

On the coast, and in such places as the Outer Hebrides, the otters use holes in the rocks or small caves, often difficult of access. Though these animals spend most of their time by the sea, they are not sea-otters. They eat a lot of crabs and shellfish and probably do not travel far from their birth place, perhaps no farther than the length of the short rivers. Travelling otters will pass over high ground and have been recorded in this country at 1200 feet.

TEACHING OF CUBS

The strange thing about the cubs of the European otter is that they do not willingly take to the water; they have to be coaxed in, or pushed in, and it is some little time before they become expert at catching their own food. The bitch otter may swim around withholding food to persuade her young to leave the land and enter the water. Young otters do not, however, require any teaching once they are in the water. After the first ducking, they swim as inevitably and naturally as a dog does. A bitch otter with cubs in the water is a delightful sight and it is here that the angler, going quietly about his sport, often sees much that is denied to the casual seeker.

SEA-OTTERS

Our common otter is found throughout Europe, and into Asia, and is frequently found by the sea. The true sea-otter is more highly specialised in its aquatic life than any other species. It measures about four feet from tip to tip and the hind feet closely resemble a seal's flippers. This otter lives in kelt beds near the shore. In colour it is a warm brownish-black, with white-tipped hairs. The sea-otter was for a long time persistently hunted in the Bering Sea, the Kuril Islands and Alaska, by the Russians, Japanese and Americans. As a result, it came very close to being exterminated, but the actions of certain governments led to its protection and the species is now increasing again. It has recovered greatly in numbers in California.

As you would expect, this otter lives on marine creatures, mainly sea-urchins and shell-fish. It can dive down to a depth of 300 feet. It has powerful cheek teeth for crushing its prey.

Otters are notoriously playful even when adult, and it is not unusual to find a family tobogganing down the muddy or snowy banks of a river. Winter tobogganing is, in fact, a favourite pastime.

The sea otter is the most highly specialised of the family. Once almost extinct, it has recovered because of protection.

The hunting of otters for their skins by primitive peoples, does not endanger the species as does commercial exploitation.

23

FROGS AND TOADS

Frogs and toads are amphibians which deposit their eggs in water, spend the early part of their lives as tadpoles, and, when fully developed, can live either on land or in the water. When the fully-developed frog or toad is under water, respiration is carried on entirely through the skin which plays a greater part even than respiration through the lungs. Breathing through the skin, therefore, is necessary even on land, for it has been established experimentally that oxygen taken through the lungs alone is not sufficient to maintain life ashore over a long period.

You must have noticed, when watching toads or frogs, how the throat pulsates in constant rhythm. This rhythm is connected with lung breathing. Frogs and toads have no ribs, so that they cannot expand and contract their chest as birds and mammals do. Air is drawn in through the nostrils,

and, by muscular contraction associated with the throat pulsations, it is sent to the lungs. When frogs are hibernating under water they breathe entirely through the skin.

The life cycle of the various species of frogs and toads follows a similar pattern. Let us take first of all the common frog. After hibernation, frogs make their way to their favourite pond for spawning. They know exactly to which pond they want to go, and will not be turned aside, as you will soon see if you turn them about and face them in the opposite direction. Very soon they will alter course and head again for their chosen destination.

HOMING AND SPAWNING

Some years ago an experiment was carried out in America with the Carolina toad, when 444 individuals were taken from a big pond and turned loose at varying distances away from it. Eighteen per cent. of those released a mile away were re-taken at the pond at varying times afterwards; those released 300 to 900 yards away were back in a very short time, some of them within twenty-four hours.

When the frogs have assembled at the pond and the weather is right, spawning begins. The frogs may be present at a pond for some time before there is any sign of real breeding activity. This quiescent period, which has been called the pre-spawning period, is probably the result of a number of factors, one of which may be the absence of a food supply for the tadpoles. The main food of frog tadpoles in the early days is algæ, and if these are not mature, spawning does not take place. Low temperature in itself doesn't delay breeding, as frogs will be found spawning when ice covers the water. Unripeness of the female frog may be another factor, for in certain species the pre-spawning period is lengthy and regular.

EXPLOSIVE

When breeding begins there is much activity, and croaking becomes general among the males. Soon the spawn is deposited and, taking up water at once, becomes the gelatinous mass with which everyone is familiar. The actual business of spawning is an explosive one, the entire mass being extruded by the female in one burst. The spawn is fertilised by the male immediately it is deposited and if there is any delay the eggs may remain infertile.

The spawn is not a solid mass; water and oxygen can pass through it so that tadpoles hatching in the centre of the mass develop at the same speed as those hatching from eggs on the outside. The number of eggs laid by a female frog varies greatly, estimates ranging from one thousand to four thousand. Development from tadpole to the tiny frog ready to leave the water takes about three months, although it may be completed in ten weeks.

In mountainous areas, where spawning takes place later and the spawn is subjected to greater degrees of cold, one may find the developing frogs over-wintering as tadpoles. On the other hand, tadpoles can tolerate drought to a remarkable extent, and some hatched in Scotland at an elevation of 1500 feet have become complete frogs by the autumn,

The spawn of the common frog quickly absorbs water and then floats in jelly-like masses on the surface.

Shown here are the various stages of development, from tadpole to fully-developed frog.

despite the fact that the casual pool in which they had been hatched dried up frequently.

ENEMIES OF TADPOLES

Frog tadpoles have a great many enemies to contend with, notably the larvæ of water beetles and dragonflies in the water, and such birds as dippers, wagtails and magpies which snatch them from the water. The enemies of the adult frog are legion. Despite its prodigious jumping powers, it falls regular victim to hedgehogs, stoats, weasels, otters, badgers, snakes, hawks, owls, gulls, ducks, crows, herons and others. Certain species of frog are also eaten by man. The common frog is not eaten in this country, although it fills the gap in France and Belgium before the Edible frog has come out of hibernation. In this country, the common frog is used by man for other purposes, notably in biological laboratories for dissection and research.

The common frog in this country usually goes into hibernation in October, although you may see individuals about in November and even in December. During a mild winter frogs may be found hopping about at any time. Frogs hibernate usually in or near water, burying themselves in soft mud at the bottom of ponds and ditches. They may hibernate in the ponds in which they breed, but this is not always so, and frogs show the same determination to reach their hibernation quarters as they do to reach their spawning grounds.

The common frog varies a great deal in colour and it is almost true to say that no two are exactly alike. The commonest colours are greys, greens, yellows, browns, and reds, variably blotched and marked with black, brown, or red. In Scotland, red-coloured frogs are very common.

The edible frog is common in France, Belgium, Holland, Italy, Germany and other parts of Europe. Over much of this area, notably in Eastern Europe, the Marsh frog is also common, and it is often considered that the two are simply geographical races of the same species. In certain circumstances they will interbreed quite freely.

The edible frog has been introduced into England from time to time, and successfully established, but in each case the frogs have eventually died out. In some cases herons have been responsible for the disappearance, but this is not the whole explanation. The main breeding colonies of edible frogs in England were in Kent and Middlesex.

The croaking of the common frog, while it is distinct enough, cannot be called loud. Both the edible and the marsh frogs are noisy, their croaking being loud and crackling. They have vocal sacs bigger than peas, and the croaking is brought about by air from the lungs passing into the throat and sacs.

A LATER BREEDER

The edible frog breeds later than the common species, the main spawning period being in May and early June, but there is much variation from place to place and even between ponds only a few miles apart. In certain parts of Europe, spawning takes place in April. The eggs of the edible frog are smaller than those of the common frog, the tadpole hatching after about ten days, and development is complete after about fourteen weeks. It appears to be the case that tadpoles of the edible frog grow more slowly in England than on the Continent. The tadpoles, like the adult frog, are highly nervous creatures wriggling quickly into cover at the first hint of danger. Adult edible frogs hibernate in, or close

The male midwife toad carries the eggs about with him.

The edible frog is found in Europe, Asia and Africa.

The croaking frog of the United States reaches a great size.

The common toad comes out in search of food, mainly in the evening. It captures its prey with its tongue.

The American toad has a large vocal sac which balloons out in an extraordinary way when the voice is used.

to, water. Young frogs of the year, on the other hand, hibernate on land.

In France, the edible frog is a favourite item of food. The method of catching them is similar to that used by small boys in this country for catching sticklebacks—namely with rod and line but without a hook. The bait used for the frogs may consist of no more than a piece of coloured material, such as flannel or cotton. The bait is moved constantly in the water and as soon as the frog takes hold it is pulled straight out. Only the hind legs of the frogs are eaten, and about twenty frogs are necessary to make a meal for one person.

Green is the general colour of the edible frog, although there is considerable variation. Adults emerging from hibernation often appear more brown than green, but the green colour soon comes up after emergence.

The marsh frog, which in England is found only in Kent, is common in Spain, North Africa, Germany and Eastern Europe. In Europe, it frequents marshes, lakes, and rivers,

Frogs are considered excellent food by many people. They are sometimes captured at night by hunters using torches.

rather than ponds. It is a large frog, which emerges from hibernation in April. At spawning time, the male frogs choose a particular vantage point where they may be seen daily croaking and driving away rival males. They do not mass together like the common frog, and it is unusual to find more than a few close together, although there may be great numbers in the area. The eggs and tadpoles of this frog are rarely seen because the spawn doesn't float on the water and the tadpoles are hidden by weeds. Late in the year, however, when the dykes are being cleared, vast numbers of young frogs are caught up among the vegetation.

The marsh frog is the biggest species found in Europe. Males, when fully mature, measure three-and-three-quarter inches in length and females up to six-and-three-quarter inches.

TOADS OF EUROPE

There are three species of toad in Europe—the Common Toad, the Natterjack, and the Green Toad. The common toad in the British Isles is found throughout Scotland, England and Wales, but is absent from Ireland, the Outer Hebrides, and certain other islands. The natterjack, sometimes referred to as the running toad, is severely restricted in distribution, being found mainly in Southern England. The common toad is squat, brown in colour, with warty back and golden eye. The toes are only partly webbed.

Toads will eat almost anything they can catch and hold—caterpillars, worms, molluscs, ants and beetles. They are voracious feeders and Boulenger has shown that individuals will swallow so many earth worms in succession that some of them are voided still alive. Individual toads sometimes find their way to a beehive where they will squat at dusk catching up straggler bees.

The common toad will be found spawning in the same pond as the common frog. Where the two species are found together, the toads are later in spawning. Toad spawn is laid in ribbons wound round water weeds and not in masses. This winding is not deliberate, but is simply the result of the female toad moving about during spawning. Toads habitually spawn in deeper water than frogs.

Though the two species tend to keep apart during spawn-

The common tree frog, which is brilliant green in colour, is found throughout Europe. It sleeps through the winter.

The horned frog has a rough skin and a horn over each eye. It is found in large numbers in the forests of Brazil.

ing, individuals do wander, and it is not uncommon to find a common toad and common frog clasped together in the amplexus position—that is the position taken up by male and female before eggs are deposited and which is concerned with fertilisation.

Unlike the common frog, the common toad tames readily, and very quickly learns to respond to the advances of the person looking after it. Tame toads have been known to live for a great many years.

The common toad hibernates on land, usually in October. Toads seen later in the year are usually younger animals. Favourite places are mammalian burrows, cellars, greenhouses, under rocks and in dry banks. Several toads may be found hibernating together.

Despite the secretion from its skin, the toad has numerous enemies, but many of those which kill it will not eat it. Foxes and hedgehogs will kill toads, but it is doubtful if they eat them. Rats, on the other hand, will tear off the skin and eat the flesh underneath, as will ravens, crows, and magpies. Stoats in captivity will kill toads but will not eat them, and it is unlikely that any mammal, wild or tame, would eat the skin.

NOCTURNAL NATTERJACK

The natterjack toad is smaller than the common toad and is usually grey or olive coloured, with red, brown, green, or yellow markings. This species is a great burrower and prefers sandy areas where it can dig itself out of sight easily. Though found in certain parts of England and south-west Scotland, it is a very local species but, because of its gregarious habits, it is usually quite numerous in those areas where it *is* found. Though mainly crepuscular or nocturnal

in habits, the natterjack is quite frequently seen about by day. Its breeding season is a long one, extending from early spring well into the summer. In certain parts of France the breeding season may extend even into September, and this has given rise to the belief that the female natterjack may spawn twice in the year. Hibernation begins in October and November, the toad burying itself in the soil to a depth of a foot or more. Food consists of beetles, spiders, wood lice, worms, and small molluscs. Like the common toad, the natterjack is easily tamed and makes an attractive pet.

MALE GUARDS EGGS

In certain species of toads and frogs it is the male who looks after the eggs. In the case of the Midwife toad, for example, the male attaches the eggs to his hind-quarters immediately after they are laid on land. From time to time he enters the water to moisten the eggs, then, when the time comes for the tadpoles to hatch, he releases his burden in the water and the tadpoles begin their aquatic life. This is in direct contrast to the usual habit of frogs and toads which abandon their eggs after laying. In a few species the development of the tadpole takes place in the egg away from the water altogether and it has been established that in these cases some kind of parental instinct has been developed.

The European Tree Frog, which is brilliant green in colour, spends most of its life in trees, as its name suggests. Like all tree frogs it is able to change colour to match its background in much the same way as the chameleon. Tree frogs have climbing discs which are adhesive and which enable them to adhere to branches and leaves. Despite their ability to change colour and to match their background, many fall victims to such birds as shrikes.

QUESTIONS AND ANSWERS

Is the bite of the shrew poisonous?

It was believed at one time that the bite of the shrew was fatal, and shrews used to be sealed into holes in ash trees, thus producing the shrew-ash, the branches of which were the cure for any person bitten by a shrew.

Strangely enough, zoologists now know that the saliva of certain shrews does contain a toxin. The saliva of the British shrew has not yet been properly tested, but seems to be harmless for all practical purposes. Anyway, the teeth of our shrews are too small and fine to break the human skin.

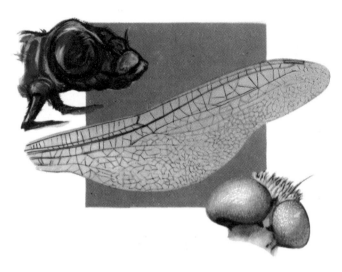

Head of the dragon-fly larva showing the mask. Centre: *wing of the dragon-fly showing fine webbing.* Bottom : *head of the perfect dragon-fly in which the huge, globous eyes are clearly visible.*

Dragon-flies, those great insects resplendent in gem-like mail, with bulbous heads and gauzy wings, are known to everybody. Striking in appearance, and frequently of great size, they are the hawks and falcons of the air, predators which live on other species of insects. Despite their sometimes frightening appearance, dragon-flies are harmless to everything except the creatures on which they feed. They cannot sting, and, though they have powerful jaws big enough to be observed chewing their prey, they cannot bite. Names like horse-stinger, stinging adder, and devil's darning needle are therefore a libel, however apt they may be as pure descriptions.

The aerial life of dragon-flies is comparatively long, lasting up to several weeks in certain species. By far the greater part of the dragon-fly's life is not spent on the wing at all, but underwater. This is during the larval stage which may last for two years or more. During this stage the dragon-fly larva, or nymph, lives the same kind of predatory life as it will when it takes the air, feeding on tadpoles, small minnows, and other pond life.

When the nymph is ready to undergo the last phase of development, it crawls up the stem of a water weed where it rests to await the final drama. Suddenly its skin splits down the back, the head of the perfect fly appears, followed by the body. Emergence continues head downwards with the insect performing a backward loop and gripping its own nymphal skin with its feet. When fully emerged, the fly rests right way up on the husk that it has left. The wings, after drying out, soon spread and rustle, and the fly is ready to begin its aerial existence.

The first man to describe the complete life history of a dragon-fly from egg to mature insect, was Professor Balfour-Brown, who reared specimens in captivity through the entire cycle. Nowadays we know much more about dragon-flies than we did when Professor Balfour-Brown began his work, but the number of species is so great that only a few can be described here.

QUICK ESCAPE FROM EGG-SHELL

There is a stage in the development of the dragon-fly where the larva resembles the pupa of a wasp or beetle. This stage used to be known as pro-nymphal: now it is referred to as pro-larval, to indicate that it immediately precedes the stage of development with which most people are familiar. The pro-larval stage may last for only a few seconds or several

Here we see a blue Aeshna, the common large dragon-fly to be seen flying strongly near pools and among trees. Like all dragon-flies, this beautiful insect is completely harmless. It lives entirely on insects.

minutes. It is now thought that the function of this stage in the life history of dragon-flies is to ensure an easy and quick escape from the egg-shell and the tissue surrounding it.

Dragon-fly larvæ vary a great deal in form, this diversity being related to their particular habitat. Functionally, however, they all behave in much the same way. There are mud dwellers, weed dwellers, and burrowers among them; the most active types being those which live among water plants. Many dragon-fly larvæ are able to change their colour to match their surroundings, even to the extent of matching the actual shade. Most of the larvæ found in Britain are weed dwellers.

The way in which a dragon-fly larva moves and feeds can be studied fairly easily in a home-made glass tank containing pond water, plants and a good cross section of pond life. It will be noticed at once that the larva of the dragon-fly lies in wait for living and moving prey which is then caught speedily and dextrously. The larva catches such prey by means of its " mask ", which is really a specially developed extensible labium. In fact, when you see this mask in operation it will remind you of two arms or pincers in its action.

WOLVES OF THE POOL

Because it has to lie in wait for its prey, the larva inevitably has to undergo long periods of fasting when no prey happens to come its way. As a result, it gorges freely when food is readily available and the great intake of food at this time is handled easily by the body and digested as quickly as it is caught. To the dragon-fly larva, nothing is prey which does not move—in other words it takes only things which move. In this way it takes tadpoles, small minnows, and suchlike creatures. Some larvæ will attack very big prey like the great water beetle (*Dytiscus marginalis*). Captive larvæ will feed on small pieces of meat, if these are moved about in front of them. An earth worm put into the tank will be seized as soon as it wriggles within range of the larva. In addition, larvæ will eat other larvæ, cannibalism being quite common in this group.

Though they have been called the wolves of the pool, dragon-fly larvæ are themselves the prey of many creatures, especially birds. Against creatures about their own size, they have special defensive attitudes which vary from species to species.

The duration of the larval period varies, but is always long. In some species it is one year, in others two, while in a great many it is even longer. Yet each year there is a group of nymphs ready to become mature dragon-flies, which will emerge at the proper season, with the proportion of sexes just right to ensure successful breeding, egg-laying, and the continuation of the species. The rate of growth of the larvæ is an aspect of the dragon-fly's life which is receiving increased attention. It has been shown, for example, that *Libellula sponsa* is one of the most rapid growers, completing his whole larval development in about two months. This compares with the rate of growth of tropical species. Other species require five years. The rate of growth depends to a great extent on temperature. In Britain, for example, most larval growth takes place between March and November: outside these months the larvæ are dormant and inactive.

FASCINATING SIGHT

The emergence of the mature dragon-fly is one of the most spectacular and fascinating sights in nature, and has been widely observed and photographed. Some little time before

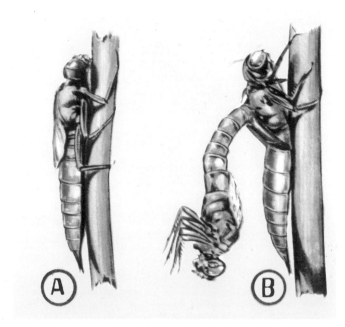

Emergence of the perfect dragon-fly from the nymphal skin. A. the nymph leaves the water; B. the dragon-fly emerges head downwards with the wings still folded.

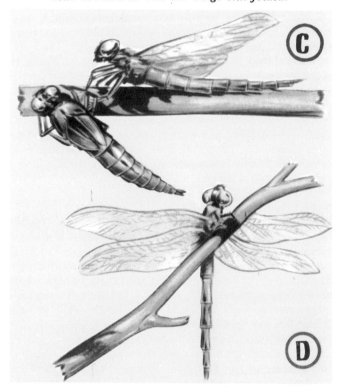

C. *another species of dragon-fly which has emerged horizontally, shown beside the empty nymphal skin. D. the perfect dragon-fly ready to take wing in the sunshine.*

the nymph is due to leave the water it chooses the stalk or stick up which it will climb. During the night, larvæ swim to these pre-selected escape routes. Some species of dragon-fly emerge at night, and the larvæ of these species can be induced to return to the water if a light is shone upon them as they prepare to come ashore.

When the larva is due to emerge, it climbs quickly out of the water, obviously determined to leave it for good. Perched on stick or reed, it begins to wriggle its abdomen violently. This violent shaking of the abdomen appears to be confined

Sometimes dragon-flies will fly out over the sea. Inevitably they are either devoured by birds or fall exhausted into the waves to be drowned.

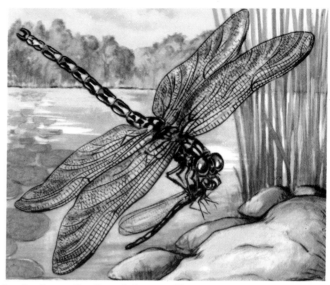

In the large family of dragon-flies are the beautiful, small, slender insects known as the damsel flies. Here we see a dragon-fly on the point of devouring a small damsel.

to larvæ which emerge in the vertical position. During this perching period, which may last up to an hour, the whole system of breathing in the larva changes. Before leaving the water it had to breathe in a special way, now it has to breathe atmospheric air and the method of respiration changes from rectal to spiracular. The nymphal skin then splits down the back and the fly begins to emerge. Once this stage has been reached, the emergence is continuous and can sometimes be explosive in the sense that everything seems to happen at once. Head, wings, and abdomen blossom out as though being inflated—in fact this happens with the abdomen due to blood being pumped into the organs under pressure. It is during the period of emergence that the motionless dragon-fly is most vulnerable to attacks by birds, although swallows catch adults on the wing.

NO COMMON NAMES

It is unfortunate that in this country most dragon-flies have no common names, unlike birds and mammals, and a great variety of less awe-inspiring insects, which have had vernacular names for a long time. This is not the case with dragon-flies, although the Japanese, who hold them in high esteem, have many such common names. We have, therefore, in most cases, to use their Latin names which, while not confusing (on the contrary they are used to avoid confusion), are not very suitable for everyday use.

The aeshnas are large dragon-flies, some of which are very common. The rare Blue Aeshna is found in Scotland. In this species the mature male is a brilliant blue and about two-and-a-half inches in length. It is smaller than *Aeshna Juncea* with which it is often found in association. Juncea is over two-and-three-quarter inches in length, but even bigger than this is the beautiful Emperor. In this country we also have the Brown Aeshna and the Norfolk Aeshna. In the libellulidæ we have our so-called Darter dragon-

flies. Our three species of libellulæ are the Four-spotted, the Broad-bodied, and the Scarce. The libellulidæ are stout-bodied dragon-flies, and *Libellula depressa*, a broad-bodied species, is the stoutest of them all. In addition to this, there are the handsome little damsel flies which may be seen in summer flying about ponds in association with the larger dragon-flies. They are slender-bodied flies. Some of them are of an intense and brilliant blue. There are also red damsel flies, like the Large Red and Small Red. Some have red legs and some have black legs, but they are all handsome and because of their small size and slender build are quite unmistakable.

ENEMIES OF THE DRAGON-FLIES

Despite its rapacity, both in its larval and perfect states, the dragon-fly has plenty of enemies of its own.

In the larval state it falls prey to birds like the dipper and the wagtail. The dipper sinks to the bottom of the pool or pond and walks along oaring with its wings, seeking such prey as caddis worms and small dragon-fly larvæ. The wagtail takes such prey in shallower water or where it has been temporarily exposed.

A small mammal which frequently preys upon dragon-fly larvæ is the water shrew.

At the time of emerging from the nymphal skin the dragon-fly is vulnerable to attack by insectivorous birds as well as by water hens and other aquatic birds. Sometimes such birds as crows and magpies, which frequent ponds on the lookout for small fry and carrion, discover the emerging dragon-flies and thus learn to look for them.

The perfect insect which is so familiar in the months of August and September is preyed upon by several species of bird, for example, the small hobby falcon and the honey buzzard. Despite its size it is frequently attacked by swallows and it is easy prey for such birds as the great grey shrike.

QUESTIONS AND ANSWERS

How many species of dragon-fly are there in the world?

Up to date about five thousand species have been identified, or described, so it can be seen that dragon-flies form only

a small part of the world's million insect species. Of the world population of five thousand species of dragon-flies, only 43 are found in the British Isles.

THE WORLD OF SPIDERS

Many people are genuinely afraid of spiders, yet most people consider them lucky and few people actively destroy them. Even in the most highly civilised countries spider superstitions are still strong, and are loosely associated with good luck. Fear of spiders is difficult to explain because even the dreaded tarantula is really innocuous. Probably it is the spider's crab-like appearance, together with the many legends of noxious spiders, which have given rise to this fear. One of the few poisonous spiders, which lives in the temperate zone, is *Latrodectes tredecimguttatus*—but its poison is of no danger to large mammals including man.

Spiders, unlike insects, have bodies composed of only two parts. In addition, they have simple eyes, no antennæ, and four pairs of walking legs instead of three. Unlike insects, again, spiders do not have a larval or pupal stage in their development.

The great class of the arachnids includes a number of creatures other than spiders, but only the spiders have abdominal spinnerets or palpal organs which the male uses at mating time.

Spiders hatch from eggs. During the growing period the young spider takes shape on the outside of the yolk. When the development is complete, the outer covering of the egg is burst open by pressure from the young spider. In some species the young spiders are helped by an egg tooth such as is found in chicks. As in the case of chicks, this egg tooth is shed after emergence from the egg. In the majority of spiders the newly born young is hairless, spineless, and without tarsal claws. It cannot eat and it cannot spin. After the young spider has completely absorbed its yolk sac it sheds its skin and becomes a real spider complete with claws, horn, spine, vision, and the power of eating and spinning.

At first, young spiders are stay-at-homes, showing little interest in food because they still have a yolk reserve in their abdomens. But, presently, they require food and they have to eat. Some species may be found sharing a fly with their mother, but there is a species where the mother actually passes food to her young from her own mouth. Some young stay in the mother's burrow for a long time, and may even feed on her body when she dies.

GROWTH OF YOUNG

Most spider mothers do not provide food for their young, so there is often a considerable amount of cannibalism until the family scatters. Where food is provided by the mother the young do not often attack each other and cannibalism is not common. Scattering of the family is important. If the young stayed close together they would soon run short of food. The emigration of young spiders is well known, the

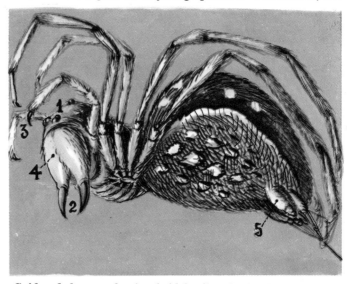

Spiders belong to the Arachnid family. In the illustration we see 1. the eyes; 2. palpae terminating in movable claws; 3. pedipalps; 4. poison glands placed in the thorax-head; 5. outlet for the threads.

The Latrodectus tredecimguttatus *is one of the few poisonous spiders which live in temperate zones. Its poison, however, is not toxic to large mammals, including man.*

The crusader spider weaves its large web between the lower, leafy branches of trees. The web is a strong trap to catch flies, or bees, under which the spider can run easily.

It is still believed to-day by many people that the bite of a tarantula can cause madness and death; in fact, the tarantula's bite is almost harmless. Behind the spider can be seen the silky cocoon containing the eggs.

young spinning silk strands on which they drift in the wind. Many die by coming down in the wrong places; many die from predation when they reach the ground; but many survive to keep the race of spiders going.

The spiders moult as they grow, their bodies becoming too big for their skins; like a boy growing out of his clothes. During the moulting period the spider is helpless, yet it takes no apparent precautions against danger, spending this time in the open or under cover in the normal way. The moulted spider is pale and soft, but the skin soon toughens. During this waiting period, between the soft and the tough, so to speak, the spider moves her legs a great deal to prevent the joints from stiffening.

Some spiders moult two or three times during growth; others may do so as often as ten times. The size of the species determines the number of moults. Spiders often die when extracting their legs from the old skin.

The spider with which most people are familiar is the house spider (*Tegamaria domesticus*). There are two other common species of house spider—*Tegamaria atrica* and

Tegamaria parietina. These species spin webs in buildings at suitable places where there is light to attract insects. They spin sheet webs, generally using corners to give anchorage and strength, and in these traps their victims are taken. *Tegamaria domesticus* is the commonest species, reaching a length of $\frac{3}{8}$ an inch. She hangs her egg sacs by a few threads from a ledge near her web. *Atrica* fastens her egg sac against the wall beside her web, while *parietina* builds her egg sac into her hiding-place. The house spiders are quick movers—so fast, indeed, that it has been reckoned that a spider of this group, enlarged to the size of man, could give the fastest sprinter an eighty yards start and win in a hundred yards.

One of the house spiders may be found in the open, the one called *atrica*, whose webs resemble those of *sylvestris*, an outdoor species. All these species weave white sheet webs. Mating takes place in the spring or early summer, and eggs are laid in early June.

CONQUERED ELEMENT

One of the most fascinating of spiders is *argyroneta*, the

Near the small windows or vent holes of cellars where insects are attracted by light, the common spider weaves her web, generally using corners for added strength.

water spider, who lives in a diving-bell of her own construction. Though not specially adapted for an aquatic existence (she is for ever rubbing herself dry), the water spider has conquered her element completely. First of all, she spins a little bell of silk under water, which will be an oxygen tent for herself and her offspring. This she has to keep supplied with oxygen. Her way of doing this is to come to the surface of the water, gather air bubbles on her legs, and to swim with them to her diving-bell. The bubbles of air are added to the existing air content of the bell, keeping it replenished and at full size. It is the air trapped by this spider which gives her the silvery appearance when she dives. In her diving-bell, the water spider can live indefinitely, breathing freely. The carbon dioxide in the tent is absorbed by the water and the air is kept fresh by the new supplies brought from the surface by the spider herself. Water spiders have been recorded biting holes in the top of their tent to allow used air to escape, after which the hole is mended and the tent re-filled with air brought from the surface. But the general opinion is that this behaviour is accidental or exceptional.

The water spider collects air bubbles and carries them under water to construct for herself her diving bell—a real house of air where she can live and breathe for long periods.

FOXES

In Great Britain, the echo of the last wolf howl has long since died away, but the Fox has survived in undiminished numbers right into the atomic age. This has its parallel in other parts of the world from which the wolf has been virtually exterminated, and there would appear to be several reasons to account for the fox's survival.

Not the least of these are its native cunning, its smaller size, its burrowing habits, and its smaller prey range. These all help in its struggle for survival, despite the fact that in areas where it attacks poultry and lambs it is constantly persecuted. Two other factors have operated in the fox's interests. In areas where its pelt is valuable it has been preserved for its fur and in modern times the ranching of foxes for this purpose has become a great industry. Then there is the influence of hunting. In Great Britain, especially in England, foxes are preserved so that they can be hunted with hounds.

Leicestershire has always been famous for its foxes, but it would be a great mistake to think that this area of England had in some way managed to acquire the cleverest and most cunning foxes. It is merely that they have been more publicised. By and large, the fox in hunting counties uses his brains most when being hunted; at other times he behaves in a fashion which might well be described as anything but cunning, because he knows perfectly well that he is in no danger outside the hunting season. In most parts of Scotland, where foxes are hunted and killed at all times and by any means, the animals are kept continually on the alert.

The greater the persecution by man, the more self-effacing and less vocal foxes become. Consequently you will hear more fox calls in a night in the English hunting counties during the calling season than you will hear in the Scottish Highlands in a week.

GREAT VARIATION

British foxes are a mixed lot, showing great variation in colour and size, with the biggest beasts coming, for the most part, from Scotland. This variation in size seems to be largely due to the fact that we have two types of fox. There has, however, been a great deal of importing and exporting for hunting purposes from Scotland to England, from the Continent to England, and from one part of England to another, so that big foxes and small foxes are liable to turn up almost anywhere. This doesn't alter the fact that Scottish foxes tend to be bigger in the skull, longer in the leg, and of far greater weight than the foxes of the English shires.

Hunting with hounds is a sport, and the fox has long been preserved for this purpose. Even to-day, when every man's hand is against them, foxes are still overtly preserved in many areas for the purpose of hunting. But the fox is hunted in many ways and for differing reasons. In most of England and a small part of Scotland, riding to hounds is purely a sport. In the Lake District where foxes are hunted because of their depredations on lambs, hounds are also used, but there the hunters follow on foot and the hunt is more of a business and less of a sport. In Scotland, except for the areas where packs of hounds are maintained, the fox has long been treated as vermin, and fox-hunting is a serious business. There, terriers take the place of fox-hounds and are sent to ground at the very time of year when English foxes are being left in peace—that is, when the vixens have cubs.

Foxes in Scotland are shot, trapped, snared, and poisoned. Any way of destroying a fox is considered a good way—which is not in the best traditions of hunting in the Anglo-Saxon sense. But all the hunting and trapping and shooting has not seriously affected the overall number of foxes in the

Fox cubs are born in spring and once they are weaned are fed on offal and insect food. Dog fox and vixen both hunt for the family.

Mountain foxes are usually bigger than those of the low country. In Britain this can be seen if Scottish Highland foxes are compared with foxes of the English shires.

long run.   Reynard we still have with us, and we are likely to have him for a long time to come.

FOOD OF FOXES

If you were to ask a number of people the question: what do foxes live on? you would almost certainly receive the answer: poultry, lambs, pheasants and rabbits.   Yet such an answer is at one and the same time only partly true and very wide of the mark.   Lots of foxes go through life without ever killing a hen.   Most foxes die without ever tasting a pheasant, and nobody actually knows how many foxes kill how many lambs.

The fact is that the fox takes a great variety of food, and the following items have been noted at dens in this country —blackcock, capercaillie, curlew, grouse, partridge, pheasant, poultry, peewit, roe deer fawn, leg of a red deer stag, hare, rabbit, rat, vole, field-mouse, mole, frog, and stoat.

The cunning of the fox is proverbial, and the foxes of Leicestershire in England have long been considered the cleverest. In fact, many foxes are imported from Scotland, by the Masters of Fox Hounds.

The blue, or Arctic, fox turns white in winter. It comes in two colour phases. It is still killed for its fur, which is of considerable commercial importance.

Some foxes can catch squirrels; others will pull the nests of small birds out of bushes.   Hedgehogs are frequently attacked and earth-worms regularly eaten.   The fox will also eat a variety of berries in season.   At a pinch he will take vegetable food.   And, of course, lambs are taken from time to time in hill country.   So it is extremely dangerous to speak dogmatically about the fox's " usual prey ".   The beast takes what he can get, and if he has a usual prey at all, that prey is far more likely to be voles, mice, rats and rabbits, than anything else.

When the rabbit was plentiful, lots of foxes killed mainly rabbits.   Some foxes made a habit of digging out every rabbit nest they found.   One beast has been recorded taking out nine rabbit nests in the same wood; another pair was recorded bringing sixty-three rats to their cubs in ten days of hunting.   Though foxes kill moles, it is doubtful whether they eat them.   Dead and dried-up moles are regularly used as playthings by cubs.   At a pinch, the fox will eat a stoat.

BREEDING SEASON

Foxes pair at the beginning of the year, which is when they are most vocal.   Dog and vixen both yap, but the vixen can also utter the most eldritch scream.   Cubs are born in March and April as a rule.   The vixen likes a ready-made den if she can find one, or she may enlarge a rabbit burrow. Some start digging from scratch.   In the Highlands, rocky slopes, or screes, are greatly favoured.   So are the dens of badgers, even when there are badgers in residence.   But most vixens cannot resist the easy digging afforded by rabbit burrows, so this kind of fox den is to be found everywhere. Many litters of fox cubs are born along our sea coasts at the bottom of inaccessible cliffs.   Others are reared in old mine workings, in quarries, or under an overhang of peat on an open heather moor.

When fox cubs first begin to play at the den mouth they are droll little creatures, all fun and capers with their heads full of fox-nonsense.   At this stage they have a great deal to learn, and watching them isn't difficult if you can sit perfectly still.   Of course, a single warning bark from the vixen will send them bolting below ground whether the cubs understand or not.   Some vixens, especially Highland ones,

The fennec, which has long pointed ears, is a native of Africa and is very largely a vegetarian. This is the species which gave rise to the story of the fox and the grapes.

The common fox, which is a carnivore living on rabbits, hares, mice, frogs, voles, hedgehogs, insects and earthworms, also eats fruit in season. It takes wild raspberries and blackberries and will eat grapes. It is perfectly true that foxes like sweet grapes and dislike sour ones. The nearest fruit we have to the grape in Britain is the wild bilberry. Foxes eat this fruit when it is ripe, but ignore it when it is not.

will let their cubs play all day in secluded places away from the actual den. Yet others will take their cubs to the open heather and keep them there. This kind of playground is easily recognised, for the cubs soon tread a maze of runways through the heather.

DEVOTED PARENTS

Vixens are devoted mothers and dog foxes are devoted fathers. Among our wild animals fathers are not usually notable for their devotion to their families but the dog fox, like the dog wolf, is a noteworthy exception. He provides the food for his vixen and cubs and continues to help his mate when she herself begins hunting. If the vixen is killed, the dog fox will rear the cubs if he can unless they are so tiny that they still require milk. Then there is nothing he can do about them. But if they are weaned, or near weaning, he will rear them.

Fox cubs, like the young of so many hunting animals, receive quite a lot of schooling. They learn to react at once to the warning bark of their parents. By being forced to find food which the vixen has deliberately hidden, they are taught to use their noses. Sometimes they are given disabled prey so that they can kill it for themselves. They are also given live prey in the form of young mice and suchlike so that they can practise the art of pouncing and striking. They make many forays in the company of their mother and quickly learn the facts of life. They begin to leave home in late summer, and at this time one can sometimes see two cubs running together. They soon part company, for foxes are mainly solitary beasts outside the breeding season.

ONE SPECIES

Though British foxes are derived from two types, we recognise in fact only one species of fox. There are less than a dozen species to be found in Europe, North America, Africa, and Asia. The best known is the European type, which is found far beyond the confines of Europe. In North America, Scandinavia, and North Russia, the fox became an important item in the fur trade and many colour phases were artificially bred so that fox-farming became a major industry. To-day, practically all silver fox skins are obtained in this way.

The Kit fox, once common in the plains of Western America, is smaller than the common fox and has been wiped out in many areas by poisoning. If its fur had been as valuable as that of the common fox, its history might well have been different.

In Arctic regions there is found the Arctic or white fox, which has also a blue phase. Recently, considerable research has been done on the distribution and feeding habits of the two types. These foxes feed on birds and eggs or stranded fish and, like the European fox, will take carrion. In lemming areas they kill large quantities of these small animals and store them for use when other food becomes scarce. Sometimes the white fox will play jackal to the Polar bear, devouring what the bear leaves behind.

In Eastern America there is a fox which can climb trees.

The Bat-eared fox of South and East Africa, is a small animal with erect ears which lives colonially in burrows and feeds on insects.

The Sand fox and the Fennec live in the desert regions of North Africa and the Middle East.

The European fox, like the rabbit, was introduced into Australia with disastrous results. One would have thought that rabbits would have been its main food, since they were so plentiful. Instead, the foxes looked for other prey items and became a serious menace to certain, rare, native species such as the lyrebird.

QUESTIONS AND ANSWERS

Do foxes and dogs interbreed?

Despite repeated reports that such crosses exist, there is no properly authenticated record of a dog/fox hybrid. Many types of crossbreed or mongrel dogs are foxy looking, but this is not enough. There is no record of a dog/fox mating under control, or the production of cubs from such a mating.

The Turkey

The turkey belongs to the order of the galliformes, and the family consists of two types. The first is found in a domestic state throughout the world but as a wild bird only in the United States of America and Mexico. The second type, called Turkey ocellato, lives only in the wild state in the forests of the Peninsula of the Yucatan.

The common turkey (*Meleagris gallopave*) is a well-built, strong bird which varies in size from eighteen inches to over three feet in length. It has four toes and the males are furnished with strong spurs. Its rather long neck is without feathers, coloured red and blue, making it rather vulture-like. The plumage is hard and compact, varying in colour from white to brown, or ash-grey, or black with metallic reflections according to the different races. The tail is rather short; the wings are reduced in size and quite unsuitable for flying.

The turkey originated in Central and North America, and at the time when Europeans reached the New World the bird was very numerous in the wild state and many were kept as domestic fowl by the Aztecs. During the day, the wild birds roamed the woods where they found abundant nourishment, the flocks often consisting of hundreds of individuals. At nightfall, the birds rose in brief flight and settled in the lower branches of trees where they remained until dawn.

With the onset of winter the flocks made short migrations to places where their food supply was assured. Early in spring the so-called turkey weddings took place.

NESTING HABITS

After mating, the females dug holes in the ground. Here they laid their ten to fifteen eggs on which they sat for a period of about thirty days. The young were raised with great care, protected from enemies by the parent, and assisted until they were able to live independently. Although hunted by wild animals, and by Indians who used their flesh for food and their feathers for making head coverings, the turkeys survived in great numbers. The arrival of the Europeans on the American continent signalled the beginning of their decline, due entirely to ruthless hunting. At the same time, however, the Europeans transplanted turkeys into the Old World, where much attention was devoted to their breeding and rearing. To-day, small groups of wild birds are still found in some parts of the United States. In Mexico they are still fairly plentiful, but the majority of turkeys of the world to-day are domestic.

The common turkey is now reared all over the world for table purposes, the flesh of its breast being of high quality. Turkey production in Great Britain is a highly organised industry. In addition, the turkey is sometimes crossed with the domestic fowl to produce a hybrid known as a churkey. While the churkey makes a fine table bird and is popular with many people, it has never become commercially important, nor at any time threatened to oust the turkey from its prominent position. Because of the turkey's strong position as a table bird its eggs are not often sold for eating. They have far greater value for setting to produce turkey poults for home consumption, or market.

While those turkeys kept for breeding may be allowed to live for several years, the vast majority of turkeys in this country have a life span of only a few months, roughly from summer until Christmas.

The turkey ocellato is found only in the wild state in the dry forests of the Peninsula of the Yucatan. Its plumage is more varied and brilliant than that of the turkey, being blue and green with changing reflections. The head and neck are quite bare and of deep blue colour. The skin around the eyes and beak, and the feet, are bright red.

The modern turkey and Christmas dinner are almost synonymous terms. It is the table bird par excellence, *and tens of thousands are reared each year for the Christmas market.*

The turkey as a wild bird is now rare. Yet, in one sense, it is the commonest rare bird in the world because of the vast numbers kept in captivity.

DONKEYS OF THE WORLD

"Fools! For I also had my hour;
One far fierce hour and sweet:
There was a shout about my ears,
And palms before my feet!"

Thus wrote the late G. K. Chesterton in his poem " The Donkey ", in which the starved, scourged and derided animal in the end stakes its claim to glory. For was it not the humble ass which carried Christ into Jerusalem?

For long centuries the ass has been a humble, uncomplaining beast of burden—in the East everybody's servant, and in the West the poor man's horse. For centuries it has been the emblem of docility, or stupidity, or stubbornness, depending on how you look at it. Yet the donkey is far from being stupid, although it is almost always docile and only stubborn when pushed beyond the limit of its endurance. Travellers from the highly-industrialised countries of Western Europe, where even the horse has been ousted by horse-power, seldom fail to marvel at the patience of small donkeys plodding along under a hot sun, carrying loads which seem far beyond the animals' strength.

The asses were probably domesticated before horses, and it seems likely that they are derived from the wild ass of Abyssinia. Though long familiar in Eastern countries, they did not reach Britain until the ninth and tenth centuries. There is only one breed of domestic ass, despite the great variety in size and colour. Body colour may be any shade of grey or brown but, unlike horses, asses never show any stars or stockings and have no chestnuts on the hind legs. The shoulder stripe varies from individual to individual in both breadth and length. Other individuals show distinct striping on the legs. The ass's long tail has hair at the end only. The ears are long and have thick hair inside them. Height varies from about two feet seven inches to four feet ten inches.

There are certain structural differences between asses and horses, but the number of teeth is the same. Generally speaking, asses live longer than horses, twenty-five years being a normal life span.

MORE PATIENT THAN HORSE

Compared with the horse, the ass is hardier, surer-footed, and more powerful for his bulk. He also has greater endurance and is unquestionably more patient. He can be depended upon to pick a safe route through any kind of

Donkeys, or asses, are members of the horse family. It is not known when they were first tamed, but the general opinion is that the Nubians of Africa introduced them into Egypt whence they spread to Europe.

The wild ass of Asia is found to-day in the mountains of Northern and Western China, the hills of Turkestan and Mongolia, and certain parts of Southern Siberia.

The onager is another species of wild ass found in Asia in both hot and cold regions. It is widely hunted for its meat and its skin.

The Nubian ass, like the Somali wild ass, belongs to a distinct group. Of low stature (it is never more than four feet tall), it used to roam the wilds of Nubia and the highlands of Eritrea. Both species are now rapidly dying out.

country. Despite hard work, he can get along with much less sleep than a horse. Normally he sleeps standing, and he has to be very tired indeed before he will lie down. Feeding the ass is not much of a problem for he seems to prefer the coarsest herbage—for example, the thistle—and this suits the poor man. He will not, however, drink anything but absolutely pure water.

The Tibetan Wild Ass, or Kiang, is really more of a horse than an ass. It stands about twelve hands high and is red brown in colour. It does, however, have a stiff, upright black mane forming a distinct dorsal line. The kiang inhabits the great plateau of Tibet down to the fringe of India, and is familiar in many Zoological collections. Kiangs are extremely inquisitive and become something of a nuisance to sportsmen because they will come in to get a close look at him and follow him in a body, thus spoiling his sport of stalking antelope and gazelle. Because they travel in parties, they have little to fear from any enemy except man, although

The Californian donkey (left), and its Sardinian relative (right) are both very small, but they are strong and sturdy animals, especially the white-coated species which is familiar to travellers in Sardinia. These donkeys are really the poor man's horses. They can survive on the coarsest food, need very little attention, and are patient and tireless workers.

wolves and snow-leopards will pull down individuals and take foals.

The Onager, which lives in the deserts of Western India, has also a broad black dorsal stripe. It is smaller than the kiang and looks more like an ass than a horse.

The wild ass of Somali, which was once found in Abyssinia, lives in the plateau country of Somaliland. The Somali is a true ass with long ears, short mane, and body coloured grey. This species requires no water, being able to satisfy its needs by eating succulent plants. The number of Somali asses has not increased in recent years despite protection afforded to them.

MULES

Asses and horses, despite differences in structure and temperament, belong to the same family group, and man has provided a closer link between them by crossing. The most common cross is the jack-donkey to the horse-mare, the offspring being known as a mule, which inherits characteristics from both parents. The mule has much of the appear-

The mule is a cross between a donkey stallion and a horse mare. It has the appearance of a donkey and the stature of a horse. Noted for its stubbornness, it also has great powers of endurance.

ance of the donkey but its stature comes nearer to that of the horse. Mules are used in teams for hard, difficult work requiring great strength and sure-footedness, for which they are better suited than horses. In the First World War, mule teams were extensively used for hauling heavy guns, and while they have gone out of use in many parts of the world, they are still bred for work in certain countries. The reverse cross—that is the horse stallion to the female ass—is not so popular and was never so popular because it had not the qualities of the mule. The word mule is used by man in other contexts. For instance, to describe hybrid cage-birds such as a cross between a finch and a canary.

Like the donkey, the mule will not drink anything but the purest water. It can survive on the same coarse food and does well on the scantiest of rations. It has almost the courage of the horse, combined with the sure-footedness and patience of the donkey, and in the days before mechanical transport came into general use, the mule was one of the most useful draft animals ever evolved by man. But the mule has not the horse's will. Once it has strained at a load and found it too heavy, it will not try again.

ELEPHANTS:
SERVANTS OF MAN

Many elephants, after a long free life in the forest, are taken prisoner by man and thereafter serve him faithfully. The frightened trumpeting of the wild elephants, herded by man into great stockades is, although they do not know it, their farewell to liberty. Decoy elephants trained by man help him to capture their wild, free kin.

There are three types of elephant in existence to-day: great pondering pachyderms which have survived the Mammoth and the Mastodon and which look like survivals from some long-past geological epoch before man trod the face of the earth. The three species are—the Indian elephant, the African elephant, and the lesser African elephant.

The species with which most Europeans are familiar is that of India, where it is still used extensively for heavy work. In the big forests of Burma it is indispensable for hauling timber through the roadless forests to the rivers down which logs are floated. Despite its great size, the elephant is far from clumsy and, apart from work requiring tremendous strength, can be taught to perform tricks requiring great finesse and judgment. Though a stampeding herd of elephants, making the ground tremble with their thunder, may wreck and trample everything in their path, "clumsy" is not an appropriate word to use for these animals.

Though the Indian elephant

To-day the African elephant inhabits the wooded regions south of the Sahara Desert. The species are becoming progressively rare, owing to ruthless exploitation by man and by constant poaching.

is the one we think of as the working elephant, and though it has had a long and close association with man, the lesser African species was almost certainly trained in its heyday when much of North Africa was under forest. The elephants brought to Rome, and those used by Hannibal in his historic crossing of the Alps, would almost certainly have been African. There is no evidence to suggest that Indian elephants were ever brought to Africa as working animals.

ELEPHANTS OF AFRICA

The great African elephant stands over ten feet tall at the shoulder. The lesser species stands around nine feet. The cows of both species are smaller than the males. Bull African elephants sometimes attain a height of eleven feet and the record for the species is over twelve feet. The African elephant has enormous ears. Those of the Indian elephant are noticeably small. Ivory comes from the tusks of the males. Length and weight of tusks varies according to the area: six feet and fifty pounds

Sometimes, and especially during the mating season, bull elephants engage in fierce fights. At such times the noise they make can be heard a long way off.

A hunter finds himself confronted by a rogue elephant. Killing an elephant requires expert marksmanship as the bullet has to hit him on a spot below the ear.

Newly-captured wild elephants in a corral. The great beasts, almost maddened by fear, roar and stamp until the earth trembles, but they soon become calm and respond quickly to the commands and cajolery of the Indian who handles them. The captured beasts are mostly females. The majority of wild bulls escape before being corralled.

being normal in the north of India, with both increasing by half in the south. Tusks of Burmese elephants are smaller than the Indians. Cow tusks are so small that they are rarely more than tooth picks. The best tusks to-day come from African elephants in the Kenya area, where nine feet in length is common.

The elephant's trunk is an organ of many uses. He collects food with it, and transfers the food to his mouth with it. He drinks with it and sprays himself with it. It is a tactile organ, a scent organ, and an organ of transport. He also breathes through it.

Despite his ponderous bulk, the elephant can move stealthily, and is far from being like a bull in a china shop. He walks on the tips of his toes, as it were, and under his toes, nature has provided him with springy cushions of adipose tissue, very elastic, so that he can move over the roughest ground almost silently.

The African elephant is hunted almost exclusively for his ivory and many ways have been devised to bring about his destruction: by shooting; by driving into staked pitfalls; and by burning the cover round him so that he is asphyxiated. Ivory poaching in Africa is big business despite the strict regulations. The elephants themselves, however, though protected on certain reserves and holding their own in many areas, are slowly diminishing in numbers while their range is for ever shrinking. White settlers have wiped them out in many places.

RELIGIOUS RESPECT

The position of the Indian elephant is somewhat different. In India it is viewed with a mixture of fear and religious respect. It is the emblem of wisdom. In some parts the working elephants are housed in brick stables where they are fed on cake prepared by their attendants. In other parts they are turned loose in the forest to fend for themselves after work. Besides working, for example, moving rocks and

Though elephants belonging to princes and other wealthy people are sometimes splendidly caparisoned, most have to perform hard manual work which they do uncomplainingly.

A circus elephant weighing five or six tons can perform delicate routine acts. This one has been patiently instructed by his trainer in a school for elephants.

40

In India, tiger hunting is a favourite sport, and wealthy Indian princes and their guests ride on elephants to seek out and destroy the great cat. The tiger does not really have much chance though he will attack when cornered, or wounded. When man's weapons fail, sometimes the elephant's trunk deals the tiger a knock-out blow.

timbers, carrying merchandise or people, elephants are used for hunting tigers. The elephant will readily face tigers in the jungle. The big cat is reluctant to tackle even a baby elephant, with or without its mother in attendance. Elephants, indeed, have really no enemies apart from man, the most common causes of death in India being snake bite and parasitic infestation. In Africa, many die as a result of blood-poisoning following on a bullet wound.

ROGUE ELEPHANTS

Elephants like humid forests and scrublands; arid areas do not attract them. They live in herds which, in some cases, reach a strength of 100 animals. In exceptional cases a herd may grow far beyond such strength. A male ousted from the herd is called a " rogue ", and is usually a dangerous animal, but a whole herd can be turned " rogue " by continual shooting up and persecution. In India, where even wild elephants are much more familiar with man, the animals tend to be, at one and the same time, more docile and more roguish. Thus you will find females placidly performing heavy labour, while wild animals nearby are running riot through a village knocking over huts, upsetting carts, and generally trampling the place into the ground. Animals which have lost their fear of man are always potentially more dangerous than wild ones.

Elephants are slow maturers and slow breeders, which is typical of animals with a long life span. The calf stays with his mother until about the age of three years. A cow with a calf is always a dangerous animal ready to defend her offspring against attack, real or imagined. For this reason, hunters do not like a raiding herd that contains many calves because, when it comes to tracking down the raiders, extreme care has to be used in stalking the nursing cows.

Ivory is very valuable and poaching of elephants for their tusks is still a profitable business. Good tusks will measure up to nine feet in length. Here we see negro porters carrying tusks through the jungle.

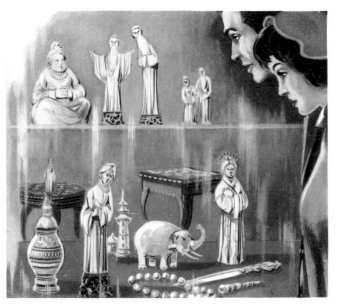

In modern workshops, steel grindstones cut the tusks into suitable shapes for working. The most common use for ivory to-day is for the manufacture of billiard balls and piano keys.

THE MOSQUITO

We usually become aware of mosquitoes and midges, not by looking for them, but because they look for us. Having found us, they pierce our skins with their sharp stylets. Attack by blood-sucking midges usually means little more than irritation; attack by certain mosquitoes can cause malaria.

In some parts of Britain it is an endurance test for a person to sit out of doors on a summer evening. This is especially true of the Western Highlands of Scotland. Mosquitoes of the genus Anopheles are another matter, and should not be confused with midges.

In Britain we have four species of Anopheles which can transmit malaria, once known as the ague.

When the mosquito settles on the skin of a human being it seeks about for a soft spot where it will make its puncture. Then it pierces the skin with its mouth-stylets to take its meal of blood. Only female mosquitoes are adapted for taking blood in this way; the males do not have suitable mouth-parts.

THE MALARIAL MOSQUITO

The disease known as malaria is spread by the Anopheles via their saliva, but it has to be understood that it is the human malaria victim who infects the mosquito in the first place. If a " clean " mosquito attacks a " clean " human being, there is no malaria transmission involved. If an affected mosquito pierces a clean human, the human can develop malaria. If a clean mosquito pierces an affected human being the mosquito contracts malaria, and thereafter becomes a carrier of the disease. It is a notable fact, of little comfort to human beings, that the mosquito appears to suffer more than the human being as a result of the disease!

Once it was understood that the mosquito became infected by man and that, thereafter, it transmitted the disease by means of its saliva, victory over malaria became a possibility. The discovery was made in 1897, by Ronald Ross. Since then, the mosquitoes have been attacked in their breeding quarters, and every effort has been made to keep them from contact with human beings. There is some truth in saying that malarial mosquitoes assisted the collapse of the Greek and Roman Empires, and closed Africa for centuries to white settlement.

The actual mechanism by which Anopheles introduces her saliva to the puncture is called the hypopharynx, a stylet which arises in the floor of the mouth, and carries the salivary channel. When the mouth stylets have been forced into the skin, saliva begins to flow down the hypopharynx, carrying the malarial organisms which will cause the disease in the victim.

BREEDING IN WATER

Mosquitoes need water to lay their eggs in. Like the larvæ of dragon-flies and water beetles, those of the mosquito live in the water. The larva of Anopheles gets its food from the underside of the surface-film of the water; larvæ of Culex, on the other hand, hangs upside down and takes its food from deeper water. The larva of Anopheles has a rotating head, with which it " sweeps " the under-surface of the water.

The feeding brushes of the mosquito larvæ are placed, one on each side of the head, like a moustache. The vibration of the brushes sets up a current, which is directed towards the mouth of the larva. The brushes filter the water, trapping any particles of food, and the mouth bristles comb these out and collect them. The larva, although legless, is able to move about with considerable agility by simple wriggling movements of the body.

Mosquito larvæ are perfectly adapted for their life in the

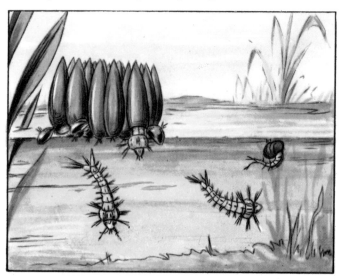

The eggs of **Anopheles maculipennis,** *the mosquito which transmits malaria, are laid on the surface of the water. Under water can be seen the larvæ of this mosquito, against which man wages constant war.*

The eggs of the **Culex pipiens,** *a mosquito which is very similar to* Anopheles, *but which is harmless. The difference between the two types is important in the study of malaria.*

In his war against mosquitoes, man concentrates on their larvae, spraying their breeding places with substances which enter their breathing pores and suffocate them.

water. The two types of larvæ—Anopheles and Culex—have big heads, a swollen thorax, and long abdomen. They have breathing pores, placed on the eighth abdominal segment, but in Anopheles the pores are on the segment while, in Culex, they are carried on the end of a breathing tube. The breathing tube of Culex opens just above the water, with flaps spread on the surface. The Anopheles larva, on the other hand, rests just under the surface-film of the water, with the breathing pores just breaking the surface. Water cannot enter the pores, because it is repelled by an oily exudation.

WAR AGAINST MOSQUITOES

The breathing apparatus of Anopheles has provided one of the main centres for man to attack. Since the larva must come to the surface, sooner or later, to breathe and collect food it becomes the victim of any substance on the water which can find an entry to the breathing pores. Water cannot do this, but petroleum oil enters at once. There are other preparations of a similar nature now in use. These

all have one thing in common: they enter the breathing pores and suffocate the larvæ.

In Britain we have more than thirty species of mosquito, but only four of these, of the Anopheles group, can transmit malaria. The commonest mosquito is *Culex pipiens* which, though a bloodsucker, rarely attacks human beings. As in the case of Anopheles, only the females make a meal of blood, the males concentrating on fruit saps and nectar.

Though mosquito larvæ all need water, not all mosquitoes lay their eggs in the same places. There is one species which lays its eggs only in water collected in holes in trees, and its larvæ are found nowhere else. Others breed in salt water. Some are found in garden tanks. Some are found in puddles. Anopheles, the malarial type, may be found in canals, slow-moving waterways, pools or ditches, or the backwaters of rivers—where the water is static or nearly so, and there are plenty of surface weeds. A disused canal will often attract Anopheles.

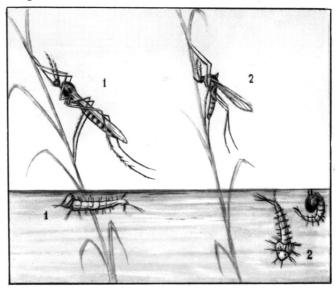

Here are the two mosquitoes, Anopheles *and* Culex, *shown with their respective larvæ. 1. mosquito and larva of the genus* Anopheles; *2. mosquito larva and pupa of* Culex.

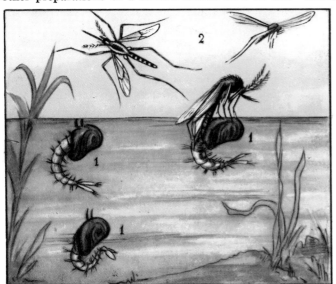

The pupa of Culex pipiens *is very similar to that of* Anopheles. *Here we see 1. the nymphs surfacing to become the perfect insects, and 2. the completion of this stage of development.*

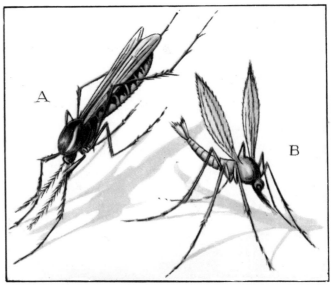

Two dangerous sickness transmitters: A. *the mosquito* Stegomya fasciata *which carries yellow fever, and* B. *the common gnat* Phlebotomus pappatasii, *which is the carrier of three-day-fever.*

THE ZEBRA

The coat of the common zebra is white with rather broad black stripes across the whole body except in the belly and the inside of the thighs.

In Southern and Eastern Africa live the Zebras, members of the horse family which have the striped coat of the tiger. It is for this reason that the zebra has often been called the horse-tiger, or hippo-tiger. Zebras, in point of size, rather resemble donkeys, from which they are distinguished at once by their short coat, fawn or yellow striped with black. Only the belly and inside parts of the thighs are without these bands, which form rings round the remainder of their limbs right down to the hoofs.

The largest of the zebras, and the one found farthest north, is the species called Grevy's. Unlike the other species, the Grevy's zebra can be tamed, and is greatly in demand for circuses and zoos. It has narrower and more numerous stripes than the others—seventeen on each side. Its ears are large and rounded. It has a stiff, upright mane and ears thickly edged with white. This zebra has a horse-like voice.

Burchell's zebra is about four inches shorter at the shoulder than Grevy's, and the flank stripes, which are broader, number fourteen. It is a fact, however, that zebras are not uniformly striped, so that one side may not be completely balanced with the other. Grevy's and Burchell's frequently associate where their ranges overlap, notably north of the Tana River, in Kenya, and at the coast near Lamu. It has been observed, however, that Grevy's zebra does not cross the river, although Burchell's is found on both sides. Burchell's is much given to associating with other ungulates like elands and hartebeest. They have a wide range extending from the Sahara to the Zambezi. Both species like high ground but whereas Grevy's keeps below 4000 feet, Burchell's thinks nothing of going up to 8000 feet.

The mountain, or true, zebras live in South Africa and are indeed very rare, being found mainly in national park areas.

One member which has disappeared already is the Quagga. This species was striped only on the neck and shoulders and used to be very plentiful in Cape Province. It has, however, been extinct since 1875.

All zebras are fast, quicker off their mark than other animals of the plains, but their stamina is not great and they soon slacken off. Their speed of thirty or forty miles an hour cannot be maintained over great distances. In general, their speed cannot be compared with that of the large antelopes. Their senses of smell and hearing are acute, and the

Zebras love to run across the high plains. They run in herds of about thirty head and pasture on the plains, or in woodland. They are quite vocal animals and whinny frequently.

Zebras are frequently preyed upon by lions and sometimes by leopards. Though they can defend themselves very well they still form a large part of the lion's prey.

man who stalks zebras has to do so with great care, upwind. The man who is stalking antelope in a herd which includes zebras, has to pay more attention to the zebras than to the antelopes. The big carnivores prefer to attack zebras when they are on the move when the sound of hoof-beats blots out lesser noises.

VALUE OF STRIPES

As in the case of other animals, boldly marked, the striping of the zebra has come in for a great deal of discussion. One theory was that the pattern made the beast invisible at night, the light and dark markings matching moonlight and shadow. The same thing has been said for the badger, but this has not stood up to examination. What does appear to be true is that in daylight a zebra standing motionless in cover is extremely difficult to pick out. But even here it is doubtful if any real advantage is conferred by their markings. While the beasts might be invisible to a lion at a distance, their great protection is their sense of smell and their acute hearing, as every person who has stalked them realises. Sometimes hunters can attract zebras a little closer by playing on their curiosity, but the white handkerchief on the end of the stick which can so often interest deer and bring them close, rarely brings the zebra very far towards the hidden hunter.

Zebras are nowhere increasing. The quagga has gone and Grevy's and Burchell's zebras merely hold their own. The mountain zebra appears to be definitely on the down grade and would almost certainly become extinct were it not for the protection now afforded it. The continued existence of animals of this type depends entirely on man, and whether or not the zebras will follow the quagga, eventually, is still far from certain.

HABITATS AND MAN

Man is forever changing the face of nature. He has been doing so since he first appeared on the earth and not always to the ultimate advantage of the earth or himself. Man has, in fact, destroyed great tracts of the world making them unfit for many species and sometimes even for himself.

In his struggle to live and to get the most out of life, man has destroyed many species directly: that is, by sheer physical destruction (for example, the passenger pigeon, the great auk, the quagga and in Britain, the wolf), and indirectly by the destruction, or alteration of habitats.

A habitat may be described as the combination of suitable terrain, suitable breeding conditions and regular food supply which any species requires for continued existence. Some species can stand disruption of their habitat, others are highly specialised and cannot. Man is the most adaptable of all animals and the most able to colonise almost any type of habitat, from the Arctic to the Equator.

The simple physical act of farming disrupts. When a farmer takes a piece of rough ground where curlews and redshanks have been nesting and cultivates it, he makes it unsuitable for these birds, so they vanish from that neighbourhood. But, in changing the function and physical face of the ground, man makes it suitable for other creatures; for example, partridges, songbirds and lapwings. Every change in land use brings about a change in types of plant and animals found on that land.

When man builds a new town this means the total destruction of vast areas of farmland or woodland. Bricks, concrete and tarmac take the place of grass and ploughland, trees, hedgerows and crops, so every form of life to which such things are necessary disappear from the scene. Here you have the complete destruction of entire habitats and such destruction is inevitable because man must have new towns to house an increasing population. The same applies in varying scale with the draining of marshes, or the building of aerodromes. In the first case, new types of wild life take over because the habitat has been changed; for example, marsh and water birds have to move out because marshes have been drained and the water table altered, so the corncrake may take over from the wild duck and the partridge from the waterhen. In the second case, practically everything disappears because tarmac is no kind of habitat for anything.

It follows, therefore, that every form of human activity upsets or changes the wild life complex of the area unceasingly and unavoidably. Man has destroyed many forms of wild life for no reasonable purpose. Small sections of the community, for their own narrow, selfish ends, have destroyed many things of general interest. Expediency has often led man to make grave blunders in land use, habitat destruction, and the extermination of many forms of wild life.

In his everyday life, man's attitude is determined in the main by purely practical considerations; ethical or moral considerations come afterwards. Looked at in this way, the disappearance from Britain of such animals as the wolf and wild boar can be more easily understood. In our intensively cultivated and over-populated country there was no room for such large mammals, the one a predator of big livestock and the other a pest to agriculture. Thus man's first attitude to animals is the result of their effect on his own survival, or what he considers to be their effect on his survival.

Then there is his concern with sport. The animals he sets aside for this purpose are given special protection and war is waged unceasingly on any other creatures that may be a danger to them. This creates many problems and man has made serious errors in his destruction of predators. Until recent years all hawks and falcons were destroyed as " vermin " by game preservers. This meant the destruction of kestrels, which are useful to the farmer; it meant the destruction of owls, which are useful to the farmer; so here you had sport acting against the interests of food production. The tragedy of all this is that all the killing of predators did not in any way improve man's sport. It has been clearly shown by modern research that eagles, hawks, falcons and predatory mammals have not the slightest effect on the numbers of game birds anywhere.

Broadly speaking, man wages war against the creatures which he considers harmful, even when his warfare makes little or no difference to the numbers of his enemies. And he encourages those creatures which are useful, even although their attacks on pests make little difference to the numbers of those pests. It would be true to say, therefore, that our attitude to songbirds, to most birds of prey and to many of our predatory animals, arises from the fact that they have either been proved useful or of no consequence. Either way from this we have developed the idea of conservation which means preserving what we have left of our heritage of wild life and even finding room for rarities which may do a little damage on the side.

The PANDA

Pandas are difficult to classify in the zoological system. They are for the most part considered as belonging to the procionids, akin to the bears. The sub-family ailuri comprises the genus *Ailurus* and the genus *Ailuropod*, each with a single species.

In the Himalayas, Nepal, and Assam and adjacent areas, at heights varying from 1500 feet to close on 5000 feet, lives a little animal of elegant and pleasing appearance, called the Lesser Panda (*Ailurus fulgens*) or the red feline bear. Sometimes it is called the raccoon. In size, the lesser panda is like a big cat, its overall length being about four feet. In build, however, it is far more robust than a cat. The head is round in shape, convex at the top, and the muzzle is pointed as it is in a bear cub. The legs are short, fat, and end in toes furnished with strong nails which can be partly retracted into their sheaths. The soles of the feet are covered with fur. The hairy coat is longer than that of a cat and is very thick and soft. The back and flanks are reddish brown with golden reflections; the chest and stomach are black; the muzzle is clear yellow except at the extremity where it is darker. The ears are well developed, covered with thick hair of reddish-brown colour outside and white inside. The tail is really very slender, but the abundant hair which covers it makes it appear very thick.

These pandas frequent zones of abundant vegetation and there they roam in couples in search of their food. Food consists for the most part of vegetable products, tender leaves and shoots, fruit and roots, but the panda will take small birds' eggs, insects, worms, and spiders, as opportunity offers. Though he may be found on the move at any time of the day or night, the panda has a distinct preference for twilight and darkness and therefore can be considered mainly crepuscular or nocturnal in habits. Pandas walk on the ground with a characteristic bouncing step, and when driven by hunger or danger they can climb trees with great agility. When resting, the panda likes to lodge himself comfortably on a forked branch or inside a hole in the main trunk of a tree.

Being very gentle animals, pandas are often captured for the singularity and beauty of their appearance. When captive they become tame very readily and freely accept food from the hand of man. When disturbed they rise on their hind legs and utter strong, loud, displeasing cries, but though they show their teeth during such demonstrations they do not attack and soon become calm again. The panda is a rather rare animal and was only discovered towards the middle of the 19th century. It is now hunted mainly for its valuable coat or for zoological collections. Its flesh, which has a strong, musky smell, is considered a great delicacy by the local people.

GIANT PANDA

To the same sub-family belongs the *Ailuropoda melanoleucus*, or Giant Panda, often called the bamboo bear. This is a much bigger animal than the lesser panda, being over three feet in length including the tail which is very short—it has to be borne in mind that half of the lesser panda's length is tail.

The giant panda looks like a bear cub. It is found in the mountains of Eastern Tibet and in neighbouring regions up to a considerable altitude. Very little is known of its habits, but it is known to frequent exclusively dense thickets of bamboo, the buds of which serve as its main food. Its awkward movements recall those of the plantigrades. The coat is thick and not very long. It is rough in texture. On the head and back the animal is white with black round the eyes and on the ears. Although exposed to very low temperatures, the giant panda never falls into a state of complete torpor.

Now an extremely rare animal, the giant panda was unknown in Europe until modern times. Before that its existence was known about only through its fur having been seen. It was only in 1939 that the first examples reached Europe. A hunter succeeded in capturing four of these animals and carrying them from the interior to the coast where they were shipped to London. There they were installed in the Zoo, arousing the most lively interest among visitors and experts. They adapted themselves to their new surroundings and to the new type of food substituted for bamboo shoots—that is carrots and other vegetables. On this diet the captive pandas appear to thrive.

The lesser panda, found in the Himalayas, Nepal and Assam.

The giant panda from the mountains of Tibet and Yunnan.

The PORCUPINE

Porcupines belong to the great family of the rodents and are divided into two groups—the Hystricidæ or Old World porcupines, and the Erethizonthidæ of the New World.

Though porcupines are notable for their armament of quills, and both Old and New World species are thus protected, there are important differences in structure which indicate that the animals developed along separate lines for a very long time. The skulls and teeth of American porcupines are different from those of the Old World species. In addition, the porcupines of North America are notable tree climbers and tree dwellers, while those of the Old World are ground-hunting and ground-living animals. In South America there is yet another species which has a prehensile tail.

Protected as they are by their quills, porcupines have little to fear from any living creature. Mainly nocturnal animals, they are coloured black and white, which may be " warning coloration " just as the badger's black and white pattern may be. In addition to their armament, porcupines can put up a further warning display by rattling the quills. When under pressure they may run backwards at an aggressor who, if he does not retreat at once, may have his face filled with quills.

Corbett has shown that many of the big cats killed as man-eaters had previously been disabled by porcupine quills. The fact that domestic dogs and many wild animals, get themselves quilled-up in this way, clearly shows that individuals of many species are always prepared to try conclusions with this redoubtable opponent. In North America it is said that the fisher, a species of marten, has become adept at dealing with porcupines by turning them on their backs with a nimble paw and then pouncing on their unprotected underparts.

Hystrix cristata, *the commonest type of porcupine, is found in Southern Europe, Asia Minor and North Africa. It is a small species of about twenty inches in length and leads a very solitary life. When molested it defends itself by striking at its enemy with its quills.*

Despite their protective armoury, porcupines are almost entirely nocturnal everywhere, and, for this reason, they are not seen any oftener than people normally see badgers or foxes. Some spend the day in holes in the ground, others in crevices, and yet others in holes in trees. The North American species, particularly, is a frequenter of holes in trees. Such locations are usually in places which provide maximum security and perhaps suit the porcupine's rather solitary nature.

The mountain porcupine is fond of sugar. With its strong incisor teeth it makes openings in the trunks of trees to suck sap which is strong in sugar substances.

In Canada, where porcupines are especially numerous, they often invade farms at night and gnaw at any wooden tools they come across, sometimes doing a great deal of damage.

The porcupine is a difficult animal to handle.

Everywhere, porcupines are vegetarians. In the Old World, a great variety of food is taken and the animals often invade fields and gardens. In winter, when snow is on the ground, the trees provide the food supply, for the porcupine stomach can deal with the toughest and harshest of fare. With incisor teeth strong enough to bite off a man's finger, the porcupine has little trouble feeding on twigs and bark. He is also addicted to the sap of certain trees and, where he has cut the bark once, he will return for the sap which gathers there later.

The Canadian porcupine, besides feeding on trees, so that he is literally never short of food so long as forests stand, has also a great liking for salt. In some parts he becomes a nuisance when he is seeking out anything with a salty flavour. Porcupines annoy humans in other ways: by eating the wooden parts of tools, by invading the foundations of houses and eating the wooden floors, by eating any kind of timber with varnish on it or which has been handled by the sweating hands of human being. Boxes which have contained salt fish are a great attraction, and in Canadian lumber camps where

salty boxes are available, porcupines are frequent visitors. The American Indians, notable for their use of, and respect for wild animals, have a high regard for the porcupine. Some of them hold it in the highest esteem, looking upon it almost as a totem animal. Others use it for its quills, which they prize greatly for ornamental purposes. Then there is its flesh which is considered a great delicacy.

LIE UP DURING DAY

Old World porcupines have their bodies heavily armed with long spines. They lie up in burrows during the day. They have thick-set bodies, powerful feet and claws, and their erect quills are sufficient to make any hunting animal think twice about attack. Though loose quills will stick in an attacker's skin, there is no truth in the belief that the porcupine can shoot these at his enemies. The main food of the Old World species is roots, bark, cultivated crops, and fruit. The Old World animals vary in size, the African brush-tail being about the size of a rabbit, while the Indian porcupine

The meat of the porcupine is edible and is said to have an agreeable taste. Here are Indians roasting a porcupine.

will reach a length of three and a half feet and weigh up to forty pounds. This latter is about the size and weight of the Canadian species.

The body of the Canadian porcupine is covered with thick hair which almost completely hides the quills. When angered or alarmed, however, the porcupine raises his quills so that they become obvious. Although his quills are short, they are barbed and highly dangerous. Any attacker which receives a few of these in his face is soon in serious trouble if he cannot rub them out because, being barbed, they work their way inwards for a considerable distance, damaging the tissues. Later, they may lodge in a joint or permanently damage a vital organ. The Canadian species feeds on bark, buds and leaves, and thinks nothing of climbing trees to get them. During the coldest weather this species is active, and it is at this time that it gets into most trouble, so much so, that in many parts of North America it is looked upon as vermin.

The South American porcupines are expert tree climbers and have stiff bristles at the root of their tails to assist them in gripping smooth trunks and branches of trees.

Here are some Indian ornaments made from porcupine quills.

The KANGAROO

The red kangaroo lives in the interior of Southern and Eastern Australia. Its strong tail acts as a prop when the animal is resting and as a balancing pole when it is jumping.

Australia has many so-called " odd " animals, not the least of which are the marsupials. The best known of the marsupials are perhaps the kangaroos.

Marsupials have reached a more advanced stage of evolution than the monotremes—for example the duck-billed platypus—but they are still primitive compared with mammals. The kangaroo, while it does not lay eggs like the platypus, does not produce fully-developed young, as mammals do. The young are, in fact, born in an immature state, hardly recognisable as kangaroos at all and little more than an inch in length. Development after birth takes place in the mother's pouch where the young kangaroo remains hidden, nursing and growing for many weeks before it is able to come out and live a separate existence.

DIFFERENT TYPES

There are in Australia many species of kangaroos and wallabies, some small, some large, the largest being the Great Kangaroo and the Red Kangaroo which are the typical animals of Australia. Estimates of the kangaroo's speed and jumping powers have been in the past greatly over-estimated, and it now seems that the maximum speed of the fastest species is about twenty-five miles an hour, which is only half the speed reached by some ungulates and a little more than a third of that recorded for the cheetah. Similarly, its jumping powers are less spectacular than was previously thought, twenty-six feet being a good jump for the big kangaroos.

Characteristics common to all the kangaroos are the small

front legs, the long, powerful, and muscular hind legs, and the thick, strong, heavy tail on which the kangaroo squats when at rest. In addition, the Rock Wallaby of Queensland has feet specially adapted for gripping rocks, for this species frequents rocky places rather than brushland or grassland. Wallaby, by the way, is a general name given to the smaller types of kangaroo.

BEAR-LIKE

The Tree Kangaroos which, despite their long tails, are rather bear-like in appearance, do not have the tremendous hind limbs characteristic of the terrestrial species. They are expert climbers, able to move with great agility in the tallest trees.

The smallest of the kangaroos is the Rat Kangaroo, which is no bigger than a rabbit.

DECLINE IN POPULATION

The coming of the white man to Australia has not had a favourable impact on kangaroos generally. Some species have been hunted down to the verge of extinction. In some areas, others are a problem because, being vegetarians, they compete with man and his domestic livestock for their living. It seems unlikely that the big kangaroos will survive unless deliberately conserved by the Australians. One species which is in great danger of extermination is the Ring-tailed Wallaby, which has a valuable pelt for which it is much hunted.

Small wallabies, like the scrub species, are like rabbits in their habits, for they frequent dense undergrowth and keep very much to their runways. They have the same habit as rabbits of thumping the ground with their hind pads at the approach of danger.

Tree-climbing kangaroos spend most of the daylight in trees. They live in the rain forests of New Guinea. This species, also found in Queensland, has the pouch which is typical of all the marsupials.

There are still in existence certain animals which appear to be survivals from a past age in the world's history (recently, for example, we had the discovery of the coelacanth). In addition, we have those apparently at a stage of arrested development, and in this class we might well consider that remarkable Australian animal, the duck-billed platypus.

Here we have a mammal which has a bill like a duck. In addition, the platypus lays eggs. Superficially, it resembles our common mole, but whereas the common mole belongs to the highly-developed group of mammals, the platypus is a very primitive mammal indeed. Highly specialised though it is, it is still a long way behind modern mammals in development, and it might well be said that it managed to get from the reptile stage and evolve no farther.

While it might be said that our common mole, with its great shovel-like forefeet literally swims through the earth, the duck-billed platypus has feet adapted to perform the

The platypus has a bill similar to that of a duck. This strange organ is covered with soft, hairless skin.

double function of " swimming " in water or earth. That is to say, it has webbed feet which enable it to swim freely in water, while it can fold back the web to allow the claws to come into use for digging when it is on land. The duck-bill has cheek-pouches in which it can store food, and there is yet another curious feature—on the hind feet of the males are spurs which connect up with a poison gland. These spurs have been likened to a snake's fangs on the one hand, and to the spurs of a gamecock on the other.

The duck-billed platypus lays soft-shelled eggs like the reptiles, and not hard-shelled eggs like those we find in birds. The eggs are dirty white in colour and about three-quarters of an inch in diameter. So here we have a mammal (a warm-blooded creature which suckles its young, is covered more or less with hair, and has a four-chambered heart) and which yet does not bring forth living young. It does, however, suckle its young, and otherwise appears like a mammal so that it can be classified as a mammal which has not developed as far as others have done.

As has been said, it most closely resembles our mole. It has the same cylindrical body, outsized forefeet, and strong claws. Despite its duck-bill, its nose is as sensitive as the mole's. It has a prodigious appetite and is an inveterate digger, being able to dig burrows up to sixty feet in length in the banks of streams. A strong swimmer, it catches its food in the water, filtering it through its duck's bill in the manner of the true duck.

The duck-billed platypus is confined to Australia, that land of many unique and bizarre animals.

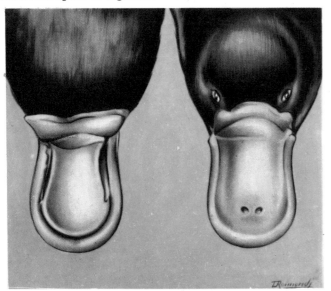
The duck-billed platypus is an egg-laying mammal. It is found in Australia where it lives on insects and shellfish.

Australia is the home of the echidna, often called the spiny ant-eater. It is toothless.

THE *Horse*

Mare with foal. Foals at birth are awkward, long-legged creatures, but they soon develop the grace of their parents.

Many millions of years had to elapse before the primitive Eohippus became a real horse. When man first domesticated the horse, using it for transport and as a beast of burden, is not clear; but the association between them is of great antiquity. In the second quarter of the 20th century, with the substitution of horse-power for horses, the horse as a working animal became more and more rare. At the present time, in highly mechanised countries, horses are seldom seen either working on farms or as draught horses in towns.

In the course of centuries, man has evolved a great variety of horses, as he has done with every other plant and animal species which he has domesticated. The varieties of cattle, sheep, poultry, dogs, and plants in existence to-day show this quite clearly. Thus we find horse breeds varying in size and

shape, from the tiny Shetland Pony to the slim aristocratic thoroughbred and the heavy work horses, like the Flemish, the Shire and the Clydesdale. The heavy draught horses are still used in many parts, but their numbers continually decline.

Yet man has not given up the horse entirely, as we shall see. While it is perhaps a sad thing to see horses disappear from the countryside, one cannot help feeling that it is as well for the horse that the internal combustion engine replaced him in the towns, for a great many horses spent their lives dragging heavy loads through city streets in all weathers. While many of these were well cared for, a great many were neglected and few of them ever had the chance to feel grass beneath their feet, except perhaps for a week or so during the summer holidays.

Chariot-racing was a favourite sport of the Ancient Romans.

One of the most famous breeds of horse is the Arab. This is the saddle horse of the desert Bedouins and has been specially bred for many years for speed and endurance. The modern English thoroughbred is descended from imported Arabian horses.

On the cattle ranches of the United States of America, the horse is indispensable to the cowboys. Even in the jet age, specially trained horses are used by the cowboys when herding the cattle.

In biblical times, horses were used by the Romans and the Egyptians for chariot-racing as well as saddle horses. Throughout recorded history man has used the horse for carrying soldiers into battle, although in modern war such cavalry units are largely obsolete except in special cases. The nomadic Arabs of North Africa, who are proud of fine horse flesh, breed the famous Arabians notable for their speed and endurance, and it was from these Arab horses that the famous English thoroughbred was derived. Fast horses were also highly prized on the plains of Eastern Europe and Russia, and for centuries the Cossacks have been notable horsemen, demonstrating their skill in countries far beyond their own frontiers. Indeed, the Cossacks are still among the most highly skilled horsemen in the world.

SPANISH ORIGIN

The horses of North America are of Spanish origin, and in many parts of the United States, particularly in desert areas,

bands of wild horses still roam. Wild, unbroken horses such as these are still used in the ever popular rodeos in the United States to test the skill of riders. These horses, when mounted, have one aim and only one aim: to unseat the rider by any means. In the great ranching areas of America, Mexico and the grasslands of South America, the horse is still used by the cattlemen, popularly known as cowboys. They, like the Cossacks, the Tartars and the Bedouins have an eye for a fine horse. Horses for cattle herding on the ranches have to be specially trained for the work, as indeed have any horses working in a specialised way.

The days of the cavalry chargers are largely over. The Crimean War and the Apache Wars are things of the past and the great chargers of the 19th century, like those of the Middle Ages, are no more; but horses of this type are still

Bronco busting! On the cattle ranges of America, horse wranglers break in the wild mustangs as cow ponies. Riding wild, unbroken horses was also a great sport with cowboys, still featured in the modern rodeo.

The cowboys of South America, known as gauchos, are born to the saddle. Instead of the lassos used by the North American cowboys, the gauchos use the bolas.

Since ancient times the horse has been used by man in war, but in modern times its place has been taken by the machine, and cavalry units have been mechanised.

Being intelligent and amenable to training, horses have been widely used as circus animals. Here we see two being taught to keep time to music.

Horse racing is a popular sport in Europe and America, and the English Derby is one of the most important events in the Racing Calendar.

much to the fore, being used for hunting and point-to-point races. By the crossing of thoroughbreds with heavier breeds, horses for hunting and jumping are produced, different types being bred for different types of country. Horses used by mounted police are largely of the same type. Others are specially bred for polo or for circus performances.

As a result of modern tendencies, lighter horses like ponies, hunters, thoroughbreds and crosses, have come into great favour, for horse-riding is still popular as an exercise and for sporting purposes. In recent years, pony-trekking has become extremely popular in the Highlands of Scotland. This has meant a great demand for the sure-footed mountain ponies called Garrons, which are really light draught horses.

HORSES STILL POPULAR

The interest of the public in racing and steeple-chasing, as well as trotting, has meant that the breeds concerned have held their own while the draught horse has become largely superfluous.

Horse shows are as popular as ever, and events like gym-khanas and point-to-point races keep the public interest in horses alive.

Horses have always been noted for their docility, intelligence, and willingness to work, but for certain types of work improvements can be made by crossing. A cross between a donkey and a horse is a mule. This cross produces a light animal of great strength and sure-footedness. A cross between a horse stallion and a female ass is called a hinny, but this has never been so popular as the mule. As a draught animal the mule has one bad feature—unlike the horse, which is always willing to keep on trying, a mule will try the strain of a load once and, if it cannot move it, will not try again. The zebra has never been used as a domestic animal, although a certain Lord Morton once succeeded in producing offspring from a cross between a zebra stallion and a mare. As a result of this experiment it was widely believed afterwards that the zebra strain remained in the mare's future offspring. This belief is called telegony, which means that once a pure-bred female has been crossed with another species all subsequent generations are contaminated. This is quite untrue.

In the sport of fox hunting, a specialised type of horse is required. Hunters are usually of mixed thoroughbred blood.

Cardinal Birds

Cardinal birds are brilliantly plumaged and the name is derived from the crimson cap which is a feature of many species. In the above illustration are some highly prized representatives of this family: 1. The blue hawfinch (Giuraca caerulea), from Virginia, Carolina and Maryland. 2. The Virginian cardinal (Richmondena cardinalis), from Virginia and North Carolina. 3. The crested cardinal (Pyrrhuloxia sinuata), from Maryland. 4. The red-crested cardinal (Paroaria cucullata), from Argentina and Uruguay. 5. Yellow-green cardinal (Gubernatrix crestata), from Argentina and Paraguay. 6. The red-crested hawfinch (Hedymelenus ludovicianus), from North-Eastern United States. 7. The Dominican cardinal (Paroaria dominicana), from North Brazil. 8. Paroaria gularis, from Argentina, Uruguay and Matto Grosso.

The cardinals are common and widely distributed in America, just as sparrows and finches are in Europe, and for several centuries these handsome little birds have attracted Europeans by the beauty of their plumage and by the ease with which they adapt themselves to human company even in climates very different from their own.

The cardinals derive their name from the gaudy red cap on their head, which is reminiscent of the crimson hat of a Cardinal. They are singularly handsome and gracious birds and it is not surprising that Europeans, seeing them for the first time, are strongly attracted to them. As a result, many

were brought to Europe long ago by sailors, and the birds are still familiar in aviaries and as cage birds in Southern Europe. In the steep alleys of the cities of Liguria, the cardinal is a familiar sight, imprisoned in a small cage above the brown sandstone doorways.

Cardinals are not only first-class as singers. Their twittering, which resembles that of sparrows, except that it attains greater variations, is a pleasant enough sound. In Europe, they are bred exclusively in captivity as cage birds and, unlike their near relatives the sparrows, thrive even in small cages, where they will sing and lay eggs and produce young.

WILD AND TAME

In the wild state, they are found all over the continent of America, preferring forests or cultivated areas. They feed on almost every type of weed seed, even those enclosed in hard shells, which present no problem to their strong, conical beaks. The European bird which most closely resembles the cardinals is the hawfinch which is smaller, with less gaudy plumage, and a poor singer. The species of cardinal kept most commonly as a cage bird in Europe, and the one most often seen in Italy, is the crested cardinal, which is common in the Argentine and as familiar a sight in city parks and roof-tops there as the sparrow is in Europe.

The crested cardinal, as its name suggests, has a crest of red feathers, but is otherwise grey-plumaged, with a white belly. It feeds on grain and seed, but likes fruit and is not averse to insects. Similar in appearance, except that it does not have the beautiful crimson crest, is the Dominican—called by the natives the "country cock". It is a native of Central America and the Island of San Domingo from which it gets its name. The smallest of the whole family is the little cardinal which frequents the forest of the Matto Grosso

The yellow-green cardinal (Gubernatrix crestata), differs notably from most of the others in its plumage, although it is a member of the cardinal family and lives in the same kind of climate.

Similar to the crested cardinal is the Dominican cardinal (Paroaria dominicana), which lives in Northern Brazil. The Dominican cardinal differs from the others in having no crest.

The Virginian cardinal (Richmondena cardinalis), *is the largest of the family. It is noted for its brilliant plumage and its pleasant song. It is found mainly in the State of Virginia.*

and rivers of tropical America. It is slightly bigger than the sparrow, but much more brightly plumaged and with a very fine voice.

Quite different from all these in colouring, but similar in size, shape and habits, is the yellow or green cardinal of Montevideo. It has a fine crest and is perhaps the best singer of the entire cardinal family.

The most striking species, both for size and plumage, is the cardinal of Virginia, which is as big as a starling: a red bird with a black mask which makes him look like a member of some gloomy medieval society. In fact he is a lively and vivacious bird, an untiring singer, and is much favoured as a cage bird by those who like cage birds.

The nests of the cardinals are round and cup-shaped and built of twigs, dry grass, and straw. The hens lay four or five eggs at a time, which are white or blue, specked with brown. The laying period is October, which in South America corresponds with Britain's March or April. The young birds are able to fly after about three months. The old birds stay together until the family is able to fend for itself. The cardinals do not migrate. They winter in their nesting areas and they are as familiar all the year round as sparrows are in Britain. They have the same urban habits as our sparrows, so that it is a common thing to see the red crest of a cardinal on the roof-tops of Buenos Aires or Montevideo.

In captivity, the cardinals soon become docile and show much attachment to their owner, so that they are often given

the liberty of the house, as budgerigars are. They are relatively free from disease and therefore present no problem in captivity.

The red-crested cardinal (Paroaria cucullata), *which is a native of Latin America, is one of the most noted members of the family. It frequents river banks in Uruguay and Argentina.*

QUESTIONS AND ANSWERS

What is the goatsucker? Goatsucker is the name often used for the nightjar. The belief that it suckles goats or cows is a very old one and still persists among some country people. Aristotle was the first man to give it this name and even its Latin title conferred by the great *Linnæus* perpetuates the legend, for legend it is. It is perfectly true that nightjars can often be seen flying around goats and cattle at night, but far from being interested in their milk it is hunting the insects often found in association with these animals. Therefore, the nightjar is the friend of man and beast.

Do hedgehogs suck cows? The belief that hedgehogs suck cows is about as old as the one about nightjars sucking goats, and it is a fact that hedgehogs are frequently found where cows are resting at night. Observation shows, however, that the beast is mainly interested in the small prey often to be found where cows are lying. In addition, it has been observed that the hedgehog will lick the milk droplets which have been pressed from the udders of heavily stocked cows during the night. These droplets often lie on the pressed, damp grass for a long time before filtering away.

The remarkable variety of warbles and trills, and the richness of the notes uttered by canaries, have made these birds popular for a long time, and connoisseurs have always been prepared to pay high prices for the best singers.

Nowadays, the canary is not as popular as it once was, its place as a household pet having been largely usurped by the budgerigar.

Nevertheless the "Fancy" still has a large and devoted following, and in certain Mediterranean countries canaries are as popular as they ever were. In some parts of the world there are still competitions for singing canaries, and in certain parts of Italy, for example, you will find rows of cages in a garden or on a large veranda, all containing canaries waiting to be judged. Round these cages, grave-faced men walk in silence as though deep in philosophical speculation. They are, in fact, giving all their attention to the trills and twitterings coming from each cage. They are judges of canary singing. The Italians are still great devotees of the singing canaries, considering them the tenors of the bird world, and after such a singing competition will often pay high prices for the best birds.

The canary as we know it to-day is a yellow-plumaged bird about the size of a young sparrow, but with a relatively slender beak. In the wild state, however, the plumage is green-speckled, with grey on the wings, and gold only on the back and breast. This is the plumage of the wild canaries of Madeira and the Canary Islands. The predominantly

The best singers in the canary family are not always the handsomest in appearance. Illustrated are the Belgian and Dutch canaries.

yellow colour with which we are familiar is the product of selective breeding, which began about two centuries ago.

There are now several varieties of canary bred in captivity, and these show much variation in plumage-colour, size and shape, these differences having been produced by selective breeding in those countries to which the wild stock was imported. Birds bred in Holland are big specimens, slightly humped, with long legs and ruffled plumage. The Belgian variety is similar, for it, too, has a curious humped back, but the plumage in this type is smooth. English breeders have produced the Yorkshire, which is a long slender bird; the Lancashire, which is bigger but of normal shape; and the Norwich, which has a sort of cowl on its nape.

ATTRACTIVE SONG

It was not the beauty of the birds' plumage, or their graceful form which induced the first European visitors to the Canary Islands to capture specimens in the 16th century; the attraction was the bird's song, notable for its freshness and variety and considered by some people to be second in quality only to that of the nightingale. This is, of course, entirely a matter of taste, and there can be no rules about it.

Three other canaries which send connoisseurs into raptures (from left to right), the Scotch Fancy, the Norwich with its black cowl, and the Yorkshire. All of these are British bred.

The wild canary is not yellow like those with which we are familiar. It is a green-plumaged bird.

Among our native birds the greenfinch is most similar in type to the canary. It is about the same size and sings well. It thrives in captivity.

Two domestic canaries intent on constructing their nest. Their colours, as you can see, differ from the traditional yellow or golden. These small birds, even when living in cages, tend their offspring with great care.

As in the case of the nightingale, only the cock canary sings, and it has been claimed that the varieties bred by the Dutch and Belgians are the best performers.

Breeding canaries in captivity does not present any great difficulty as the birds adapt themselves very well to confinement. They will breed three or four times a year, and require no more than a simple nesting box placed in their cage. In this box the pair of birds will build their nest of cotton threads and feathers. The eggs require about thirteen days to hatch, and the young begin to fly after three weeks. A month later, they are able to feed themselves and are self-supporting.

LEARNING TO SING

It is at this time that breeders separate the young ones from the parents and isolate them. This helps to produce accomplished singers, for the young birds are placed one to a cage, and are allowed to hear only an adult male in perfect voice singing. The idea is that if they hear only the *maestro*, they will copy him.

As far as feeding is concerned, the canary is not difficult to please. During the growing period, the birds do very well on soaked bread and seed. Later, the birds will take almost every kind of seed, as well as lettuce and juicy fruits. They are especially fond of figs.

Canaries can be and often are, crossed with native birds of similar size and type, for example, the goldfinch. Young birds produced from such matings are referred to in Britain as mules, indicative of their infertility and inability to breed.

Through the centuries these small song-birds from the Canary Islands have had a large and devoted following. In many countries, and especially in Italy, singing competitions are organised at which diplomas are awarded to the best birds. The prices paid for these champion singers are often very high, but enthusiasts feel that the birds with the golden voices are worth the price. In Britain, canaries are exhibited by fanciers who compete with each other in producing the best specimens.

Giraffes

The neck of the giraffe, despite its length, has no more bones than the human neck.

Early comment on the giraffe was: " There ain't no such animal "—which is another way of saying that those who saw it for the first time could not believe their eyes.

Yet the animal was common enough in Roman times when the strangest and most bizarre species of tropical fauna, destined for circus games, turned up in the Levantine bestiaries. Later, the giraffe disappeared even from the memories of most Europeans, taking on the character of a mythical animal. Fantastic descriptions of them given by explorers were seldom believed. The animals were constantly confused with the unicorn, the non-existent monster which adorned the crests of medieval chivalry.

One of the first, perhaps the very first of these gentle animals to make its appearance in Europe in recent times was that owned by Lorenzo the Magnificent. The giraffe which was sent by the Pasha of Egypt to Charles X, King of France, and which travelled from Marseilles to Paris on foot, created such a sensation that for many months it was the subject of discussion in scientific journals and pamphlets.

Zoologically the giraffe is a ruminant, belonging to the great family of cud-chewing mammals which includes antelopes, deer, and the domestic ox. It is the tallest animal living in the world to-day. In the case of the male the distance between the ground and the top of its head may be eighteen feet or more. The female is considerably smaller, being around sixteen feet by this system of measurement.

The giraffe's head is very small in proportion to the size of its body and is elongated, with flexible lips which are both extensible and prehensile. The tongue, which is used to pull

Giraffes are still quite common throughout the Equatorial region of Africa, especially in Tanganyika and Rhodesia.

away the leafy growth from trees, is black and extremely long. On the forehead are two little horns covered with skin. In males there is a marked bone protuberance between them. The long neck, which is proverbial, is the most striking characteristic of the giraffe family. But, despite its great length, it is made up of only seven vertebræ, as in man himself. The vertebræ of the giraffe are cylindrical and very elongated.

DOWN BEHIND

All four legs of the giraffe are of the same length, but because of the slope of the back, and the strong muscular system of the neck, the fore legs appear to be considerably longer. The giraffe, in fact, looks " down behind ". Three toes are present, two of them forming a strong hoof similar to that of cattle. The mane is short and bristly, tawny or black in colour. The tail, which is relatively short, and ends in a tuft, is used by natives as a fly whisk. The giraffe's handsome coat shows considerable variation from region to region. Most commonly it is reddish, dark or even black, varigated with white or yellow, which gives it a mottled appearance. The belly is always white.

Not so very long ago giraffes were numerous throughout Equatorial and Southern Africa. Unfortunately, indiscriminate hunting by European settlers, from which they have suffered greatly, has drastically reduced their numbers. This hunting made a quick impact on the number of giraffes because they are not very prolific animals. As a result, they are not so often seen to-day, and their distribution is much more restricted than it was. Nowadays, the great national parks of Uganda and Rhodesia provide sanctuaries for them, and there they live more or less undisturbed because hunting is completely prohibited. In the national parks it is possible to observe giraffes with little difficulty.

There are two species of giraffe in Africa to-day—the Somaliland reticulated species, which lives in North Kenya

Here is a giraffe caught by a lasso. Before long it will be the inmate of some zoo.

and Somaliland; and the Common Giraffe, which is a native of East Africa. The Somali giraffes frequent low ground, seldom moving higher than the 3000 feet contour while the common giraffe habitually moves to twice that height. The common giraffe is usually about a foot smaller than the Somali species.

The main food of both species is the flat-topped acacia,

The giraffe is a swift runner and when young animals are required, they are chased in motor vehicles and caught by lasso.

59

the leafy growth of which they can reach easily with their long necks. Their great height also enables them to see long distances, even in thick bushy country, so that they receive plenty of warning of a hunter's approach. Once they break away their action warns other wild animals within a wide area. In areas where they are protected they become very tame and are often a nuisance to motorists when they block the roads. The only enemy of the giraffe in the wild state is the lion, which can kill the young.

Giraffes, when fighting, bang their necks together until one of them retreats after being knocked dizzy. When defending themselves against enemies, however, they use their feet—either cow-kicking with the hind legs or dabbing with the forefeet as red deer hinds will do when chasing a fox.

Giraffes live in small herds of twenty or thirty animals, although groups of fifty strong are not uncommon in Kenya. The most common size of herd is a dozen animals or less. Such herds are usually made up of younger age groups because the really old animals tend to live apart in isolation.

THE LONG NECK

There used to be a lot of discussion as to whether giraffes grew long necks to enable them to reach the tops of trees or whether they turned to feeding on the tops of trees because they had long necks. It is certainly true that they would find it extremely difficult to graze as cattle do, and you can get some idea of this if you watch a giraffe drinking, or when he does decide to pick something from the ground with his mouth. When he does either, he splays his front legs widely apart and arches his neck with great difficulty. The posture looks so uncomfortable that one realises immediately how completely adapted he is for browsing on trees.

The wide ears which fan out from under the horns, and the large mobile nostrils, indicate that the giraffe's hearing and sense of smell are highly developed. These compensate

him for his lack of offensive weapons and, together with his swiftness, enable him to escape from lions and man. The giraffe can run faster than any horse, with a gait which is peculiarly his own, and his jumping powers are tremendous. As with so many other " weaponless " animals the giraffe can defend itself vigorously when attacked or cornered. Its kick can knock down a wall, and the lion, despite its great power, rarely attempts to kill an adult giraffe.

In captivity (nowadays almost every important zoo has at least a pair of giraffes), the giraffe lives for up to twenty years under good conditions and management, and will breed readily in captivity. Yet many visitors to a zoo have the feeling that it is wrong to keep in a restricted enclosure this tall animal with the long neck and the sad-looking face, whose real home is the wide plateaux and forests of Africa.

UNGAINLY RELATIVE

A close relation of the giraffe is the Okapi, which stands about five and a half feet at the shoulder and has a much shorter neck and legs. The okapi, an ungainly animal, is found in the wet forests of the Eastern Congo. It is even more strikingly patterned than the giraffe, its body being almost purple in colour, its neck and face light brown, and its under-parts white, while there are several bars on its face.

Like other animals of retiring habits, okapis were for a long time considered much rarer than they really are. Because they live in dense forests they are not often seen, but they are not uncommon and are frequently killed for their meat and hides by African tribesmen. Despite the fact that the okapi in the wild state lives in tropical rain forests, it thrives in zoos, and in countries where the climate is completely different.

The okapi was " discovered " by modern science only sixty years ago, and is thought by many to be the survival from an earlier period—perhaps the forerunner of the giraffe as we know it to-day.

The wooden cages in which giraffes are transported have to be strong to stand up to their kicking.

Giraffes, probably because of their bizarre appearance, are always a great attraction for children at the zoo.

THE PASSERINE BIRDS

The passerines, or perching birds, form a vast family, and only a few common European species can be dealt with here.

Crows of one kind or another are common in Europe, and some species occur in most countries. Though generally noted for their black colour, not all members of the family are sombrely plumaged. The brightly-coloured jay is a notable exception. The magpie is white-bellied and white-shouldered, with long tail and wings of blue, bronze and green.

The largest of the crows is the raven, which is found practically throughout Europe except for Italy, the French Plain, and the Low Countries, part of central Europe and Scandinavia. An early nester, the raven prefers mountain crags, where its croaking can be heard throughout the year. In some localities the birds nest in trees. They feed largely on carrion, and in the Scottish deer forests large numbers of ravens move in during the stalking season to feed on the paunches and entrails of deer left on the hill. Often a neighbour of the golden eagle, the raven is a sore trial to the great bird of prey, harrying it for apparently no reason and driving it off viciously during the nesting season.

The Carrion Crow, which is all black, is absent from Ireland, Scandinavia, Eastern Europe, and the Mediterranean; but the Hooded Crow, which is black and grey, is found in Ireland, Scandinavia, Eastern Europe, Italy and the Balkans, and is generally absent from England. Yet these two species are considered to be mere geographical races of

The rook is the commonest of the crow family. It nests gregariously in high trees.

one species. Where their ranges overlap they interbreed from time to time, and hybrid offspring have been frequently observed and reported. Both species are largely scavengers, but they take small mammals of many kinds, small birds and nestlings. On grouse moors the hooded crow is a confirmed predator on grouse eggs.

The Rook, another black member of the family (with a white face) is a gregarious bird and a colonial nester. Nests are placed usually in the topmost branches of trees and a colony, once established, does not readily desert the rookery. Each year, early in March, the birds return to patch up old nests and build new ones and from then on, until after the young birds are in the branches, a rookery is a noisy place. Young rooks are commonly infested with parasites known as gapeworms, which give them a bronchial wheeze.

SMALLER CROWS

The Jackdaw is a small crow with a silver eye and a grey nape. Jackdaws may nest singly or colonially in holes in masonry, rocks, burrows in banks, or trees. Ruined buildings are a favourite site. Like rooks, jackdaws show no hesitation in nesting close to human habitations.

Magpies are distinctively plumaged. They are found all over Europe. The nest of the magpie is as distinctive as is the bird, being a bulky structure with a roof. It may be placed in a thorny hedge only a few feet from the ground, or high in the branches of a tall forest tree.

The jay is an alert, wary bird and is often referred to as the " watch-dog of the woods."

The nutcracker lives in coniferous forests in mountain areas. It is a member of the crow family.

The lesser grey shrike is an inhabitant of South and South-Eastern Europe.

The Jay is the most brightly coloured of all the crows, with brilliant sky-blue on its wings. It is a tree nester, an alert watch-dog of the woods, which betrays intruders at once, and it is found throughout Europe except for Northern Scandinavia and the extreme north of Scotland.

The Chough, which is a red-legged, red-beaked crow, is extremely rare in the British Isles, and is mostly found in Spain and the Mediterranean area.

The Nutcracker, which is found in Central and Eastern Europe and Southern Scandinavia, is about the size of a jackdaw but is brown in colour, speckled with white. The flight is jay-like. This species nests mainly in coniferous woods and mountain areas and is a colonial nester.

STARLINGS

The Common Starling is a well-known European bird, being widely distributed throughout the area except in Spain, Italy and along the Mediterranean coastline. This bird thrives equally well in town or country, nesting in buildings, corn stacks, nest-boxes and holes in trees. It is a first-class mimic, incorporating in its own song the notes of other birds, and individuals can give excellent renderings of the chuckling of fowls or the cry of the lapwing.

The Spotless Starling, which is found mainly where the common starling is not, is to the uninitiated almost indistinguishable from the common species.

The rock thrush breeds in rocky regions up to 8,000 feet.

The Rose-coloured Starling on the other hand, in its plumage of rose-pink with black head, wings and tail, and its obvious crest, is a very distinctive bird. It breeds in south-east Europe. Outside that area, its movements are unpredictable, and in autumn it shows a tendency to break out westward.

THE BUTCHER BIRDS

The shrikes are familiarly known as butcher birds because of their habit of impaling prey on thorns until it is required. In such a larder you may find, according to the size of the shrike, anything from bees to small birds or tree frogs.

The Great Grey Shrike, which is the largest of the family, is found in Spain, Northern and Eastern Europe. To the British Isles it is a straggler. This species will nest in bushes or tall trees and kills mice and lizards as well as small birds and insects. It has a habit of hovering and is also much given to tail-fanning.

The great grey shrike likes the covered country of woods or orchards or thick scrub. In the north of Spain it likes to nest on wooded river banks, where it may be seen perched in a tree watching for lizards, slow-worms or frogs.

The starling is well-known for its close association with man.

The Lesser Grey Shrike has a more restricted range than the great species. Its flight is direct and it hovers frequently. It prefers more open country, such as commons with scattered trees and bushes, and frequently nests in roadside trees.

The Red-backed Shrike is a summer visitor to England, nesting in the southern half of the country. Like its relatives, it impales small birds and insects on thorns. In England, the bird nests in bushes and other thick cover, and may be seen in hedgerows or perched on look-out post or tree, from which it pounces on its prey.

SPARROWS AND FINCHES

The sparrows of Great Britain and the Continent are similar in appearance, but the House Sparrow of Britain is as distinct from the Italian and Spanish species, as it is distinct from the Tree Sparrow. The house sparrow is found throughout Europe: the Italian Sparrow in Italy and also in Greece, the Spanish Sparrow in Spain; while the tree sparrow is found in most of Europe, and the Rock Sparrow in about the same areas as the Spanish sparrow. As a result, one has to be careful when looking at sparrows along the northern Mediterranean coast when trying to sort out which is which.

The common house sparrow is familiar in almost every town in the British Isles, nesting frequently about houses, under tiles, in holes in walls, or in ivy on walls. It also nests in trees, and when it does so is frequently assumed to be a tree sparrow when, in fact, it is merely a house sparrow nesting in a tree. Though sparrows have conical beaks adapted for crushing grain and weed seeds, the young birds in the nest are in the first instance fed on insect foods. Later they become as omnivorous as the parents, when they will take all kinds of grain and seeds and many kinds of fruit. Sparrows are frequent visitors to the bird table in winter when they will accept almost any food laid out for them.

Like the sparrow, the finches are birds with beaks specially adapted for crushing seed. The chicks, however, are fed animal food in the form of insects in the early stages.

In Britain, the most familiar finches are the Greenfinch, and Chaffinch, the Bullfinch and the Goldfinch.

The Hawfinch is confined almost entirely to England but is widely distributed in Europe. The Siskin, on the other hand, is found in Scotland and Ireland but not in England, and is absent from most of Mediterranean Europe and France.

The ring-ouzel is often referred to as the mountain blackbird.

The Linnet is distributed throughout the British Isles, but the Twite, sometimes known as the mountain linnet, is absent from most of England.

The Crossbills, which are forest finches, have crossed mandibles which enable them to rip pine cones with ease. As a British breeding bird, the crossbill is confined to Central and Northern Scotland, but in some years there are crossbill invasions, when great numbers of birds turn up in other parts of the country. In recent years, the crossbill has been extending its range in Scotland and is now nesting in considerable numbers far south of the Cairngorm area.

The Pine Grosbeak and the Scarlet Grosbeak, similar in appearance, are not natives of Britain but turn up occasionally as vagrants.

THE THRUSH FAMILY

In Britain, the commonest member of the thrush family is the Blackbird which is also found throughout Europe except Northern Scandinavia. In this species the male is black with an orange beak; the hen is sooty brown with a dark beak and shows the typical thrush mottlings on her breast. As a result she is frequently mistaken for a dark song-thrush. The cock blackbird has a rich, melodious voice, and is

The blue rock thrush is found in Spain and along the Mediterranean coast-line.

deservedly placed high on the list of song birds. In spring and summer he has a habit of singing at dusk, when his rich, flute-like notes are a delight to the ear.

Blackbirds nest two or three times in a season but the earlier clutches are often devoured by raiders like magpies, jays, and crows. The nest may be placed in a bush, a hedge, a wall, or even on the ground. In their first suit of feathers, young blackbirds are sooty-brown with mottled breasts, and resemble the adult hen.

In the nesting season, blackbirds feed themselves and their young almost entirely on earth worms, caterpillars, and adult insects. Earth worms, in fact, are fed to chicks in large numbers. Outside the breeding season the birds will turn to berries of many kinds, and in some areas do a certain amount of damage to fruit.

Also widely distributed, though absent from most of Spain and the Mediterranean coast line, is the Song Thrush, called in Scotland the Mavis. Its habits are similar to the blackbird's, but in the breeding season it is more conservative in its choice of nesting sites, preferring shrubs and hedgerows to walls and buildings. The eggs of the song thrush are bright blue, freckled with black. Unlike the blackbird and the other thrushes, the song thrush finishes her nest off with a plaster lining which she works smooth with her breast by turning round and round. Very occasionally the plaster

The golden oriole is a rare visitor to England.

Sparrows are common birds throughout Europe. The Italian sparrow, illustrated here, is very similar to the Spanish sparrow and the common sparrow of Britain. All sparrows are notable for their cheery chirruping.

The greenfinch is a common member of the finch family in Britain, easily recognised because of its distinctive plumage. The male illustrated here is a bright, dark green with a yellow wing band.

The fieldfare is a large Scandinavian thrush which moves southward in winter. From early September onwards large flocks of fieldfares are a common sight in the British Isles.

lining is omitted, while on some of the outer isles of Scotland the finished lining may be of moss. Young thrushes when fledged are pocket editions of their parents.

The Mistle Thrush is a larger and bolder bird than the song thrush, and in the nesting season will not hesitate to fly at human intruders, slapping with its wings, and knocking one's hat off one's head. This species prefers to nest in trees—usually on a high branch, sometimes in a crotch, but nests in bushes are not rare. In most years the mistle thrush is the earliest nester of the three.

THRUSH VISITORS

Besides the resident thrushes, Britain has visiting species. In summer we have the Ring Ouzel, often called the mountain blackbird, which has a conspicuous white gorget, more striking in the male than in the female. The ring ouzel likes mountains and moorlands and may be found nesting in old stone walls or on heather slopes. In Scotland, a favourite nesting site is under a boulder just above a sheep or deer path on a steep slope. This species is shy, and when disturbed at the nest, may fly right out of sight before pitching, returning stealthily after the intruder has gone.

The cock ring ouzel has a clear piping song and an alarm call reminiscent of the blackbird's.

In the breeding season the bird occurs in hilly and moorland areas of Scotland, Northern England, Wales and Ireland. It also nests in Norway, the mountains of Spain and southern Europe, except Italy.

In winter we have two common visitors, the Fieldfare and the Redwing, both of which nest in Scandinavia and in certain parts of Central and Eastern Europe. Fieldfares occur commonly in flocks from September to February or March; redwings are not such common visitors, and are more usually to be seen in much smaller groups. The redwing is easily identified by the chestnut slash on its flanks and by the buff striping round its eyes. The fieldfare is a large, striking thrush with grey head and rump, chestnut back, and near-black tail. When in flight, the grey rump and the white beneath the wings are very noticeable.

RARE VAGRANTS

To the British Isles the Golden Oriole is mainly a vagrant, but numbers of birds turn up in South-East England each year, and occasionally a pair nests there. As a result this species has been given special protection by law in Great Britain. On the Continent the bird frequents orchards, river banks and well-wooded parklands, and is seldom seen far from cover. The nest is usually near water, set in the forked branch of a tree. The male oriole is a handsome bird, brilliant yellow in colour with black wings and tail. The black tail is boldly edged with yellow. Female and young birds are yellowish green with dark wings. Orioles live in most parts of Europe except the extreme north and the Mediterranean islands.

The Rock Thrush and the Blue Rock Thrush are birds of Spain and the southern half of Europe. Both are haunters of rocky and desert regions. The rock thrush habitually nests high, from 3,000 to 8,000 feet; the blue rock thrush nests in rocks, cliffs and buildings.

In the rock thrush the tail is chestnut with a brown centre, while the male in summer has a slate blue head, neck, and mantle. The blue rock thrush is easily distinguished by his overall blue-grey plumage which, in winter, looks much darker.

THE FAMILIAR ROBIN

Few birds could be better known throughout Europe than the common Robin or Redbreast which, in Great Britain, is a familiar garden bird. In Britain, especially in winter but also at other times, robins habitually thrust themselves upon the notice of man, and are regular visitors to bird tables and kitchen windows. In many respects, the continental birds tend to be much shyer and wilder. While the British birds tend to make a habit of nesting in suitable gardens, continental birds show a preference for remoter woodlands and glades in deep forests. Robins have a very strongly developed territorial sense and, each autumn, individuals take over their chosen area, which they defend strongly against other robins. About the end of the year, the birds begin to pair and territories are shared. British robins habitually rear two broods in a season and sometimes three, and it is not unknown for them to be reared in the same nest.

During the nesting season, robins not only seek out gardens and lanes near houses; they will invade the actual buildings. Thus one frequently finds nests in tool-sheds, potting-sheds, and such places, as well as jacket pockets, and old kettles thrown in the rubbish heap. At this time the birds are not averse to being watched at close quarters, so that the most casual observer can stand close by observing them. The cock bird feeds the hen when she is brooding and helps to rear the brood. When his hen goes on to lay her second clutch he will be seen taking care of the first family. It is a good plan if you wish to keep track of the robins in your neighbourhood or those in your garden to place coloured rings on the legs of the young birds before they leave the nest. However, if you have no experience of ringing birds you should do this only under the supervision of an experienced person.

The so-called American robin is ten inches long; the upper parts being dark and the entire breast brick-red in colour. Male and female resemble each other very closely, but the male bird has a blacker head. The American robin is far more thrush-like than our own much smaller bird. It frequents woodland and scrub and, like our own blackbird, is much given to nesting near human habitations. This New World bird is a rare vagrant to many parts of Europe.

THE POETS' BIRD

Poets have written, and continue to write about the song of the Nightingale, which is a common enough bird in Western and Southern Europe, but rare north of the English Midlands. The bird has, however, recently nested in Scotland. The song of the nightingale is notable for its variety of notes, delivered with great power, but there are many harsh phrases in its song. The nightingale draws attention to itself by singing at night when other birds are silent. Its song is not so noticeable during the day when it has so much competition from other species. Many people consider the blackbird a finer singer than the nightingale. Others consider the Sedge Warbler or the Blackcap in the same class. None of this alters the fact that descriptions of the nightingale's song as " unique " are justified. The plumage of the nightingale is inconspicuous, the bird being more or less uniformly brown—russet above and grey-brown below with a suggestion of brighter red on the tail. Its movements suggest the robin but it is not such a dumpy bird. It is more retiring than the robin and, except when singing, tends to stay low in cover. The nightingale nests in woods, thickets, or roadside spinneys where there is plenty of ground cover.

The American robin is really a member of the thrush family.

The song thrush, or mavis, is a notable songster.

The pied wheatear is easily distinguished from other wheatears.

Arrival time in England is from April onwards, and nesting begins early in May. Only one brood is reared each season, and the chicks are tended by both parents in and out of the nest.

The Bluebird of eastern North America is only a little larger than the common sparrow. It is also the only blue bird with a red breast. Its song consists of three or four notes.

THE EARLY BIRD

Wheatears are migrants which begin to arrive in Britain in the early part of March, so that it is not unusual, when the winter has been long, to see them skipping over the snow drifts. The common wheatear frequents rocky hillsides, high moors, barren and upland pastures, inland or on the sea's edge. The birds draw attention to themselves by their *chacking* call. The cock is a distinctive bird, grey above and white tinged with buff below, with black wings, black patches around the eyes, and a grey-and-black tail. These bold markings do not make him as conspicuous as you might think, for when he is flitting among rocks or when he perches on a grey, lichened boulder, he becomes almost invisible.

Wheatears may be found nesting in rabbit burrows, rock clefts, old walls, or among scree. When the nest is in a burrow system, the fledged young may be seen appearing at several exits when the parents arrive with food. During feeding spells they will wait at the mouths of such burrows, but when disturbed they will go below until called out again. The wheatear normally rears only one brood in a season but will produce a second clutch of eggs if it loses the first one. The common wheatear is found all over Europe and winters in Arabia and North Africa.

The Pied Wheatear, which breeds in Rumania, is only a vagrant to Scotland and Heligoland and Italy. Females were recorded in Scotland in 1909, and in 1916, on the Isle of May in Orkney.

The Black Wheatear has been recorded in England as a rare vagrant. Normally it breeds in Spain and the Mediterranean area as far as Italy.

WHERE THE GORSE GROWS

The Stonechat is common in Europe. In the British Isles many birds are resident while others appear to move out after the nesting season. This is not a bird of arable country, preferring, rather, waste-ground and gorse-covered commons, or stony hillsides, especially near the sea. If there are stonechats in an area you will find them where there is gorse, because the species seems to prefer this kind of cover to any other. The male stonechat has a black head and white patches on the sides of his face. He has also a white wing patch and a white rump. In breeding plumage his chest is bright chestnut.

Stonechats are quick-moving, nervous little birds, which are ever bobbing and flicking their tails. They are also very vocal. They like perching on the topmost twigs of gorse bushes or other vantage points where they may be heard scolding incessantly.

The nest is usually built in the bottom of a gorse bush or other such cover, most frequently touching the ground but sometimes a foot or two above it. Ground nests have a distinct runway leading to them. Egg-laying commonly begins in April, and breeding continues throughout the season, as many as three broods sometimes being reared. Although the hen bird incubates alone, leaving the eggs to feed herself, the chicks are cared for by both sexes. There are isolated records of the male bird taking a turn on the eggs. Young and adult feed almost entirely on insects although seeds are occasionally eaten.

The Whinchat is less conservative in choice of habitat than the stonechat, and may be found in rough pastures, lowland meadows, marshes and hedges, as well as on hillsides. It has the stonechat's habit of perching on the topmost twig of bushes, but will also perch in trees. In the autumn, whinchats can sometimes be seen in family parties, when they will visit arable fields. This bird tends to be most active very late in the evening.

The whinchat is absent from much of Ireland, most of Spain, and all of Italy and Greece. It is, however, generally distributed in Scotland and England. In Britain the bird is a summer resident, the first birds putting in appearances at the beginning of April.

The nesting season is in the second half of May and into June. As in the case of the stonechat, the hen alone incubates the eggs, but the young are fed by both parents. In England, two broods are sometimes reared, but in Scotland single broods appear to be the rule.

The common robin is the bird emblem of Great Britain.

The nightingale is the most noted of all bird singers.

THE RHINOCEROS

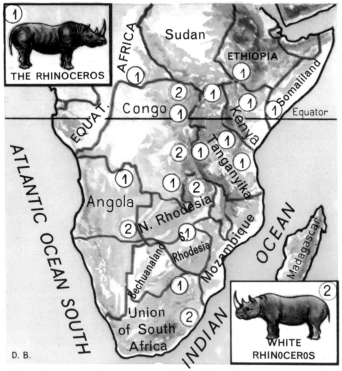

THE RHINOCEROS

WHITE RHINOCEROS

D. B.

The rhinoceros is represented in Africa by two types, the black and the white, both of which are found south of the Sahara desert.

Rhinoceroses, because of the structure of their skulls, are grouped with the horses and tapirs, although it would be difficult to imagine anything less horse-like than the rhinoceros with its short legs, barrel body, thick hide and horned snout.

It seems incredible that in this modern age the rhinoceros

should still be hunted—even relentlessly persecuted—because of the supposed therapeutic value of its blood and horn and other parts of its body. The Chinese are blamed for starting this superstition. Be that as it may, the body of the rhinoceros is so valuable that poachers find it profitable to hunt the animal despite the protection afforded it and the heavy penalties imposed on those who kill it. Rhinoceros horn, among the superstitious, is considered a cure for many ills, though in fact it has no known therapeutic value. But the magic of the rhinoceros horn is still believed in over great areas of the East. The horn is composed entirely of

O. BERNI

The Sumatran rhinoceros has two horns on its snout, one placed behind the other. It is the smallest and hairiest species. The greatest recorded length of the front horn is $32\frac{1}{2}$ inches.

The Javan rhinoceros is a smaller and more slender animal than the Indian rhinoceros. It is hairless and almost black in colour. The single horn is from 9-11 inches in length and is often absent in females.

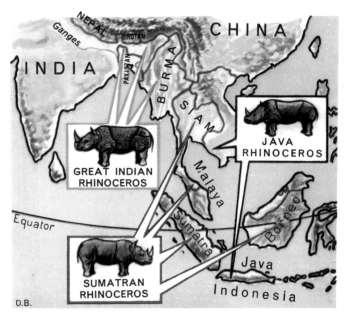

A map to show the distribution of the Indian rhinoceros, the Javan rhinoceros and the Sumatran rhinoceros.

they were much more widely distributed over the Old World and were found even in Siberia. The Siberian species, now extinct, was the only one which carried a single horn in the middle of its forehead. All rhinoceroses are active, powerful animals, fit to defend themselves against almost all potential enemies.

The great Indian rhinoceros and the white rhinoceros of Africa, weigh about two tons and are as tall as a policeman. The smallest species is the Sumatran, which weighs less than a ton and is about the height of a red deer stag. Between these two, in size and weight, comes the rhinoceros of Java. Persistent persecution has made the Indian rhinoceros a scarce animal. Despite all the protection afforded it, it is still relentlessly poached, mainly for its supposed therapeutic value. The blood is collected in tiny bottles and fetches high prices. The carcass of the animal in India may be worth as much as 2000 rupees.

agglutinated hairs, and it would be difficult to imagine anything less therapeutic than hair. Yet powdered horn is greatly in demand, and some people even believe that holding a horn in the hand is beneficial, like the lucky rabbit's foot.

REPUTATION FOR SAVAGERY

Rhinoceroses to-day are confined to Asia and Africa and vary, according to species, from a ton to two tons in weight. Tremendously strong and powerful animals, they have long had a reputation for savagery which derives from the fact that a wounded rhinoceros will charge his tormentor with great fury. The belief still persists that the hide of the rhinoceros is like armour plating and proof against a bullet from a modern rifle. The skin, in fact, is pliable during life and toughens and hardens after the beast is dead. It can be pierced by a rifle bullet.

There are five species of rhinoceros in the world to-day, three of them being Asian and two African. At one time

The Indian rhinoceros is the largest species found in Asia. It can reach a length of 12 feet, plus two feet of tail and will stand over six feet tall at the shoulder. The skin is divided into the so-called " armour-plating " by deep skin folds. The length of the horn in this species is about one foot long, but twice that length has been recorded.

The African rhinoceros differs from the Asiatic types in having no " armour-plating." There are two species in Africa, the black and the white, both of which have two horns placed one behind the other on the snout. Rhinoceroses are mostly nocturnal in habits—they feed on leaves and grass, and frequent either open country, or scrubland near water.

The Tube-Noses

The term tube-nose is often used to describe a group of birds known scientifically as Procellariiformes. The families making up the group are the petrels, shearwaters, and albatrosses which are oceanic birds ranging in size from the very small to the very large. They have tubular nostrils on top of the culmen. The horny covering of the bill is usually clearly marked off in plates surrounded by grooves.

Of the small petrels the best known is probably the storm petrel, usually illustrated dancing on or skimming over the waves of the sea. Petrels are pelagic birds, which means that their lives are spent at sea except when they come ashore to breed. They are only found inland when driven by severe storms, and this happened a few years ago when storm-driven Leach's petrels and some storm petrels were picked up dead or dying in many parts of Scotland, including the central Highlands.

The storm petrel is about six inches long, sooty-coloured, long-winged and white-rumped, closely resembling the house martin. During the breeding season, it comes ashore to turfy or boulder-strewn island slopes. It breeds in colonies varying in size from a few pairs up to great numbers, but the nests are not always close to each other.

NO NESTING MATERIAL

Individual birds excavate their own nesting burrows in peaty soil. More frequently, the nest is placed under boulders, in stone walls, or among loose stones. As a rule, no nesting material is used, but occasionally the birds use a grass or reed lining. One egg is usual. Where two are found in a nest, one of them is usually an addled egg from the previous year. Both sexes take their turn on the eggs, incubating for two or three days at a time. The chick is fed by both parents by regurgitation, but the parents' visits are irregular, and the chick may be untended for two or even

three days at a time. The fledging period is between eight and nine weeks.

Though active by day when at sea, storm petrels are entirely nocturnal during the nesting season, flying into their nests after dark. The food of the storm petrel appears to be mainly marine plankton or floating oil, but stomach examination has shown that the birds also eat fish liver, fish, small molluscs, and crustaceans. The thick, oily contents of the stomach are regurgitated for the young, but may be ejected by the nesting bird in the face of an intruder.

The storm petrel ranges from the eastern North Atlantic to the Mediterranean, and breeds in Iceland, Northern France, the coast of Spain, and many Mediterranean areas. Its range extends to Africa, the Red Sea, and the eastern coast of North America.

LIKE A SWALLOW

Leach's fork-tailed petrel is a larger bird, being about eight inches in length with a distinctly forked tail. It breeds in parts of North America, Greenland, Ireland, and the Faroes, as well as many parts of the Pacific. Though white-rumped, the white patch is split down the middle by grey feathers. This species is a buoyant and accomplished flyer which can dart like a swallow or glide like a shearwater.

For nesting purposes, it frequents the same kind of habitat as the storm petrel, but in America will also breed in woods, nesting among scrub or tree roots. The nest is placed in a burrow in peaty ground or under boulders. The nest chamber is sometimes lined with dry grass, reeds and moss. Like the storm petrel, Leach's lays only one egg, on which both sexes take their turn. Incubating birds may sit for four days or more without being relieved. During this period they do not leave the nesting burrow and go without food. The chick is fed at irregular intervals by both parents, and

The light-mantled sooty albatross, is ash-grey in colour, with a sooty face. It is darkest around the eyes and has a pronounced, broken white eye ring.

The wandering albatross is the largest bird of the ocean, having a wing span of 11 feet. Its colour is mainly white, but it has black wing tips.

The Manx shearwater is dark above and white below, which distinguishes it from all other members of the family.

then, when fledged, is deliberately neglected so that it is compelled to leave the nesting burrow and fend for itself.

The stomach content is like that of the storm petrel, food being derived from marine plankton and from the excreta of whales and from marine mammals. Small fish, crustaceans and molluscs are also eaten.

The Madeiran forked-tail petrel, which frequents the Atlantic and Pacific oceans, has a less obviously forked tail than **Leach's** petrel, and a white band across its rump. The two species are, however, extremely difficult to separate on sight. In addition, they closely resemble each other in habits. One possible help to identification is that the Madeiran species habitually follows ships, while **Leach's** petrel does not.

OTHER PETRELS

Similar in size is Wilson's petrel which breeds on cliffs and hill-tops and the islands of the Antarctic. It closely resembles the storm petrel.

The Frigate petrel, about eight inches in length, is an

***Leach's** fork-tailed petrel is about 8 inches in length. It is distinguished from the storm petrel by its fork tail and greater size.*

Atlantic and Australasian species which has only been twice recorded in the British Isles. It is an erratic flyer with unusually long legs which dangle conspicuously when the bird is treading water.

The Kermadec petrel is a much bigger bird, measuring about fourteen inches in length. It breeds in the sub-tropical zone of the South Pacific. Vast colonies form at nesting time on Kermadec and Lord Howe Islands, where they breed among rocks and bushes. Burrows are not used, the nest being placed on the ground in the shelter of ferns or other such cover.

The Capped petrel is larger than the Kermadec. It is a rare species which formerly bred in many parts of the New World, but there are no available accounts of its nesting habits.

The Fulmar petrel, about eighteen inches in length, has received much attention from ornithologists in recent years, and " The Fulmar " by James Fisher is the most detailed and exhaustive work on the species yet available.

A FOLLOWER OF SHIPS

The fulmar's breeding range extends from Baffin Land to

The fulmar petrel has spread spectacularly in recent years and is now found right round the coasts of Britain.

Novaya Zemlya. It has also occurred in the Baltic area, and south to Portugal and Madeira as a wanderer. In the British Isles the fulmar formerly bred only on the island of St. Kilda, which is now uninhabited and a nature reserve. It first bred in the Shetlands in 1878. In recent years its spread round the British coasts has been spectacular. At one time it was thought that the spread was due to the fact that predation by St. Kildans had ceased, but it has been clearly shown that there is no connection between the depopulation of St. Kilda and the spread of the fulmar.

In superficial appearance, the fulmar is rather like a gull, but the narrow wings without black tips are a distinguishing feature. Its flight is also quite distinctive, consisting of long glides on stiffly extended wings, with intervals of flapping like the shearwater's. It has a habit of banking steeply with the lower wing almost touching the water. It habitually follows ships.

On the island of St. Kilda more than 20,000 pairs of fulmars come each year to breed. Steep slopes and coastal cliffs are favoured for breeding, but occasionally pairs will be found nesting in buildings. Most nests are on the coast

The frigate petrel is an accidental visitor to Britain. The entire under-surfaces of wings and body are white.

The Great shearwater, 18 inches long, breeds on Tristan da Cunha in the South Atlantic. It is pelagic.

but, in some parts of Europe, breeding colonies have established themselves twenty miles from the sea. The single egg may be laid on bare rock; more often it is in a hollow of some kind or under an overhang. Both sexes sit on the egg for periods of about four days. The young are brooded and fed by both parents at irregular intervals. The chick is apparently fed only once a day, but there is a possibility that the male feeds it by day while the hen does so during the night. The chick is fed by regurgitation.

The food of the fulmar petrel varies slightly according to area. In the Arctic it lives to a large extent on floating material such as oil and blubber from the carcasses of whales and seals. It will also take dead or wounded birds. In warmer seas it will feed on fish, fish offals, crustaceans and molluscs. It has been seen drinking oil floating on the surface of the sea and has been recorded eating dead birds.

THE MANX SHEARWATER

The Manx shearwater is fourteen inches long, black above and white below, and is resident in Britain. It breeds in the Scilly Isles, off the coast of Wales, in the Orkney and Shetland Islands, the Inner and Outer Hebrides. There are colonies on Eigg, Canna, and St. Kilda, and a remarkable mountain-top colony on Rhum.

At sea, the Manx shearwater flies low over the waves on rigidly extended wings, tilting from side to side as it weaves and circles, and almost touching the water with the tip of the lower wing. During the breeding season the birds gather off-shore in daylight, just before sunset, flying in to the breeding grounds after dark. The flight inland usually takes place two hours after sunset. On nights of bright moonlight most birds do not fly in at all. On arrival, the birds mill about in the air uttering their weird cries. They leave the breeding grounds again about half-past two in the morning. The nest is placed at the end of a burrow excavated by the birds, and where large colonies nest the ground becomes honeycombed. Male and female take spells on the egg for periods up to four days or more at a time. When the chick hatches, it is visited and fed by the parents nightly. When it is fledged, it is deserted by them and it may remain in the burrow for a period of up to a fortnight before taking to the sea to fend for itself.

The Balearic shearwater is a vagrant to Britain, but breeds in the Mediterranean area. The Madeiran Little shearwater, which is about eleven inches long, breeds in Madeira and the Canaries, while the Great shearwater, which is eighteen inches long, breeds only in Tristan da Cunha, although it ranges over the entire Atlantic ocean and is a summer and autumn visitor to the British Isles. It turns up most frequently in the seas off the Hebrides, the west coast of Ireland, and Devon and Cornwall.

The Mediterranean shearwater, which is about the same size, has appeared only once in Britain—in Sussex. It breeds along the Mediterranean coast and from the south of Spain to North Africa.

The Sooty shearwater, which is slightly smaller, is an occasional autumn visitor to Britain. It breeds in the Southern Hemisphere in the area of New Zealand.

OCEAN WANDERER

Albatrosses are probably best known from Coleridge's poem " The Ancient Mariner ", and are looked upon as the great wanderers of the ocean. They are distinguished from other sea birds by their enormous size, great wing span, and gliding flight. The Black-browed albatross has a wing span of nearly eight feet.

Like petrels and shearwaters, albatrosses are pelagic birds, coming to land only to breed. The rest of their life is spent at sea gliding above the waves on outstretched, almost motionless wings.

The black-browed species has turned up only once in Britain: in Cambridgeshire. Its breeding range is in the seas of the Southern Hemisphere. Outside the breeding season it turns up occasionally in the North Atlantic. It nests in colonies, sometimes small, sometimes large. Large colonies may number up to many thousands of birds. Colonies frequent marine islands and nests may be found up to the 1800 foot contour.

The nest is made of mud, which is dug up round the chosen site. In this way the nest when completed is surrounded by a trench. Because the same site is used year after year, the nest will reach a height of three feet. Where mud is not available, dry earth and moss are used for nest building. One egg is the rule, but two have been recorded. The breeding season is in October, November, and December. The female black-browed albatross undertakes the entire task of incubating and is fed by the male on the nest, which she does not leave throughout the period.

DUCKS

Man has domesticated the goose and the duck, and now has many varieties kept either for egg production or for their carcasses, but it is with the wild relatives of the duck that we are concerned here.

Ducks belong to the same family as geese, and are usually easy enough to distinguish. The popular distinction, however, cannot be maintained scientifically. Ducks are much greater water-lovers than geese. They are smaller, have narrower wings and shorter necks. In flight their wing beats are much more rapid. In ducks, there is usually considerable variation in plumage between male and female—that is between drake and duck—whereas in geese and swans the sexes are alike. In ducks, the males take very little part in the rearing of the family.

The garganey is very slightly larger than the common teal. This duck breeds in long grass or other vegetation, near water.

Ducks are divided into several groups. First of all there are the surface feeders which take most of their food in shallow water; then there are the diving ducks which have short legs set far back on their body and are stouter birds than the surface feeders. They are mostly birds of the open water and some live an entirely marine life in the winter-time. Lastly, there are the sawbills, which are recognised by their tapering, slender bills and the conspicuous crest of feathers at the back of their heads.

GOOSE-LIKE DUCKS
A duck which is goose-like in many ways is the Shelduck, with its plumage of black, white and chestnut, and bright red bill. This species likes low-lying, muddy coasts or estuaries, and sandy bays. During the breeding season it will often leave the waterside and nest in thickets on hillsides, many miles inland. Shelducks will not often be seen singly. They are sociable, and during the breeding season, duck, drake, and their brood may join up with others until there are several families living together.

The shelduck's routine is determined by the rise and fall of the tides. When the tide is ebbing the birds feed in the wake of the receding water and sometimes they can be seen tap-dancing to bring up the worms. When the tide is in, the birds will rest on the shore or on sand-dunes. It is not unusual for the shelduck to up-end in water like the mallard when feeding.

The shelduck's favourite nesting site is in a rabbit burrow or other such hole, but quite often it will be among rocks, sometimes in open heather, and sometimes in gorse or brambles. The nest is composed of the bird's own down mixed with some grass and, where it is in a burrow, it may be from six feet to eight feet from the entrance. The young shelducks, when they leave the nest, are looked after by both parents, but when several families unite, as they do

where the birds are plentiful, the family identities become lost.

The Ruddy Shelduck, which is an orange-brown bird with black tail and wings, is only a rare vagrant to the British Isles, breeding in Spain, the Middle East, Russia, and into Tibet and Mongolia, spending the winter in Arabia, India, China and elsewhere.

DUCKS WILD AND TAME
To most people the most familiar duck is unquestionably the Mallard, often referred to simply as " wild duck ". The mallard will nest almost anywhere where there is water, will interbreed freely with domestic ducks, and breed in captivity itself. Where mallard drakes interbreed with domestic ducks the most notable effect is on the egg production of the female offspring: it falls below the normal for the domestic variety. Mallards bred in captivity become perfectly tame and, apart from using their powers of flight, behave in much the same way as ordinary domestic ducks. Large numbers are reared in this country each year for sporting purposes.

Crossbred domestic ducks are frequently like mallards. They differ only from them in point of size, the wild duck being as a rule smaller.

The mallard drake has a dark green head with a white collar. His breast is purplish brown and his back pale, vermiculated grey. The female is mottled brown and buff. Both sexes have a purple speculum edged with black and bordered with white. In eclipse plumage the male resembles the duck. The mallard duck usually nests in thick cover under bushes, or in hedge bottoms or among rushes, but she will also nest in holes in trees, on islands, and in ruins, and even in the old nests of other birds. In a domesticated state the mallard will breed twice in the year; in the wild state she probably breeds only once. However, in some seasons even the wild birds nest early and late, and it is not unlikely that a duck which lays her first clutch in February may breed again before the autumn. Young mallards leave the nest when their down is dry and are tended mainly by the duck, although there are many cases where the drake will be seen in company with the female. British-bred mallards are almost entirely sendentary. Abroad, the species breeds throughout Europe into Finland and Russia as well as Asia, right into Japan. It also breeds in North Africa and the Middle East and in North America.

LESSER DUCKS
Rather smaller than the mallard is the Gadwall, which breeds in certain parts of England and Scotland and has bred in Ireland. The bird appears to be increasing in numbers and spreading its range in the British Isles. Abroad,

it is widely distributed over much the same area as the mallard.

The drake gadwall is a grey/brown bird with black tail, and has dark and light crescent markings on his breast. He has a white speculum, dark grey bill and orange/yellow legs. This species usually nests in very thick cover close to water. The nest, built by the duck, is composed of down mixed with grass or sedges. The nesting season is late May and early June, and the duck alone incubates. The young are taken to the water by the duck after their down is dry, and there is no evidence that the male takes any part in looking after the family.

The Common Teal, which is a small duck about fourteen inches in overall length, is well known and distinctive. Its size alone distinguishes it from all other European ducks except the garganey. The teal is a fast-flying, active duck which rises almost vertically when flushed and swerves and wheels when in flight. The teal breeds on dry ground among bracken, heather, or gorse, but will also be found in pollarded willows. The nest is composed of dead leaves, bracken and down. Though the duck alone incubates the eggs, the drake often helps with the young.

The Green-winged Teal has turned up only occasionally in the British Isles, its real home being the New World. It breeds in Alaska down to California, in Mexico and parts of the United States. The males resemble the common teal but do not have the horizontal white stripe on their sides and have a vertical white mark on the side of the breast in front of the wing. The females are indistinguishable.

The Blue-winged Teal is also a New World species which appears only rarely as a vagrant in the British Isles.

The Garganey looks the same size as our common teal and is, in fact, only slightly larger. It is an uncommon breeder in parts of England, and has bred in Scotland. In Europe it breeds north to Iceland and Sweden and into Asia. The main feature which distinguishes the garganey drake from the teal drake is the broad white band which extends from the eye to the nape.

WHISTLING CALL

A larger duck than any of the teals is the Wigeon. The drake has a chestnut head and a white mark on his flanks. His body is mostly grey. His whistling call, which is uttered with the beak open, is most distinctive and should identify the wigeon drake at all times. He is a rapid flyer, though not as swift as the teal, and rises straight up from the water in twisting, swerving flight.

The wigeon breeds on moorlands, rough pastures and bracken-covered slopes, and the nest is usually built among heather or bracken, and lined with grass mixed with feathers. The breeding season is in May. The duck incubates alone, and is rejoined by the drake after she has led her ducklings to the water. Originally introduced to Scotland, the wigeon has spread its range and now breeds in many parts of Scotland and certain parts of England.

The American wigeon drake is easily distinguished from the common wigeon drake by his grey head and white crown. The habits of the two species are similar, except that the American species shows a greater liking for fresh water. This species breeds on the lakes of North Dakota where there are no trees and on high ground in Alaska in the shelter of conifers.

The American wood duck, or Carolina duck, is a great favourite on ornamental waters.

The wigeon breeds on moors, marshes, islets and lochs. In winter it is mainly a sea duck.

The teal is the smallest European duck. It breeds on moors and marshes, often far from water.

The mandarin duck, introduced into Europe as an ornamental species, now breeds wild in many places, including England.

One of the most striking ducks is the Shoveller, with his great spatulate bill, which is very obvious when the birds are at close quarters on the water. In addition, the drake is boldly plumaged, with dark green head, black breast, and vermiculated grey upper parts. The duck is dull brown except for the area about the bill, cheeks and throat, which is near white.

The Common Pochard breeds in Europe as far north as Southern Sweden and Germany. It also breeds in Russia, Asia and from the south of Spain into Algeria and Tunisia.

The Red-crested Pochard is only a rare vagrant to the British Isles. The drake has a crimson bill and a chestnut head.

A common species in certain parts of England and Wales, and in the West of Scotland, is the Tufted Duck, most distinctive in its contrasting plumage of black and white. The drake has a tuft from which the species derives its name. This duck likes to nest on islands on large lakes, although at times it will be found on quite small ponds. Sometimes large numbers of tufted ducks nest close together. The breeding season is usually in June when the duck will lay up to fourteen eggs in a hollow lined with grass or rushes, thickly padded with down. When the ducklings leave the nest they are at first fed by the duck, who dives for them, but within a few hours of leaving the nest the ducklings are able to dive for themselves. Only one brood is reared in a season.

The muscovy duck is widely kept as an ornamental fowl. It often roosts well off the ground.

The shoveller duck is a surface feeder which frequents marshes and ponds.

FAMOUS FOR THEIR DOWN

Ducks famous for the quality of their down are the eiders, and the Common Eider provides the down for the more expensive, lightweight sleeping-bags used by mountaineers and others. This duck nests chiefly on islands near the coast or along the foreshore in the western isles of Scotland. However it will be found nesting inland and even on hillsides. This is also the case in Iceland where the birds may be found on river banks many miles from the sea. The nest, which is built by the duck, is thickly lined with down and feathers. The usual clutch of eggs is from four to six but there is great variation in clutch size, and up to ten eggs have been recorded. Where more appear in one nest, this is usually the result of two ducks laying together. The common eider nests in Europe as far south as France and Holland, and in north Russia.

A smaller species is Steller's eider which has been recorded only twice in England and breeds in Siberia, Alaska and northern Finland.

Bigger than Steller's eider and almost equal in size to the common species, is the King Eider. The king eider male is readily distinguished from the common eider drake by his black back and orange bill, apart from the broad shield which forms a conspicuous knob on his face during the breeding season. It resembles that of the mute swan, rises level with the bird's crown and is bordered with black feathers. The king eider is a rare vagrant to the British Isles, breeding in certain parts of northern Europe, Asia and North America.

THE SAWBILLS

Goosanders, mergansers, and smews are the so-called sawbills. In these ducks, the bill is narrow and slender and the upper mandible does not overlap the lower. Along the edges of both mandibles are saw-like sharp teeth directed slightly backward, from which the group derives its name.

The Goosander is twenty-six inches in overall length, three inches longer than the common Red-breasted Merganser and the largest species in the group. The drake has a bottle-green head, white breast and sides, and black back. The head is not noticeably crested. The bill is blood red. The flight of the goosander is typical of that of the merganser, the bird travelling close to the water and following almost every bend of a river, although at times it will fly high. In Britain, generally speaking, wooded areas are preferred for nesting, but abroad the goosander will be found breeding far beyond the tree limit. Some nests are close to water and the same site may be used year after year. A very common site is inside a hollow tree.

In the case of the red-breasted merganser, the drake has a chestnut breast and a striking crest. He has the bottle-green head and the red bill of the goosander. In the breeding season mergansers frequent rivers and lochs on the sea coast. Unlike the goosander, which nests only beside fresh water, the red-breasted merganser nests on islands, sea lochs and estuaries, as well as inland. In the case of this species, the nest is usually on the ground under cover among rocks, or a hole under tree roots. The bird is widely distributed in the British Isles and breeds in Europe to North Sweden and North Finland as well as in parts of Russia and North America.

The Hooded Merganser, a North American species, which winters in Cuba and Mexico, is a very rare vagrant to the British Isles, less than half a dozen specimens having been certainly recorded.

The Smew, which is about sixteen inches long, has a shorter beak than the other sawbills. The adult drake is mainly white plumaged but has a black patch on his face. The smew is an uncommon winter visitor to the British Isles, but does nest in many parts of Europe and Asia and is found occasionally in North Africa and Egypt.

GEESE

Geese, ducks, and swans belong to the same large family, representatives of which are found all over the world. Though they differ considerably, and sometimes markedly, in appear- *ance, it is not always easy to tell a swan from a goose or a goose from a duck. It is impossible to maintain any strict scientific division between the groups.*

The geese most familiar to Europeans are the greys: for example the Greylag goose, the Bean, and the Pink-foot. Large numbers of these birds hailing from Arctic areas, winter in other parts of Europe down to the Mediterranean or North Africa. In some years one species will be found predominant in a given area; then for a short period its place may be taken by another. Similarly, the numbers of wintering geese are subject to great fluctuation over the years, and in some years an area may have no wintering geese at all. The reasons for these fluctuations are not understood.

Perhaps the most familiar species in this country is the greylag goose which breeds in Iceland, Scandinavia, the Baltic States, Russia and Poland. Two hundred years ago the greylag was breeding in Yorkshire and other parts of England and Scotland. Nowadays, British breeding birds are to be found in the North of Scotland and in the Outer Islands, but not in great numbers.

THE GREY GEESE

Unlike the other grey geese, the greylag will be found nesting on small marine islands, but its main habitat is the moor and loch country of the far north. Outside the breeding season the species flocks to marshy grasslands, bogs, moors and estuaries. At this time the flocks will flight to stubble fields and other cultivated areas to eat grass, grain and potatoes left over at harvest time. A flock of geese feeding by day in open fields is difficult to approach and it has often been said that the birds deliberately post sentinels; but this is perhaps reading too much into observed geese behaviour.

At any given moment some geese will be walking about or feeding with their heads down, while others will be standing upright watching. The position of individual birds is continually changing, and the most that can be said is that the birds with their heads up are sentinels for the moment; but there is nothing to suggest organisation or the delegation of this function to individual birds in the flock.

Greylag goose in flight. Note the regular chevron formation adopted by these birds. Greylag geese fly south in autumn and north in the spring, and their flight calls have been likened to the music of fox hounds.

The greylag goose breeds on northern moors, marshes and islets. In winter it frequents grasslands, arable fields and estuaries, and in some parts of the country its depredations on young grass are quite serious.

Geese feeding. It has often been said that the wild geese post sentinels when feeding. The truth seems to be that at any moment individual birds can be seen standing with their heads up.

The greylag goose is the largest species. It has no black on its bill, and the forewing and rump are pale grey. The colour of the forewing is noticeable in flight, or during wing-stretching when the bird is on the ground.

Scottish greylags breed on heather moors or islands in fresh-water lochs. The nest is built of heather, moss and grass, and liberally mixed with down and small feathers. Eggs usually number from four to six. In Scotland, the laying season begins in April. In other parts of Europe, however, the season is earlier. The goose broods the eggs by herself but the gander is always in the vicinity. The goslings are able to pick up food as soon as they leave the nest and are looked after by both parents.

Greylag geese normally feed by day on land, although birds will sometimes be seen in shallow water up-ending like ducks. Where the birds are constantly shot at, however, they will reverse their routine—resting by day and feeding by night.

WHITE-FRONTS

The White-fronted Goose is a smaller bird than the greylag,

The white-fronted goose breeds sociably in the tundra. It is smaller and darker than the greylag.

The bean goose is browner and usually darker than the other "grey" geese. It is also less vocal.

easily recognisable by the white patch on its face and the black barring on its breast. The black barring may be very extensive. The white-front breeds in North-East Russia, Siberia, Arctic North America, and parts of Greenland. It is a winter visitor to Britain, where birds will often be seen lingering as late as May. The main wintering grounds of the white-front in Britain are the Inner and Outer Hebrides, the Severn, and Ireland.

This species, which breeds in the Arctic tundra, prefers river islands as nesting places, and tends to be gregarious. The nest is a hollow in the peat, made of heather, lichens and grasses mixed with down and feathers. The clutch size varies according to place, four eggs being usual in Siberia, while up to seven are common in Canada and Alaska. The goose incubates the eggs while the gander stands guard nearby. When the goslings leave the nest they are tended by both parents.

The Lesser White-Front is smaller than the previous species, but the white on the face covers a greater area, extending to the top of the head and between the eyes. It has a much smaller bill and a prominent yellow ring round its eye. This species breeds in Scandinavia and Siberia, usually at a much greater altitude than is typical of the other grey geese. The nest is usually on a hummock, although the birds sometimes choose willow and birch thickets. The materials used for the nest are typical as is the mixture of down and feathers. The breeding season of this species begins in early June. As in the case of the white-front, the goose does the incubating while the gander stands guard. The lesser white-front is only a rare vagrant to Britain.

WINTER VISITORS

The Bean Goose breeds in Norway, Sweden, Finland, and Russia. It prefers thin cover of birch or pine, always within easy distance of water, and sometimes birds will be found nesting on river islands in woodland. Many bean geese, however, breed well beyond the tree limit. The nest is typical. Breeding begins in early June in Scandinavia but in the Far North may be three weeks later. As with other geese, the female alone incubates, but both parents attend to the goslings.

The bean goose is a winter visitor to the British Isles: the main concentrations being found in the North of England, West, and South-West Scotland. In some years the bean goose will be found in company with greylags in areas which are normally considered purely greylag territory. This species is much darker coloured than the greylag, its appearance often being quite sooty. It is a slim goose with a longish neck. Its legs are orange or orange/yellow and the beak orange/yellow and black. Two phases of the bean goose occur, one with the black of the bill predominating and the other with the yellow predominating.

The Pink-footed Goose breeds only in Greenland, Iceland, and Spitzbergen, and flies south for the winter as far as Belgium, Holland and Germany. Wintering flocks begin to arrive in Britain in August and arrivals continue until September. The main concentrations are on the east coast from the Dornoch Firth to East Anglia but flocks occur in the west, notably in the Solway and Clyde areas and some of the Scottish islands. In other parts of the country the pink-foot is uncommon and unpredictable.

Smaller than the greylag, the pink-foot has a dark head and a pale body, pink legs and a slender black bill with a pink band. Its forewing, though pale grey, is not so pale as in

The snow goose is the easiest of all to recognise because of its pure white plumage. It has black-tipped wings.

The pink-footed goose regularly frequents arable fields in winter time. It breeds in the far north, usually among rocks and hillsides.

the greylag but this feature is not much of a guide in the field. The pink-foot is often found in great flocks which roost on coastal and estuarine sand banks. This species is not usually found on the same ground as the greylag. In winter, mixed flocks do occur in some areas. The pink-feet frequent arable fields when feeding, and in Wales may do so on hillsides.

To the British Isles, the Snow Goose and the Greater Snow Goose are uncommon visitors. The former breeds in Siberia and Arctic North America. The latter has been recorded in Greenland and North Baffin Land. Both species winter in more southerly parts of the United States of America.

In the field, the two species are indistinguishable, both being pure white birds, identical in appearance with only about two inches between them in overall length.

CLIFF NESTER

The Red-breasted Goose breeds in the Arctic from north-western Siberia eastwards, migrating in the autumn to Hungary, the Caspian Sea, Persia and Iraq. It breeds along the shores of the rivers in the Arctic where there are cliffs or steep banks. Outside the breeding season it flocks to grasslands and cultivated areas in the Caspian area, spending the night at sea. This is an easy goose to recognise because of its bold, colourful markings—black, white and chestnut red. Unlike the grey geese, which are notable for their flight formations, the red-breast flocks straggle along in undisciplined array. The flying flock may have no more shape than a flock of rooks and the nearest the birds ever get to formation flying appears to be in line abreast (according to Zhitnikov).

Russian observers have noted that the red-breast makes a habit of nesting close to the eyrie of peregrine falcons or rough-legged buzzards, the nest of the goose being usually on a river bank or scrubby slope. To the British Isles, the red-breast is classed as a very rare vagrant, but it is a favourite bird of ornamental waters. Because some of these semi-domesticated types wander it is often difficult to tell whether any red breast is an escapee or a vagrant from abroad.

On ornamental waters the Egyptian goose is also a favourite as it was with the Ancient Egyptians. It has long been acclimatised in England; it is a handsome goose, mainly chestnut-brown in colour with black and grey on its upper parts and yellow-brown, barred with black and white, on the underparts.

INTERBREEDING

Wild geese, when kept in captivity as pinioned birds or when bred in captivity, frequently interbreed with each other and most if not all of the offspring appear to be fertile.

Some years ago, Dr. John Berry produced all sorts of first-and second-generation hybrids. The greatest collection of geese and other water fowl in the world is at Slimbridge in Gloucestershire. Anyone interested in this group of birds should make a point of visiting this remarkable collection.

DOMESTIC GEESE

The greylag goose is the progenitor of all the common grey domestic geese. Popular varieties of domestic geese are the Chinese, both grey and white, the Roman, the Toulouse and the Embden. The lightweight Chinese are kept usually for egg production; the others being heavy are reared for table purposes. All will interbreed freely among themselves as well as with domesticated greylags.

QUESTIONS AND ANSWERS

Is the title " silly goose " justified?

By any standards the term is a libel. Geese are more intelligent than any type of domestic fowl. In captivity they become very friendly. They are easily disciplined and easily managed. They learn quickly and many people consider them as intelligent as any member of the crow family.

How many eggs do geese lay?

In the wild state most geese lay from 4-6 eggs, perhaps up to 7. Domestic breeds like the Chinese, however, will lay a sequence of 4 or 5 dozen in the best strains and if they are not allowed to go broody. The heavy breeds are not notable egg producers.

THE BADGER

Though badgers are common enough animals, they are seldom seen unless by people who make a point of looking for them, even where the location of a sett is known. And such setts are obvious enough. Badgers are seen by most people usually as a result of accident, for not only is the animal shy and retiring—it is, for the most part, nocturnal in habits.

Badgers spend the greater part of their lives underground, emerging only for the purpose of finding food, when mating or visiting, or to use their outside latrines. Their time of emergence is fairly well related to the setting of the sun. The later the sun sets the later will be the emergence of the badgers—so that in Scotland, for example, on a June night, the watcher may have to wait until midnight before the first badger shows itself.

This is not to say that badgers are never active in daylight. In quiet areas, especially in remote mountain areas, badgers do at times lie out in the open, well hidden from view but in a place which catches the sun. It is a habit with some mountain badgers to take their cubs, once they are strong on their legs, out on to the open hill where they will play and forage by night and lie up in deep heather during the day. This explains why badgers are sometimes put on foot in such places in the middle of the day, far from the nearest known sett.

BADGERS IN DAYLIGHT

Adult badgers have also been seen during daylight, in March, playing in forest glades, and this may well have been connected with mating. Still, if you want to see badgers, the surest way is to visit an occupied sett before sunset and wait till after dark for the beasts to emerge, for that is the standard pattern.

It must have occurred to anyone who has looked at a picture of a badger that the animal's face is very boldly and strikingly marked in black and white, whereas most other animals are notable for the way their colours merge with their backgrounds. It has been said that the badger's black and white face matches the pattern produced by the moon shining through trees, a kind of black and silver barring. The late Mortimer Batten, who was an excellent observer, made out quite a case for this idea but the circumstances in which he saw the badgers which gave him the idea were exceptional. Familiarity with the badger, in normal conditions of either darkness or moonlight, more and more compels one to incline to the opposite view. A badger's face is a strikingly obvious thing from the moment he pokes his head from the sett on a dark night. It is like a ghostly apparition rising from the dark earth. On very dark nights the badger's face is, in fact, the only thing the observer can see. Moonlight has little effect on this. Probably the badger's face is meant to be obvious, as the skunk's striping makes him obvious, and for much the same reason. The badger is a powerful animal and fears nothing that roams the woods, except man himself. The bold black and white pattern is, therefore, possibly a warning pattern.

WEASEL FAMILY

Badgers, though superficially they may not appear so, are members of the great Mustelidæ family: the family of the weasels. More bear-like than weasel-like, the beast is often referred to as the last of the British bears, yet once you see him moving he is all weasel, for he has the typical rippling, hump-backed run. He has been called cumbersome and clumsy, yet his speed is remarkable once he has been put on foot. This is not to say that he has the coursing abilities of

The badger's striking black and white face is very obvious even on a dark night. Once thought to have something to do with matching moonlight and shadows, this is obviously untrue, as any watcher can see for himself.

Young badgers are born early in the year in February and March, and as soon as they are old enough they go foraging with their parents. They are extremely playful and make a great deal of noise.

the fox, for he has not. But he is a far more nimble beast than is generally realised.

Though a true weasel, he is more omnivorous than carnivorous. While he will take any flesh food that he finds or that he can catch, he is perfectly well able to get along on a largely vegetarian diet. Thus he will eat berries of many kinds, especially dog-hips in season, the bulbs of the wild hyacinth, the roots of many plants, and grass if he has to. He will take rabbits from snares or traps, catch them on foot if he can, and makes a habit of digging out rabbit nests as he does the nests of wasps—although the techniques are different and distinctive. A wasp's nest he merely rips out with his bear-like claws: when it comes to rabbits, however, he digs down vertically on to the nest instead of following the burrow from the mouth.

FOOD OF BADGER

In farming areas he is not above cleaning up food left by domestic stock—for example poultry mash and pellets; and fish remains tossed on a farm midden are a sure attraction for any passing badger. He kills rats and mice when he finds an occupied burrow, again digging out the occupants with his powerful claws. When foraging, his pace is most often a plod, for he prefers to regulate his movements to the dictates of his nose. As a result, highly mobile prey like hares or full-grown rabbits is beyond him.

It would be true to say that he habitually takes what is in front of his nose. Tiny leverets in their forme are an easy prey for any hunter who stumbles on them, but these aren't easily found by mere searching and it is doubtful if many are killed by badgers. Hedgehogs, who hunt when the badger is hunting, are sometimes caught and killed, the hedgehog not being fast enough to escape the plodding brock. The hedgehog, once caught, is torn apart and eaten right down to the quills. It is unlikely that badgers go looking for birds and their eggs, but they do stumble on ground nests from time to time. If they find eggs they will eat them, but probably the average badger destroys few nests or nesting birds in its lifetime. Pheasants often get away with a brood next door to an occupied badger sett.

It is commonly stated that badgers will not eat carrion, but we should be clear about this. The badger will not eat putrefying flesh, but he will eat dead animals which are comparatively fresh. Badgers kept in captivity will eat almost anything—hare, rabbit, horse-flesh, cow meat, mutton, eggs, milk, oatmeal, wheatmeal, dog biscuits, dehydrated meat, cooked maize, bulbs, tubers, potatoes, grain, tomatoes, sugar, mice, worms, and almost any kind of insect.

DELAYED IMPLANTATION

In the badger there is the phenomenon of delayed implantation which also occurs in roe deer. Implantation of the fertilised ova takes place at the end of the year, and badger cubs are almost always born in March, whatever the time of mating. For many years there was great speculation as to when badgers actually did mate, then Ernest Neal, who has done the most exhaustive work on badgers in Britain, provided ample evidence that mating takes place in the autumn. It now seems clear that mating also takes place in the spring. A spring mating explains those cases where badgers have been a year in captivity before producing young. The number of cubs varies from one to five.

When badger cubs begin to emerge from the sett they do not at once go hunting with the adults. You will find them

The badger is fond of rabbits. The young ones he digs out of their nest. Full-grown rabbits are usually too fast for him, but he will take them from traps and snares.

playing about the sett and digging burrows all round it. At play, they are extremely noisy, crashing through the undergrowth and often running over the feet of a watcher if he sits still enough. They are often noisy by day as well, and if the observer approaches the sett quietly he will hear the thudding of the cubs underground. Badger cubs, like fox cubs, are not as suspicious or alert as the parents. An adult badger emerging from his sett pokes his head in and out several times critically, testing the wind, before he finally makes his exit. Young cubs, on the other hand, simply crash about in the direction they happen to be facing.

A badger sett in which a whole family is living has many well trodden runways radiating from it; but you will not find the rubbish lying around that you will find at a fox den, unless there happens to be a fox in the same burrow system. Where a sett is adjacent to a cornfield, the badgers will sometimes tread a track through the corn, which naturally displeases the farmer very much.

BADGERS AND FOXES

The relationship between fox and badger is a strange one. By human standards the badger is a meticulous animal, while the fox is the opposite. The badger will not carry food into his den, or leave remains lying about the entrance, whereas the fox habitually does both. Why, then, should the cleanly badger put up with the fox's dirty housekeeping? This is a problem to which no one knows the answer. Probably the badger puts up with the fox so long as the lodger does not get directly in his way—for example, where the fox lives in a different part of the sett and uses a different entrance. Recent observation at a big sett containing both badger cubs and fox cubs showed that the families were located in different parts of the sett, and the adults used different exits and entrances.

Badgers can and do kill fox cubs at times, and any full-grown badger is more than a match for the biggest fox. A full-grown badger is also well able to stand up to attack by even the biggest dogs, although he will make a point of breaking away and getting underground as quickly as possible. Where terriers are put to ground after foxes living in a badger den, the badger has often to face up to the assault and, being the powerful fighting machine he is, he mauls

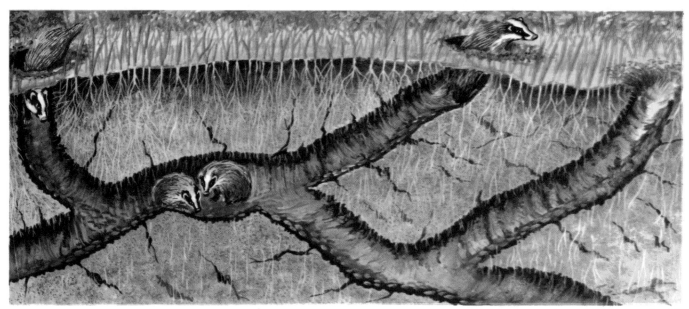

Badgers are forever digging, and a thriving sett soon becomes a series of mounds and craters above a labyrinth of tunnels. The animals spend the greater part of their lives underground, but do not hibernate in Britain.

and maims many a terrier. In such cases he is not, of course, deliberately fighting the fox's battle; he is merely defending himself and his home because his home has been invaded and he is being attacked. Careful fox hunters do not allow their terriers to enter known badger setts.

DO NOT HIBERNATE

Badgers do not hibernate, although it is frequently stated that they do. What is true is that, in the worst weather, they may not come out for several nights in a row, but this kind of behaviour is not confined to winter-time. The badger will lie up at any time if he is well fed or alarmed. He likes to gorge and then go to sleep—the bigger the gorge the longer the sleep. Though he does not like to be out during storms or periods of lashing rain, you will find his tracks in the snow, even in the mountains, and often at great heights. He is active in every month of the year.

Since they spend most of their lives underground, many badgers must die underground. What happens to them? Probably the other badgers in the sett dig a hole and seal the dead one in. But Brian Vesey-Fitzgerald has observed badgers dragging out a dead member of the clan and burying it outside the den altogether. Considering the badger's cleanly habits, such behaviour is not altogether surprising.

From June onwards, badgers may be seen carrying in a lot of bedding to the sett. This may be either grass or bracken. Some beasts take in bundles of fallen leaves in late autumn. Bracken or grass is balled up and trundled forward between chin and forepaws, but I have seen a badger moving backwards when the bundle was loose, as in the case of an armful of leaves. Old bedding is rolled out and stuffed into a convenient hole or cavity near the den. At bedding time, a badger can be followed quite easily from his " hayfield " to the den because of the bits and pieces he leaves in his wake.

BADGER DIGGING

There are two reasons why people dig badgers out of their dens. One reason, the commendable one, is because someone wants to introduce badgers to another part of the country. The easiest way to do this is to dig out the animals and transport them. The other reason is " sporting ". The

old English sport of badger digging is a brutal business. Terriers are put down the pipes to prevent the badger digging away while men dig down to him. Once the men reach the badger he is caught with tongs, put in a sack and hit over the head. This has never been made illegal.

Badger baiting, which consists of turning a badger loose in the open and turning terriers on him, is illegal, but it still goes on in parts of England. Thus a brave animal and small, brave dogs are brutally used to amuse human beings.

In the " sport " of badger digging many small, courageous terriers are mauled, maimed and killed underground by badgers, but this aspect is rarely publicised when reports of such " meets " are published in the local press.

The only possible justification for killing badgers is when they are doing damage and since badgers do little damage anywhere at any time, the situation seldom arises.

BADGERS AS PETS

Badger cubs taken young before their eyes are open make excellent pets and are not difficult to rear.

There is little justification, however, in rearing badgers simply and solely for the purpose of making them into pets. The justification arises where a sow badger has been killed leaving behind small cubs, or where a small cub has been injured. In other words, one rears the young badgers for the benefit of the young badgers and for no other purpose. Badgers so reared can subsequently be put into some sort of den, in or near a garden, where they will soon settle down and live a normal life; normal that is in all respects except that they have lost their fear of man. It is only too true that the lives of young animals when they have lost their fear of man frequently end in tragedy.

BADGER WATCHING

Because of their sedentary habits badgers are easily watched at night if the watcher takes certain precautions. These precautions consist mainly of sitting still and in such a position that the wind is blowing from the den to the watcher. If the watcher fulfils these conditions and is in position an hour before the badger is due to emerge, he will almost certainly see badgers.

Martens AND Weasels

A century ago pine-martens could be killed in Scotland in hundreds, and the polecat was also common. On the Glengarry estate, some one hundred polecats were killed in the three years 1837 to 1840. Even assuming these figures to have been exaggerated, as they probably were, the arithmetic is still frightening. While to-day the marten is not as rare as it once was, it is far from being a common animal even in areas which suit its requirements and where it has protection, as in Wester Ross.

In the 19th century, martens were destroyed as a matter of course by sportsmen and all who preserved game. At that time it was thought we had two species of marten—the pine and the beech—but this was incorrect. We had and have only one: the pine-marten.

The pine-marten, often called the sweet marten to distinguish it from the polecat or foul marten, is about the size of a cat, but leaves a track like a hare, so that tracks alone are an uncertain indication of the beast's presence unless you are very expert. Though a forest animal, the marten was for long compelled to live on bare mountains in Scotland where it bred among rocks or in trees or in the old nests of crows or squirrels' dreys. Its food consisted of frogs, insects, fruit, rabbits, squirrels, lizards, birds, wasps and honey.

A marten can kill the fawn of the roe deer, which is the biggest animal in its prey range. A specialist predator on squirrels, the pine-marten is quick and agile in the trees and has the squirrel habit, when it sees an intruder, of moving from rock to rock or round the trunk of a tree, keeping the intruder in view while itself remaining hidden.

The American marten is smaller than our native pine-marten and has a redder pelt. The other North American marten, which is larger than our pine-marten and sometimes almost black in colour, is the fisher or pecan. It is one of the most powerful of the weasel family and, besides killing what you would expect, can even kill porcupines. It tips them over with a furry paw before tearing at their unprotected undersides.

The sable, which is a marten with an extremely valuable pelt, ranges from European Russia to Japan, but has become rare because of persistent hunting. The fur of the sable, always expensive, was greatly prized in the court of Imperial Russia and it was the hunting of the sable that led trappers far into Siberia. Now that it is on the rare list, attempts are being made to farm it for its fur and to re-establish it in many of its former haunts.

The mink, which also bears a valuable fur, is now farmed extensively in North America and Scandinavia, although many wild animals are still trapped. Mink-ranching is now an established industry in Britain, and escaped animals have settled down in some parts of the countryside to become a pest to poultrymen.

POLECATS AND FERRETS

The polecat, now rare in Britain, is found in Europe and Asia. It has creamy buff fur and dark guard hairs. It is probably the ancestor of the domestic ferret. Ferrets and polecats interbreed freely and, indeed, the domestic ferret comes in two phases—the white or albino, and the dark or polecat variety. Under stress, this member of the weasel family can launch a most nauseating gas attack, which gave it its old name of foul marten. It is a considerable predator on rabbits when left alone to hunt them.

It is extremely difficult to tell a polecat ferret from a wild polecat and, since polecat ferrets can survive in a wild state and frequently escape to do so, this gives rise to great difficulties. It is impossible to tell one from the other by looking

The common weasel is a mouse hunter and a killer of rats. It has a short, smooth tail with no black tip and is thus easily distinguished from the stoat, which is larger.

The American mink is similar to the Old World species, but is a bigger animal with a softer fur. It is extensively farmed for its fur in North America and Europe.

The beech-marten occurs in Europe and Asia.

The sable is a valuable fur-bearer.

Many mutations of the mink have been bred in captivity.

at them and even the anatomist in the laboratory cannot be sure, although at one time he thought he could. Therefore, while there are what you might call right polecats and wrong polecats, nobody knows right from wrong. There are polecats on the Island of Mull which are the descendants of gone-wild ferrets but are not considered the real thing. But it seems reasonable to accept that a polecat which looks like a polecat, acts like a polecat, and breeds polecats which look and act like polecats, is a polecat for all practical purposes. You know that if one raids your henhouse: right or wrong kind, the result is the same.

If we compare the pine-marten with the polecat we will find that the first measures about twenty-two inches in length plus twelve inches of tail, while the second will measure under eighteen inches with seven inches of tail. In the pine-marten the fur is thick, fine, and sable-like; the tail is thick and bushy, while throat and chest are yellow in varying shades. The polecat's fur is long, almost black, with a purple sheen, and it has light patches over its eyes. Probably the pine-marten breeds only once a year and the polecat twice. Both species spit, hiss and chatter, and have a loud cry.

THE WOLVERINE

The largest of the family is the wolverine, sometimes known as the glutton or Injun devil. It is found in the extreme north of Europe and Asia and in the northern half of North America. It is four feet long, dark brown in colour, with a pale brown stripe along each side, and resembles the badger more than it does the typical weasel. It will kill anything it can catch and hold. It is savage and completely fearless. It is an expert at robbing traps and finding and scattering food caches hidden by hunters.

Despite its reputation for savagery, it is worth noting that Peter Krott managed to tame wolverines in Northern Europe, returning them later to the wild state where he was able to study their life cycles under natural conditions. This is one of the few instances where a wild animal, having lost its fear of man, could be depended upon to behave naturally while being observed closely.

Our smaller native weasels are the common stoat and the common weasel. Though the least of the weasels in point of size, they are not the least in any other way. Relentless hunters, they often kill when they are no longer hungry, a habit which, from the human point of view, is good or bad depending on what they are killing. If the prey killed in excess of needs happens to be voles, rats, mice or rabbits, no one is likely to feel annoyed with them. The stoat is not nearly as plentiful as it used to be, and probably the gin-trapping of rabbits has had much to do with this. The weasel is by far the commoner of the two species.

THE STOAT

The stoat is considerably larger than the weasel—a really big animal measuring up to fifteen inches or more in length and weighing up to eleven ounces. Some of the stoat's length is accounted for by its tail, which is over four inches long, bushy like a squirrel's, and tipped with black. Male stoats are bigger than females. Apart from the mountain hare, the stoat is the only other British mammal which turns white in winter; but the change does not take place all over the country, and white stoats are more common in some years than in others. In the south of England stoats may turn white, make only a partial change, or no change at all. In Scotland, the change to white is normal, though in lowland areas specimens are sometimes seen which have made only a partial change.

Stoats kill rabbits, mice, voles, rats, leverets, and birds. They will also remove eggs from nests whether on the ground or in trees. Individual stoats will make a store of eggs, sometimes in a rabbit burrow, sometimes in an outhouse. The stoat will invade any burrow that he can get into.

Stoats breed only once a year, the young being born in early summer. The nest may be in a hollow tree, a hole in a wall, at the foot of a bank, in a rabbit burrow or in a thicket, and it may be high up on a mountain side. The female drags her prey to the nest to be eaten and she can haul prey two or three times her own weight. When she is moving eggs she rolls them along the ground under her chin. The stoat family sticks together as a unit for some time, thus forming so-called summer and autumn packs. Winter packs may be no more than a single family, but a very large pack may be made up of two or more. Packs of up to seventeen animals have been noted hunting together and such a gathering will face almost any living thing that gets in its way.

Though dogs, and even people, are liable to be attacked at such times, such attacks are not a common habit of the stoat.

THE LEAST WEASEL

There is in Europe and Eastern Asia a small weasel called the Least weasel, but so far no specimen has ever been recorded in Britain. This does not alter the fact that many small weasels in Britain are referred to as Lesser weasels or Mouse weasels. They are, however, females of the common weasel in which species the females are notably smaller than the males. Every so-called mouse weasel in Britain turns out to be a female, which illustrates the point.

Our common weasel is smaller than the stoat, being from seven to eleven inches in overall length, which includes two inches of tail. Weasels weigh only from two to four ounces, their tails are not bushy, and they do not turn white in winter. Unlike the stoat, weasels breed twice a year, giving birth to four, five or six kits. Small family parties of weasels are not an uncommon sight in summer or autumn.

When hunting, the weasel sits upright from time to time in listening attitude just as the stoat does. It darts about at incredible speed, but often bounds in the same fashion as the stoat. When a weasel is making its final rush at a rat or a mouse it does so with its short tail stiffly erect, and the hairs on end. All weasels may not behave in this fashion, but there are no records of any which behave otherwise.

The weasel makes her nest of grass or leaves in a hole or wall or bank, in a tree stump or corn stack. The animal is much given to hunting on and in corn stacks, where it catches such prey as mice and sparrows.

Outside the breeding season, weasels are great travellers and no matter where they are disturbed they seem to know every convenient hole in the neighbourhood. They spend as much of their hunting time below ground as above ground, and mole-runs are commonly used for getting from one place to another.

Both stoat and weasel are extremely curious, which is often the death of them. If you disturb either and it seeks refuge in a wall or bank, it will come out soon if you stand by and watch. In the same way they will return time after time to their prey, even when you are standing a few feet away, and it is a fact that if one of the family is killed, say on a road, the others will come out to drag the body away. Habits like these make the animals easy targets for the man with a gun.

The wolverine is the most powerful of weasels.

The beech-marten is often found hunting about farms.

The polecat is now a rare animal in Great Britain.

WINGED PREDATORS

Among birds these are the lordly ones—the bold and the mighty—the hunters—the highwaymen of the air. And they are beautiful, the lordly ones—some of them aristocratic, and not one of them ignoble. They kill to live—bird, mammal, frog, or insect, according to their needs and powers—and who are we to say that they are cut-throats or vermin?

The truth is that birds of prey exercise little, if any, effect on the numbers of the creatures they kill as food. They do not determine the numbers of their prey; it is really the other way round. If you think about it for a moment, you will see that it could not be otherwise. Surely the amount of food available to a species determines the number of mouths that can be fed?

In Britain, the extermination and killing down of many species of predators has been due almost entirely to the actions of game preservers. In this respect we have probably the worst record in Europe. Yet, at one time, most British birds of prey had an honoured place in sport. For centuries they were the pride of kings, nobles and prelates. But that was in the age of falconry, before the days of gunpowder. Then, the peregrine falcon sat on the fist of kings; in the 19th and 20th centuries its place was the gamekeepers' vermin board, hanging by the neck—dead.

So, in Britain, birds of prey fell on evil days. The osprey and the sea eagle vanished altogether; the golden eagle and the harrier were thinned down to danger level; the peregrine and the merlin disappeared from long-familiar places; the kite, once numerous, was reduced to a handful of birds which still exist precariously in Wales. To-day all British birds of prey are protected—except one, the dashing sparrow-hawk.

GOLDEN EAGLE

In Great Britain, the Golden Eagle still nests mainly in the Highlands of Scotland, although a few pairs now breed in the southern uplands and the bird has once more gained a footing in Northern Ireland. So far there has been no re-colonisation in Northern England.

The nest of the eagle is called an eyrie. In Britain, most eyries are under two thousand feet and many are under one thousand. In the Outer Hebrides, however, nests are common about five hundred feet. The breeding season is from late March, when the eggs are laid, until mid-July when the young birds fly. Two eggs are usual, but often there is only one and occasionally there are three. Where there are twin eaglets in an eyrie the stronger chick, usually a female, sometimes kills her nest-mate. This almost always occurs where hunting is bad and there is a scarcity of food in the nest. Eaglets normally fly at between eleven and twelve weeks of age, but are supported by their parents for some three months afterwards. Young eagles have a great deal of white in their tails.

In Britain, the food of the golden eagle is mainly mountain hares, grouse and rabbits. But the birds also take crows, fox cubs, ptarmigan and plovers regularly. In addition, you may find in eyries, wood pigeons, gulls, curlews, ravens, blackcock, red deer calves, roe deer fawns, and carrion of several kinds.

Much of the animosity against the golden eagle in many parts of Europe arises from its predation on lambs which are, of course, economically important animals. It is, however, very difficult to obtain exact information about the extent of this predation in Europe. In this country, where much work has been done on the subject, it is quite obvious that lambs are not commonly killed by eagles. A great many eagles will, however, take dead lambs readily enough. On the other hand, there are eagles in many parts of Scotland

The golden eagle nests mainly in remote mountain areas.

The sea-eagle no longer breeds in the British Isles.

which will not touch lambs, living or dead at any time.

PREY RANGE

A great deal of misunderstanding exists regarding the weight-carrying ability of eagles. While it is true that an adult female can lift a considerable weight if she can take off with it down a slope, her abilities are much poorer if she is lifting prey from level ground. In the case of red deer calves, these are carried to the eyrie in pieces, for no eagle could lift such a weight. As a matter of fact, it is very doubtful if golden eagles kill many red deer calves. Available records tend to show that red deer calves are taken when they are already dead. The fawn of the roe deer is, however, well within the prey range of the golden eagle.

One is always liable at any time to come across a golden eagle feeding on a dead deer, and there are plenty of reports of eagles harrying small herds of deer. Occasionally a deer is killed, or kills itself during such a stampede, by falling. It is extremely doubtful if the eagle's assault is a deliberate means of achieving this end. I have a record of an eagle harrying red deer in this fashion. The beasts ran off but were not obviously afraid of the bird. Later, the eagle turned her attention to a roe buck grazing in the open, but the buck, instead of running, as the red deer had done, reared up on his hind legs and boxed back at her until she broke off the assault.

An eagle survey was carried out on the Island of Lewis, in 1955, by Dr. J. D. Lockie and David Stephen. It was found that the main prey animal was rabbit, although on the ground the sheep stock was one of the densest in Britain. The rabbit, plus the constant supply of carrion mutton, maintained the high density of eagles, which was something like nine breeding pairs to 100,000 acres.

Most golden eagles have two or more nesting sites which they use in succession but sometimes you will find the same eyrie occupied year after year. In Great Britain, the bird and its eggs are now specially protected by law.

SEA EAGLE

The Sea Eagle, properly known as the White-Tailed Eagle, does not now nest in Britain, although individual birds are seen from time to time on passage. The adults, as the name suggests, have white tails. Most nests in Scotland were on sea cliffs, but no sea eagle has nested since 1908. The second bird of this pair disappeared in 1918 after sitting each year in an empty nest. The place was Shetland.

This species preyed on much the same food as the golden eagle, but also took a great deal of fish and offal as well as many sea birds. It was reputed to be a great killer of lambs (which we have now no way of establishing) and its destruction was largely due to the actions of sheep interests. Although it is a non-breeding bird in Britain, it is given special protection by law, so it may well re-establish itself as the osprey has done.

The sea eagle breeds in Iceland, Norway and Sweden into North Russia. It nests also in North Germany, Czechoslovakia, Hungary and Greece, as well as many parts of the Middle East. In these places the bird nests quite commonly in trees and far from the coast, in marshes, reed beds and estuaries. With this species two eggs are usual, but three are occasionally recorded. As with the golden eagle, the male provides the food which is fed to the young by the female. European records show that prey includes dogs, foxes, roe deer, squirrels, moles and hedgehogs, as well as

The condor is the giant vulture of South America.

The secretary bird is a noted killer of snakes.

The eagle was the battle crest of Imperial Rome.

The spotted eagle is found in Eastern Europe. In appearance it resembles the golden eagle, but in flight it is a far more sluggish bird.

many species of birds. Young white-tailed eagles are fledged at ten weeks old but remain with their parents for several weeks after leaving the nest.

SPOTTED EAGLE

The Spotted Eagle is only a very rare vagrant to the British Isles and Western Europe. It breeds in the Baltic States and Russia, Hungary and the Balkan Peninsula. It is a dark-brown eagle, smaller than the golden eagle, taking such prey as rabbits, voles, frogs, lizards, hares, hamsters, rats and mice.

IMPERIAL EAGLE

The Imperial Eagle of Spain and Eastern Europe is about the same size as the golden eagle, but it is sluggish in behaviour, and a heavy-looking bird. The Spanish type has noticeably white shoulders, which give the bird a white leading edge to the wing when in flight. In colour, the adult imperial is blackish-brown, with yellowish crown and nape. In old birds this yellow may be near-white. The imperial's tail is square-cut, with five or seven grey bars. This species frequents plains and marshes, or steppe land, and builds a bulky nest in some isolated tree, where it can be seen from a great distance away.

PEREGRINE FALCON

The Peregrine is the king of British falcons and is now specially protected by law. Though no longer a rare bird it is by no means common. It is a bird of wild sea coasts and inland crags, and nests year after year in the same rock or cliff. The male is called the tiercel; the female, called the falcon, is considerably bigger than her mate.

The peregrine is a fine, bold falcon who hunts high and fast and does almost all of his killing in the air, up in the open where everyone can see him. He kills by dropping on his prey from above in a breath-taking stoop. Grouse, duck, and pigeons are common prey, but the peregrine will take almost any kind of bird including very small ones.

In some parts of Scotland the cuckoo is a favourite food and as many as half a dozen have been seen in one eyrie. At other eyries, prey as small as newly-hatched mallard ducklings has been recorded. Periodically there is an outcry against the peregrine falcon in Britain by pigeon fanciers who claim that the bird kills vast numbers of racing pigeons each year. This claim is not borne out by the facts, and in a great many parts of Britain peregrine falcons hardly ever see a racing pigeon. The claim that the peregrine falcon endangered the war effort in 1939–45 by killing racing pigeons carrying important messages is one which can hardly be taken seriously.

This falcon has almost a world-wide distribution, and is a great wanderer outside the breeding season.

THE PRIDE OF KINGS

At one time it was highly prized in the sport of falconry, when a pair of birds might have been worth £1,000. Falconry still has its devotees, particularly in the Middle East, and the peregrine is still the favourite bird, but for many reasons the sport is not what it was. It takes time and skill to train a falcon, and the man has to have a great deal of the right kind of ground to hunt over to make the keeping of falcons worth while. Then there are the protection regulations which make it illegal to take a young falcon from the nest without an official licence.

The behaviour of peregrine falcons at the nest varies from bird to bird and at different periods of the breeding season. When the falcon is sitting on eggs she may slip off quietly at the approach of an intruder, or she may make some kind of vocal demonstration. When she has young she is much more likely to come screaming round your head with or without the tiercel as company, and there are individual birds which will swoop very close to your head as the hen harrier habitually does. Once the peregrine falcon starts screaming at you, you need never be in any doubt about its identity. Though cliffs and crags are the normal nesting places in Britain, the birds will nest on the ground on wild moorlands in certain parts of Europe. This latter habit has, in fact, been recorded in England.

The nest is a simple, unlined scrape on a rock shelf. Nesting time is April to May—roughly April in England and May in the north of Scotland. Eggs usually number three or four. The chicks hatch in just over four weeks and leave the nest at between five and six weeks of age. They are fed for some time afterward by their parents. While the falcon is brooding chicks, the tiercel does the hunting. Not often seen, and rarely recorded, is the " Pass ", when the tiercel passes prey to the falcon high in the air. The falcon turns over on her back and receives the prey in her feet.

MERLIN

The Merlin is the smallest falcon on the British list, the male being scarcely larger than a Mistle-thrush. He may measure no more than ten-and-a-half inches from beak to tail tip.

This species is not plentiful in Britain to-day and for that reason has been given the same special protection as the eagle and the peregrine. It haunts heather moors, sea cliffs, and coastal sand-dunes. On moors it is not liked by game preservers and there it is incessantly harried despite legal protection. Yet, in fact, the bird takes few grouse chicks and all observers of the nesting merlin in this country know that it preys hardly at all on grouse.

Most merlins nest on the ground, but some nest in cliffs and some use the old nests of hoodie-crows or carrion-crows. In Scotland, the great majority of nests are in deep heather

The hobby is a small, migrant falcon which hunts dragon-flies, beetles and other insects. It is uncommon in Britain.

in a scrape lined with some heather twigs and moss. Four or five eggs are usual, and the chicks leave the nest before they are a month old.

The merlin is a bold and persistent little flyer, fit to take even a strong lark in the air. In summer it can be seen pursuing such birds as the meadow-pipit, yellow hammer, thrush and linnet, but it will come to ground for such mammals as voles and shrews, and takes far more insect food than is generally realised. It is bold in defence of its nest and will drive away such birds as hoodie-crows.

In the British Isles the merlin is a resident but we do have visitors from other parts of Europe in winter. Birds of the European race breed in Iceland, Norway, and Sweden.

HOBBY

The Hobby is a pocket peregrine and only very slightly bigger than the merlin. It is a summer visitor to Britain, and winters in North Africa.

The hobby is a rare falcon in Britain and nests in England. There is only one nest recorded from Scotland but several from Wales. But England usually has all the British nesting hobbies. Birds of passage, they are sometimes seen in the northern Highlands of Scotland.

Like our other falcons, the hobby builds no nest. In England it uses the old nest of crow, magpie, wood-pigeon, or sparrow-hawk. Three eggs are usual but the chicks fly in something over a month from hatching. The hobby is specially protected by law in the British Isles.

This small falcon in flight has all the characteristics of the peregrine. It will swoop on birds from above, take them in straight flight, or bind on to them from underneath. It has no trouble catching such birds as swallows and martins, and can fly down even the swift. It catches a great many insects and beetles in the air, passing them from foot to beak in flight. Such strong flyers as dragon-flies are no trouble to the nimble hobby, and lumbering beetles are taken with the greatest of ease. Small birds of many kinds are also preyed upon, one of the most frequent being the meadow-pipit, although in some districts the skylark is the favourite. At times the hobby will pursue birds that seem far too big for it, like the wood-pigeon and the partridge, but it is doubtful if in normal circumstances the bird could kill either of them.

The hobby breeds in many parts of Europe from Norway

to Andalusia. It spends the winter in Africa and perhaps North-West India.

KESTREL

The Kestrel is a common falcon in Britain and a killer of mice, voles, young rats, shrews and frogs. As a result it has been protected for many years in most parts of Britain. Since 1954, the bird and its eggs are protected at all times.

This is the falcon you see hovering above fields and commons as if suspended from an invisible wire. Hovering thus, it scans the ground below for mice and voles and such small creatures. When it sees one it plunges vertically to earth, opening its wings at the last moment and clutching with its feet.

Like so many birds of prey, the kestrel is conservative in its nesting habits, returning to the same locality year after year, and quite frequently using the same nest—usually the old nest of crow, magpie or sparrow-hawk. Up to six eggs are usual, and a pair feeding six chicks has been known to carry to the nest three hundred and twenty mice, voles and shrews in twenty-eight days. Although the main food of kestrels is obviously small mammals, they do take insect food and a variety of small birds, but there is no question about their preference for fur over feather. This can be easily checked if you examine the pellets cast up by the birds. These contain all the indigestible matter like fur, bones, teeth and feathers. In these pellets you will find a dozen mouse skulls for every bird's claw.

Young kestrels fly at about four weeks old. In the early stages the male provides all the food, which is fed to the chicks by the female. When the male arrives with food he may call the female off and transfer it to her or fly to the nest with it in his beak. Kestrels do not carry prey to the nest in their feet.

LESSER KESTREL

The Lesser Kestrel, a smaller bird than the common kestrel, is found in Portugal, Spain, Italy and the Mediterranean region. Although smaller than the common kestrel, it closely resembles it. The lesser kestrel is a gregarious bird which may be found nesting in colonies about old buildings and sometimes in town and villages. It is mainly an insect feeder, although it does take small birds and mice.

HARRIER

There are three species of harrier nesting in the British Isles,

The kestrel is perhaps the most familiar falcon in Britain. It can be seen hovering above fields on the lookout for mice.

the rarest of these being the Marsh Harrier which is confined almost entirely to Norfolk. In recent years the Montagu's Harrier has nested in Central Scotland. The third species, the Hen Harrier, which became very rare in the period between the two world wars, has become re-established in many parts of the country.

Harriers are long-winged, long-legged, hawks which nest on the ground. Their food is mainly small birds and mammals, frogs and lizards and, in the case of the marsh harrier, fish. All three are specially protected by law in Great Britain.

THE BUZZARD

The Buzzard is a large, rather ponderous bird of prey which is frequently mistaken for the golden eagle. It is widely distributed in Britain and is common in the Highlands of Scotland. In Europe, it breeds from Norway and Sweden, south to Spain, France, Italy and Greece.

In the British Isles, before myxomatosis almost exterminated the rabbit population, the main food of many buzzards was young rabbits. The birds, however, take all kinds of small mammals and though game birds are rarely molested, the bird is quite capable of taking them. It is unusual, however, to find game birds of any kind in a buzzard's nest. In some parts of the country, carrion is a frequent item, especially dead sheep or lambs. One of the most astonishing records of buzzard food comes from the island of Eigg, off the West Coast of Scotland, where buzzards were noted carrying to their chicks nestling blackbirds and pipits only a few days old. This is the only record in Britain of buzzards raiding the nests of small birds.

It is customary to look upon the buzzard as a weak bird, and it is true that it has not the dash of the falcons and gives the impression of being slow. It is also true that it does not normally go out of its way to hunt " difficult " prey. Nevertheless, it can, when it wishes, kill hoodie-crows, pheasants, grouse or partridges.

Unlike the falcons and like the golden eagle, the buzzard builds a substantial nest on cliff ledges or in trees. Unlike the golden eagle it is inclined to be vocal and its mewing call can be heard for long periods when the bird is soaring and wheeling.

Several buzzards can often be seen flying together and these are often reported as " many eagles ". Aerial circuses of this kind are a buzzard habit not an eagle one. In Southern Europe the buzzard is much more given to raiding poultry yards than it is in Britain.

THE KITE

As a British breeding bird the Kite is confined entirely to the mountains of Wales. Only a few birds breed there now and these are constantly protected during the breeding season against egg collectors. They have also special protection in law, but the kite in Wales fails to multiply, and this is one of the dangers once a species sinks to small numbers: it is difficult to build up again. But although it is rare in Britain to-day, it is widely distributed in Europe and common in the Mediterranean countries. In Spain, the bird kills all kinds of small mammals and birds like cuckoos, larks, and pigeons, as well as frogs, snakes, lizards, slow-worms, fish and insects. As in Britain, it is also given to raiding farmyards for chickens and ducklings. In the nesting season it is liable to pick up anything for nesting material, including part of the washing strung out on a clothes line.

The peregrine falcon kills by swooping on its prey.

The kite nests in forest trees. In Wales, it shows a preference for slender oak trees on hillsides, but in Scotland, before it became extinct, pines were the favourite nesting site. All sorts of odd materials are used in the building of the nest, including wool, hair, rags and paper.

OSPREY

Until 1959, the Osprey was properly classified in Britain as a visitor. The bird was once common in Scotland and used to nest in almost every suitable loch, but it was severely harried during the 19th century and, by 1908, it was extinct as a breeding species. From 1908, until 1959, no osprey was known to have bred in Britain. In 1959, the bird bred successfully at Rothiemurchus, due largely to the well-organised watching teams sent by the Royal Society for the Protection of Birds.

In North America, the osprey is called the Fish Hawk, and it is common enough there. In Europe, it is found in Norway, Sweden, Finland, and North Russia, also in the Mediterranean area, the Balearic Islands, Corsica, Sardinia, and Sicily.

The staple diet of the osprey is fish; for example, sea-trout, brown-trout, bream and perch. European birds, as well as taking fish up to four pounds in weight, have also been recorded carrying small mammals. Jackdaws, cuckoos, and wounded birds have also been recorded, and pheasants are occasionally taken.

Though nesting sites in Scotland were almost always on rocky islets in lochs, mostly in pine trees but sometimes on ruined buildings, the birds in Europe are not so conservative. Some breed on cliff ledges, some in bushes, some on sandy flats or among rocks, but always near salt or fresh water. In some parts of Europe the bird has a tendency to nest in small colonies. The nest often reaches a great size because it is occupied for many years in succession. Three eggs are the usual clutch and these are incubated mainly by the hen. The hatching period is 35 days, but chicks are fed by the hen for about six weeks, after which food is simply deposited in the nest and they have to feed themselves. The young birds leave the nest at from eight to ten weeks of age.

SPARROW-HAWK

The Sparrow-hawk is the only British bird of prey which

has no protection in law. It is widely distributed in the British Isles and throughout Europe from Norway to the Mediterranean. Where woodlands are scarce the sparrow-hawk is scarce because it is a woodland hawk.

The case against this hawk is that it kills game chicks and song birds, the inference being presumably that if the sparrow-hawk were not checked we would be left without game birds or song birds. This is manifestly absurd, especially in these days when we are realising more and more that birds of prey make no significant difference to the numbers of creatures on which they prey.

The sparrow-hawk builds its own nest of twigs and branches, usually high up in a tree against the main stem. In some areas it shows a distinct preference for larch trees. The nesting season is May. Four or five eggs are usual and the chicks leave the nest any time between three and four weeks old. The male bird, who is very small compared with his mate, kills all the food in the early stages, bringing it either to the nest or to a plucking place where he gives it to his mate. These plucking places, often a tree stump or small boulder, sometimes a simple knoll, always betrays the sparrow-hawk because of the feathers scattered around. Once a gamekeeper has located a plucking place it is a simple matter for him to lie in ambush and shoot the bird on arrival.

There are odd records of two female sparrow-hawks sitting in the same nest but whether this means that the sparrow-hawk· is at times polygamous is not in any way certain. The scarcity of records of this habit suggests otherwise.

The species is also notable for the fact that if a hen is killed off the nest the male very soon finds another mate.

Sparrow-hawks are bold, active hawks which favour a low-flying attack—the hidden, swift approach over hedges or walls right into midst of feeding birds. They will pursue such birds as starlings and sparrows into buildings and even into netted poultry runs. They have been known to stun themselves, flying against glass when pursuing their quarry.

The main food is certainly small birds, but female sparrow-hawks kill many wood-pigeons which are a great pest to the farmer. The remains of thirteen wood-pigeons have been found lying along the edge of one wood where a pair of sparrow-hawks was nesting.

VULTURES

Vultures are large, eagle-like birds, unfeathered on head and neck. At close quarters they are unattractive birds; on the wing they are large and graceful, even majestic. In Europe there are four species: the Griffon, the Egyptian, the Black, and the Bearded or Lammergeier, and they are found along the Mediterranean, from Spain to Eastern Europe.

The Lammergeier nests in remote caves in high mountains, and is an imposing bird, three and a half feet long, with wedge tail and falcon-like outline. It has a black beard, and is rust-coloured on the breast, with underparts buff, and dark underwings. It is found in the mountains of Spain, and a few mountainous regions along the Mediterranean.

The Griffon is found in Spain and other Mediterranean areas, mainly in mountains, where it breeds sociably in caves or rock ledges. The Egyptian vulture, conspicuously white underneath when in flight, is found in much the same areas, and nests in cliffs or in trees, being often found scavenging in villages. The Black Vulture, which resembles the griffon in size and flight, is dark all over and does not have the downy white head of the griffon. It nests in remote mountain areas or plains, usually in trees, occasionally on cliff ledges.

The red kite, rare in Britain, is common in Europe.

The osprey, or fish hawk, is nesting again in Britain.

The dashing sparrow-hawk preys mainly on small birds.

You could find no greater contrast, for example, than that between the fan-tail on the one hand and the magpie on the other. Or between the small Oriental frills and the strong-flying, heavy-nosed racing pigeons which are so popular and so widely kept by fanciers.

The racing pigeon is, perhaps, the most widely known and certainly the most extensively kept in Europe. Each year, tens of thousands of birds compete in races, up to and over five hundred miles, and British pigeons are flown each year in great numbers from Rennes and Dol in France, which give their names to important races.

All wild pigeons are fast flyers, but the domestic pigeon can put up incredible performances both in speed and stamina. It would be a great mistake, however, to imagine that racing

The homing pigeon is widely kept by fanciers in Europe, both for racing and exhibition purposes. Thousands of these birds are sent to France each year from Britain to compete in the famous Rennes Race. These birds face wind and storm on their way home, and many fly distances of from five to six hundred miles. The type illustrated here is popularly known as the blue-bar, because of the wing markings.

Pigeons and doves are one and the same thing; generally speaking we refer to the bigger specimens as pigeons and the small, slender types as doves. For example, the turtle-dove is never called the turtle-pigeon, while the ring dove, which is a big species, is more usually referred to as wood-pigeon. There is, however, no general rule.

Man has done with pigeons what he has done with so many other species: he has, by selective breeding, evolved his own varieties, which he keeps for sport or amusement.

There are a great many handsome varieties of pigeons. The brightly-coloured specimen illustrated here is a native of tropical Africa.

pigeons are infallible, or that they always return home. Apart from casualties during the races, many birds either do not come home or cannot come home. They go astray, and may turn up in someone else's loft or go feral altogether.

Varieties like the fan-tail, which come in several colours, are kept simply for decorative purposes or for exhibition, and the modern fan-tail with its chest sticking above the level of its head is a rather grotesque bird. Others like tumblers and tipplers, which are homers in every sense of the word, are kept for amusement, but varieties have been bred entirely for show which do not have much opportunity to tumble or tipple, and which are seldom allowed free flight. Most of the others are purely exhibition varieties.

EXTENDED NESTING SEASON

Generally speaking, wild pigeons have an extended nesting season, but this is surpassed by their domesticated relatives some of which would breed throughout the year under proper conditions, if allowed to do so. It is the practice,

The wood-pigeon, or ring dove, is a large, wild pigeon which has become a farm pest.

therefore, especially with racing stock, to separate cocks and hens, except when the owner wishes breeding to take place. Furthermore, it is on the connection between cock and hen, and that between the birds and their nests, that the whole fabric of homing from long distances is built up. In other words, the birds do more than simply fly home; they have responsibilities of a kind which provide an almost irresistible attraction.

Domestic pigeons which go feral are quickly absorbed into the already feral population, and in time assume the characteristics of the typical rock dove. In many places they will interbreed freely with the rock dove and, in fact, a great many so-called rock doves, indistinguishable from the real wild species, are not genuine rock doves at all. Even in remote areas, far from contact with human habitations, the pedigree of wild rock doves is often suspect. This confusion is rendered more complete by the fact that many fanciers keep true rock doves under domestic conditions. This means cross-breeding at home and, when individuals go feral, the existence of " rock doves " which are of domestic origin.

In those domestic pigeons where there is no selection, and breeding is not controlled, the birds soon conform to a type with definite colours and markings, the principal types predominating being the barred and the chequered. The same markings are found in the red varieties, and, in addition there is the so-called mealy, which is the result of colour crossing.

WILD PIGEONS

In Europe there are five species of wild pigeon. The Wood-Pigeon, or ring dove, is perhaps the best known of them all because it is to be seen almost everywhere except in completely treeless regions or the extreme north. A woodland species, it prefers established woods or forests, although it will nest in hedges and bushes down to within four feet of the ground. It is greatly attracted by larch and pine woods, and in such places may be found breeding in great numbers. In the same places winter flocks may also be found roosting.

This brilliantly-coloured dove is a variety from Cuba.

The wood-pigeon is larger than the other European species, being about sixteen inches in overall length. With its white wing bar, and its small white patch on each side of the neck, it is distinctive apart altogether from its large size. Young ring doves, when first fledged, do not have these neck markings.

Wood-pigeons breed early and late, from February to October and even November, and may rear two or more broods in a season. The nest, if built from scratch, is a small, simple, latticed platform so loosely constructed that in some cases the eggs can be seen from the ground. Quite regularly, however, wood-pigeons will adapt the old nests of crows or sparrow-hawks. Despite its frail appearance, the nest built by the wood-pigeon serves its purpose well. It is strong enough to last through the winter, long after the young pigeons have flown. It is true that the young pigeons sometimes fall out of the nest, but this is not a common occurrence.

The turtle dove is the smallest of the British wild pigeons, being about eleven inches in overall length. It frequents open country with rough hedges and spinneys, and nests in bushes. It has a soft, purring voice. Its tail is black with white edges, it has black-and-white striped neck patches, and its upper parts are brown, laced with black.

Wild domestic pigeons revert to type in a few generations, the type being the original wild blue rock dove which has a white rump and two broad black bands across the wings. This type is abundant in towns and cities and will be found nesting in buildings and ruins. The true rock dove frequents rocky sea cliffs and nests in crevices, or caves.

Two eggs are laid in almost all cases. Being white, and laid in flat, open nests, they are conspicuous in the early part of the year when the trees are bare; unless, of course, the nest happens to be in a dense spruce or other evergreen. Where the nest is in a thorn or other deciduous tree, the eggs are easily seen and early clutches are often eaten by such birds as crows and magpies.

SERIOUS PROBLEM

When the chicks are very small, they are covered with thread-like golden down which is gradually replaced by quills and then by feathers. Feeding is by regurgitation. The chicks push their beaks into the mouth of the parent bird who pumps food from her crop for them. When the chicks are very small this food is in the form of curd, often called pigeons' milk, but as the young birds grow they receive more and more solids until they are taking grain, weeds, and greenstuff freshly gathered, but all food is fed by regurgitation —the adult bird bobbing up and down during the process. Practically every kind of grain, weed seed, fruit and green-stuff is eaten by wood-pigeons, and they can be a serious problem for the farmer, as when they eat turnip tops in the spring or dibble in the drills where oats have been sown. They will take peas, beans and most kinds of garden produce. Caterpillars are eaten in small numbers. An idea of the wood-pigeon's food consumption can be gained from the fact that the crops of individual birds have been found to contain 88 peas, 40 beans, 1350 grains of oats and 1400 grains of wheat.

From late summer onwards, wood-pigeons begin to form into flocks and it is at this time that they can do a great deal of damage in fields of ripening grain. They take the grain (before cutting) by straddling down the stalks; and when it is stooked after cutting they will flock in great numbers to the stooks and do great damage. It is for this reason that the wood-pigeon is not protected by law in Britain, and may be killed or taken at any time of the year.

SPORTING BIRD

A shy, wary bird, blessed with exceptional vision and powerful flight, the wood-pigeon is a difficult target for the shooting man, who, generally speaking, expects his lowest

This quaint dove with the ornamental head-dress is a native of New Guinea.

The stock dove nests in old trees, rabbit burrows, buildings and such places.

ratio of kills to cartridges with this species. The bird is equally difficult as a photographic subject because it will desert eggs or young chicks readily at the slightest intrusion. Here, of course, we are speaking about wood-pigeons in the country and not the birds (more or less approachable), nesting in town gardens or public parks where they are not molested. Nowadays, shooting-men construct hiding-places in woods where wood-pigeons come to roost, and in this way manage to destroy more of them, but all the shooting has made no notable impact on the number of wood-pigeons generally.

The main enemies of the wood-pigeon are the peregrine falcon, which is able to out-fly it and kill it without difficulty; the female sparrow-hawk which kills it occasionally and with some difficulty; and the golden eagle, which takes pigeons when available. In addition to these birds, there are two mammal predators which sometimes kill young birds in the nest. These are the stoat and the rat, both of which will climb to nests in hedges or ivy.

THE STOCKDOVE

The Stockdove is smaller than the wood-pigeon (about thirteen inches in length) and darker in colour. In flight it is easily distinguished by the absence of the white wing bars and the white neck patches. Instead of a white patch on the neck the stockdove has one of glossy green. Similar in behaviour to the wood-pigeon, the stockdove often associates with it in winter. After you have picked out a stockdove in wood-pigeon company, you will notice that its flight is more rapid. The voices of the two species are similar—the stock-dove's cooing being even more monotonous than that of the wood-pigeon. Close attention will show that while the stockdove accents the first syllable of its song, the wood-pigeon accents the second. Thus, stockdove: *ooo*-roo-oo; wood-pigeon: coo-*coo*-roo-coo-oo.

While the stockdove may be found in much the same places, and has an equally wide distribution in Europe, it prefers more open woodland. In addition, it will be found nesting in rocks as well as trees, and on the ground in rabbit burrows. You will also find it nesting in old buildings. Like the wood-pigeon, the stockdove is black-listed by law in Britain, and for the same reasons.

The tufted dove, common in Australia, is a fast flier.

The fantail pigeon is the result of selective breeding by man.

As in the case of the wood-pigeon, the stockdove normally lays two eggs only, but a clutch of three is not uncommon, whereas in the wood-pigeon three eggs are most exceptional. The chicks are fed in exactly the same way—first on pigeon's milk, and then on food similar to that of the wood-pigeon. Two or three broods are reared in a season. Young stockdoves leave the nest when about a month old.

SMALLER DOVES

In this country, the true wild Rock Dove is a bird of rocky coasts, where it nests in caves and rock fissures. In other parts of Europe, birds reputed to be wild breed inland but, as has been said earlier, there is much confusion as to which are truly wild rock doves and which are not.

About the same size as the stockdove, the rock dove is recognised by its distinct black wing bars and its white or grey/white rump. This dove is a bold, dashing flyer often to be seen skimming low over water and sweeping about cliff faces as gracefully as the fulmar. Only very occasionally will the rock dove pitch in a tree. It is more likely to do so on the ground or on rocks. Like the wood-pigeon, it may occasionally be seen settling on water for no apparent reason. The rock dove is found in Scotland and Ireland, and in southern Europe from Spain along the Mediterranean coast to Turkey.

The Turtle-dove is notably smaller than any of the three pigeons already mentioned, being just under eleven inches in overall length. Widely distributed over Europe, it was in the British Isles formerly confined to England, but it has spread remarkably in recent years and is now nesting in Scotland. This dove nests in bushes, orchards, and scrublands and may use the old nests of thrushes and blackbirds. In plantations, it will occasionally use the old nest of a rook. The species tends to be gregarious and several birds may be found nesting quite close together.

The turtle-dove cannot be confused with the wood-pigeon, the stockdove or the rock dove. Apart from its smaller size and more slender bill its colour and markings are distinctive, the tail being long and graduated, black with white tips to the outer feathers. The wings and shoulders are rufous, also with black centres to the feathers. The head and neck are ash-grey, and there is a patch of black and white feathers at the sides of the neck.

NEWCOMER

The Collared Turtle-dove, which is about the same size as the common turtle-dove, was formerly absent from Britain as a breeding species, being found in eastern and southeastern Europe. In recent years it has been recorded breeding in the British Isles and is still spreading its range. It is distinguished from the turtle-dove by the black half collar on the back of its neck. It has red eyes, pale blue-grey shoulders which are displayed in flight, and a tail which shows a great deal of white. This species frequents mostly towns and villages. It nests commonly on buildings and sometimes on the ground.

QUESTIONS AND ANSWERS

Can pigeons swim?

The answer is that they can, but nobody knows why a pigeon should want to swim. The wood-pigeon has been watched by a number of observers swimming slowly with gently flapping movements of the wings, but whether it is actually bathing, swimming for pleasure, or trying to rid itself of parasites is not known.

What is acorn disease?

In some years there is often high mortality among wood-pigeons, which occurs about the time the birds are feeding on acorns. Affected birds are unable to swallow food, and as a result they lose weight quickly and are often found in a dying state. Because " piners " are usually found at acorn time the disease has been popularly called acorn disease.

BUTTERFLIES AND MOTHS

Butterflies are insects, with all the usual insect characteristics and others besides. One notable difference is in the form of the mouth, which is not used for biting at all, but for sucking. The ordinary insect mandibles have become modified in the case of the butterfly into a sucking proboscis.

In no group of insects will you find such a wide range and variety of colours, and butterflies have been rightly called the most beautiful of them all. If we look at the wings of a butterfly we shall find that they are covered with tiny scales, easily detached, showing a wide range of colours. In fact, the scales will rub off on to your fingers like dust if the insect is too firmly grasped.

The scales vary in shape—round, oval or serrated—and are arranged in such a way as to give the impression of small enamel plates. The colours of the scales may be due to their structure or the pigment in them. In other words, the colours may be produced by materials in the scales, or by outside factors. Structural colours are produced in the same way as the colours of a soap bubble, by outside factors.

In the majority of butterflies, the coloration of the underside of the wing is sombre and uniform. When the resting butterfly raises its wings it is difficult to see, so that the coloration of the underside has been called " protective ". If you watch a butterfly alighting you will see that it holds its wings erect, displaying undersides only.

The life of a butterfly is generally brief, the female dying soon after laying her eggs. From egg to insect, and then back to the egg again, usually takes place within a year; more precisely, the cycle is completed between one spring and the next. In one group of butterflies, however, the adults hibernate, and do not pair until the spring. These butterflies all belong to the Vanessidi, except the Brimstone.

NOT A SINGLE STAGE

Butterflies lay very tiny eggs, even those of the largest species being no bigger than pin-heads. From egg to perfect insect is not a single stage. First there is the caterpillar, or larva. The larval period is of varied duration, lasting from a few weeks to several

DEVELOPMENT OF A BUTTERFLY

Laying the EGGS — A CATERPILLAR develops. — The CHRYSALIS Stage — The perfect BUTTERFLY

Arrangement of the SCALES — Enlarged scales of butterfly WINGS

The birth of a butterfly begins when the eggs are laid and is completed by stages, ending when the perfect insect emerges from its chrysalis.

In Britain, the cabbage butterfly (left), can be seen in any garden during the summer. The common blue (right), is easily identified by its blue wings.

The peacock butterfly is one of the handsome Vanessa group, with " bulls-eye " markings on its wings resembling the tail feathers of the peacock.

The gaily-coloured swallowtail takes its name from the tail-like formation of its hind wings. The Apollo (right), is found in the Alps and the Appenines.

The Camberwell Beauty (left), has gold edges on its wings. The Red Admiral (right), is a dark butterfly with brilliant red markings and white spots on its wings.

The emperor moth is a moorland species. In April and May the males range far over the moorlands. The larvae feed mainly, but not entirely, upon heathers.

The skull-shaped design on the thorax explains why this moth is called the death's head. If disturbed, or handled, it often utters a squeaking cry.

Emerald green on an almost black ground distinguishes the handsome Indian priamus. When flitting among the trees it is easily mistaken for a bird.

months. The larva, which is worm-like, grows very rapidly and changes its skin three or four times during growth. In general, larvæ are not brightly coloured. The body at this stage is covered with shaggy joints, bristle and hooked cornicles. The mouth consists of two jaws with which the caterpillars devour leaves, fruit and flowers. When the larva has completed its growth it stops eating and becomes a chrysalis. In this form, the last stage of development takes place, and after some time the perfect butterfly emerges. In some cases the chrysalis stage lasts right through the winter.

Though butterflies, during their short, gay, apparently aimless existence, are perfectly harmless as far as the interests of man are concerned, this is not true of their caterpillars. Caterpillars consume great volumes of vegetable matter during growth, when they may increase in size by ten times, and are thus among the great ravagers of vegetation. Many of them become serious pests of agriculture: enemies of the farmer, the forester and the fruit grower.

Provided with short but numerous legs, often eight pairs

Butterflies of strange shapes and brilliant hues are found in India, Australia and South America. This South American species has wings of a shiny, metallic blue.

In the virgin forests of West Africa lives one of the largest butterflies in existence. It has a wing span of almost nine inches and is called Antimachus.

of them, caterpillars drag themselves slowly, and with difficulty, over the leaves and branches of trees, and the green growth of food plants. They gorge themselves to capacity, then rest to digest their meal. The caterpillar has only one purpose—to grow: its life at this stage consists of eating and resting, a period which may last from a few weeks to several months.

Caterpillars are furnished with strong mandibles, and eight or ten small eyes which give them a good field of vision, so that available food supplies are rarely missed. If we observe a caterpillar during the growing process we shall notice that the skin which covers its body very soon becomes too tight for it. The caterpillar's solution to this problem is to cast the old skin and grow a new one. The old skin bursts longi-

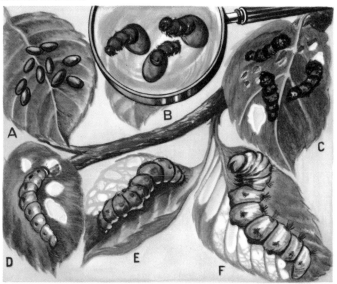

Metamorphosis of a butterfly: A. *eggs are deposited on a leaf.* B. *larvae emerge.* C. D. E. F. *four successive stages of a caterpillar's growth.*

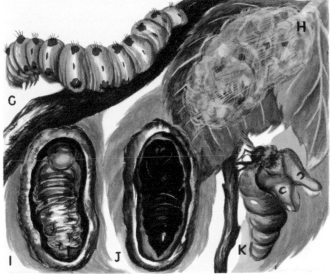

G. *growth is complete.* H. *the caterpillar weaves the fine web of its cocoon.* I. *chrysalis taking shape.* J. *chrysalis complete.* K. *butterfly emerges.*

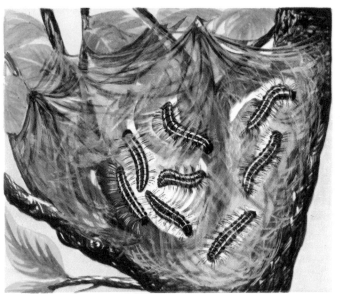

Some species of caterpillars weave silken shelters in the branches of trees.

Certain caterpillars which live in oak and pine trees, descend at night in columns of threes and fours to hunt.

tudinally and falls off, leaving the caterpillar naked. During these successive moults, which may number four or five, the caterpillars become temporarily somnolent. But as soon as their new skins are complete they go back with renewed vigour to their work of eating and growing, making up for lost time.

The skins of caterpillars vary a great deal in colour, and some caterpillars are extremely handsome, brightly coloured, silky, or adorned with bizarre little horns or tufts of hair. There are a few caterpillars which can cause skin irritation when handled; this is due to toxic agents secreted by the caterpillar.

Eventually the day arrives when this butterfly-in-the-making, full of food, has completed its growth and is ready for the next stage. This is the chrysalis or pupa stage. The larva sheds its larval skin for the last time. The skin which replaces it this time is quite different.

The pupa is at first soft and wet but it quickly dries, and hardens. This period is one of seeming death, and lasts for several weeks. But the pupa is really very much alive, as you will see if you touch it, for then it will palpitate and contract. Yet, for all practical purposes, it is not a living thing at all: it doesn't see, it doesn't move, it doesn't eat, it doesn't do anything. It dangles in the shade, rigid and lifeless, developing.

Though the pupa isn't at all like a butterfly, the form of the perfect insect can be seen, with two little stumps betraying the wings. In addition, there are organs which the caterpillar did not have, and which the butterfly will not possess. On the last segment of the abdomen there is a circle of points and hooks, and it is these which will tear away the envelope when the butterfly is ready to emerge. In the British Isles there are three main types of pupa: that which hangs upside down by the tail with no other support; that which is attached by the tail but is supported by a silken girth; and that which is enclosed in a silken cocoon.

EMERGENCE OF BUTTERFLY

A few days before the perfect butterfly, or imago emerges, its colours can be seen through the pupal skin. The colours do not all develop at the same rate. It is generally the case that dark colours, like black and brown, develop more slowly than bright ones, like yellow and red. Thus, in the

This paradise species with leafy wings lives in New Guinea.

Note the owl's face on the wings of this species.

pupal state, we can see the bright colours through the skin before we can see the dark ones. When all colours are present, the butterfly is ready to emerge.

At this point the pupal skin splits behind the head. The butterfly begins to crawl out of its husk, carefully extracting its wings, legs and antennæ. The empty pupal skin remains pretty much as it was except that there is now a hole in it, and it is empty. The butterfly crawls to a convenient spot where it can rest with wings hanging down to dry. At first they are wet and limp. But they soon dry out and the colours blossom as they spread. The butterfly is careful not to bring the wings together until they are completely dry. Emergence may take up to two hours, as in the case of our well-known Red Admiral.

The butterfly is now ready to begin its aerial life, and will now fly in the sun, and waver about in apparently aimless flight. But, in reality, its life is not aimless. It has much to do and little time in which to do it. So it visits flowers for their nectar to keep it alive, then mates, and lays eggs to produce the next generation. Its life may last no more than a few days, or up to two months.

ANATOMY OF BUTTERFLIES

Butterflies, like other insects, have external skeletons. They have four membranous wings, but whereas, in most moths, the fore and hind wings are united during flight by a coupling device known as the frenulum, this is never found in butterflies. In butterflies, the fore wings overlap the hind wings considerably. On the heads of butterflies there are two antennae, of variable length according to species, and of variable form. Laterally placed are the two large, composite eyes, each of which is composed of thousands of tiny tubular eyes. The mouth has become modified into a spiral tube or proboscis, which enables the butterfly to suck the nectar from flowers.

The anatomy of butterflies has been much studied in recent years. We may say briefly that the insect's heart and stomach are high up near the back. A single large artery, which goes from the heart to the thorax, carries the blood through the body, assisted by small auxiliary hearts like subsidiary pumping stations, activated by strong muscles which are placed at strategic points. The skin is both skeleton and armour;

The dead-leaf butterfly is a native of India and Malaya.

These brilliant butterflies are natives of India, Ceylon and New Guinea.

Magnolias are the favourite hunting ground of this species.

This Himalayan giant has a wing span of nearly twelve inches.

Small and extremely dainty are these species of tropical Asia.

From tropical India comes this flying jewel called Cyrestis thyodama.

Pholus vitis *is found in American vineyards.*

the legs are extremely strong. The frail-looking butterfly is, in fact, a well-designed insect, adapted to the life it leads.

Butterflies, like bees, have colour vision, but they have not been so closely studied in this respect as bees. The late Dr. Eltringham experimented with Small Tortoiseshell butterflies which were visiting a bed of asters made up of white, pink and purple flowers. Nearly a quarter of the flowers were white, yet the butterflies made only 47 visits to the white flowers as compared with 135 to the pink ones and 245 to the purple ones, in a total of 427 visits. Yet the pink flowers outnumbered the purple ones by four to three. It was later established that the attraction was not due to difference in the scent of the flowers.

MOTHS IN BRITAIN

There are more than ten times as many moths in Britain as there are butterflies. There are two ways of distinguishing moths from butterflies. In moths there is a coupling device called the frenulum which unites the fore and hind wings during flight. In butterflies the antennae are never feathered, but always end in a knob; the antennae of moths rarely do.

The largest British moth which often measures five inches across the expanded wings, is the Death's Head Hawk moth. The title largest is sometimes open to question because the Convolvulus Hawk moth is quite often as big. The death's head derives its name from the skull and crossbones markings on the thorax. It can squeak like a mouse and is the only moth capable of uttering such a sound.

QUESTIONS AND ANSWERS

The British humming bird?

From time to time one reads reports in the newspapers about humming birds in England. These alleged humming birds always turn out to be humming bird hawk moths. These are strong moths, very fond of bright sunshine, when they may be seen hovering before honeysuckle, jasmine and other such flowers, thrusting their long tongues into the nectaries. Their wings vibrate rapidly so that they appear to the human eye as a blur and it is not surprising that the moth should be mistaken for a humming bird.

The Chinese silk moth has inspired many artists and poets.

THE Swallow Family

For several centuries there has been speculation as to where swallows went in winter. One suggestion was that they flew to the moon. Gilbert White, the English parson, although he knew that many birds did migrate somewhere, was firmly convinced that others hibernated in England. The idea of swallows hibernating is not as far-fetched as once seemed, because one species has been found in a torpid state in the United States. However, it can be taken that the swallow with which we are familiar migrates to South Africa, while a few birds occasionally over-winter in the south of England.

The route taken by swallows to and from South Africa is now fairly well understood—due to observation of birds during migration, and on arrival, and to the recovery of ringed individuals. The route taken by birds from the British Isles is through France and Spain, then across the Mediterranean to North-west Africa, after which they follow roughly the west coast of the Congo area before cutting across to the Transvaal and the Orange Free State.

There is an alternative route taken by European birds, by which they cross the eastern Mediterranean into Egypt, whence they follow the Nile and the coast of East Africa to their wintering grounds. The return journey is made along the same routes.

As a further result of ringing it has been discovered that some swallows make this double journey many times. Yet again, marking individual birds has shown that many of them not only return from their wintering quarters to nest in the same building, but will choose the same rafter and even the same point on the same rafter. One bird at a Scottish farm nested in the same place for four consecutive years and returned on the fifth year when its nesting history was not noted.

The most astonishing story revealed by ringing was of a nestling which was ringed in the County of Ross and Cromarty in Scotland, in 1911, and was killed by a cat near Glasgow nine years later. This must have been one of the most widely travelled swallows in all Europe.

Swallows which arrive in England at the beginning of April have usually reached Spain a month earlier. They have been observed in the Cantabrian Mountains passing through on 12th March, and these were not the first birds reported flying north that year. The northward movement goes on through May and June, and birds do not reach northern Scandinavia until the end of the latter month. While swallows tend to leave their nesting areas after congregating in considerable numbers, they return in smaller groups and frequently arrive at their nesting quarters in pairs, which suggests they are mated on arrival.

Birds which arrive in central Scotland by the third week of April, may not begin nesting until the middle of May. Nevertheless, these birds usually manage to rear two broods, and sometimes attempt a third. If the third brood is very late the parents may desert it in the nest, but if the chicks are fledged at migration time the parents may, and sometimes do, wait on until they are ready to make the journey. In some years swallows may, therefore, be seen in central Scotland until the beginning of November.

At one time it was thought that swallows, when migrating, put up great mileages each day—in fact the flight both ways appears to be a leisurely one, with the birds making frequent stops to rest and feed, and the journey takes about two months either way.

SWALLOW TYPES

The Common Swallow, sometimes called the chimney swallow, is dark metallic blue above and white below, with a chestnut throat and long tail streamers. It can quite readily be distinguished from other members of the family.

The Red-Rumped Swallow, which is confined to the south of Spain and the Balkan Peninsula, presents no problem because of its tinted breast and rump.

The House Martin, which is as closely associated with human dwellings as the swallow, is a dark bird with white breast, white rump, and a slightly forked tail.

The Sand Martin, which is found about sand pits and river banks, is a pale brown bird with white breast and a brown band across its chest.

The Crag Martin is similar but has a squared tail and white flecks on the upper tail feathers, besides lacking the brown chest band.

The swifts are very much larger, and scimitar-winged —the Common Swift being dark all over, with a white chin. The Pallid Swift is pale brown all over with a much greater area of white on the chin, while the Alpine swift is bigger than either, pale brown with white chin and belly, and a brown chest band.

The swallow will rear two broods in a season and sometimes attempt a third, but the third is not always reared. The birds do not breed in their winter quarters.

The house martin is easily distinguished from the swallow by its white underparts, prominent white rump, and short tail streamers. House martins like building their nests close together in rows.

The swift is a swallow-like bird with very long wings. It is dark brown all over except for its white throat. Swifts are fast flyers and often very noisy in flight. They are neither so common, nor so widely distributed as swallows.

Though in a few parts of Europe some swallows still nest in caves and others on ledges in old-fashioned chimneys (hence the name chimney swallow) the vast bulk of European birds nest in close association with man, in byres, stables and outhouses. Occasionally a pair will nest in a porch or greenhouse or among masonry, but, generally speaking, rafters or beams in buildings are chosen, or a site at the apex of the roof. At nesting time the birds may be seen in farmyards or at field gates gathering nesting material where cattle have churned up a mixture of earth and dung. This material is carried to the chosen site and stuck on in the first instance to form the outline of the nest at the point of attachment. This is added to throughout the day, and daily, straw being freely mixed with the plaster. The material quickly sets and, being reinforced with straw, is extremely strong. The feather lining is added last. Sometimes swallows appear to choose a weak mixture, for the nest falls down when barely half-finished. A properly cemented nest will remain in position for a long time. Unlike the nest of the house martin the swallow's is open at the top.

Although both sexes carry material for nest building, the female swallow appears to sit on the eggs almost entirely by herself. Observation shows that the male bird will roost behind the female on the nest in the early stages of incubation. The eggs hatch in about a fortnight and the chicks are fed in the nest by both parents. During feeding spells the nest may be visited as often as sixty times in one hour, and it is remarkable how the parent birds, after hawking flies in brilliant sunshine, can swoop into barn or stable and cork-screw unerringly through the darkness to the edge of the nest, then leave the darkness and hunt with obvious ease again outside. This ability indicates a remarkable adjustment of vision to quickly-changing light intensities.

LIKE THEIR PARENTS

When the young leave the nest, they perch on eaves or overhead wires where they wait for the parents to feed them. This is done in a flash. At the approach of the parent the chick flutters its wings, the adult swoops up, brakes momentarily in flight to transfer food, and is away again instantly. Though the young swallows are plumaged like their parents they are easily told apart because of their short tail streamers. When young swallows have reached this stage they are a great attraction to farm cats. The parents are very much alive to the menace and they may be seen swooping time and again at a prowling cat in efforts to drive it off. Some cats retreat in the face of this assault; others have learned to turn it to good account, leaping up unexpectedly and catching the swooping bird in the air.

As the days become colder and shorter, the swallows have a tendency to gather in parties. By then most, if not all, young are strong on the wing. Parties from one farm meet parties from another, and morning after morning the augmented flock may be seen sitting on overhead wires or along roof-tops. Then one morning the flock disappears and does not return. The swallows have left on the long journey to South Africa and will not be seen again until the following spring.

HOW THE SAND MARTIN MAKES ITS BURROW

The sand martin is a tiny swallow which is able to drive a burrow the length of a man's arm in hard-packed sand. This it does with no other tools than its soft, insectivorous beak and its small feet. Both birds work at driving the tunnel and quite often work together. They loosen the sand by pecking at it with their beaks, then they scrape it behind them with their feet, often lying on their sides to do so. The work becomes harder as the tunnel lengthens because the sand has then to be pushed a greater distance to the tunnel entrance. The tunnel, when complete, will be about two inches in diameter. When the birds are feeding chicks the tunnel entrance becomes greatly enlarged to a diameter of 5 or 6 inches, or even more; this is the result of the constant traffic when the birds are feeding young. Every time they touch down at the tunnel entrance they dislodge a little sand with their feet.

There is a whole folk lore about birds which is almost as interesting as their natural history. Many of the old beliefs are concerned with luck and omens. The magpie, for example, presages good or ill luck, joy or sadness, according to the number seen at any one time. The raven has long been considered a bird of ill omen; so have owls. Many people do not like the cuckoo, and so on.

Some beliefs die harder than others. Still current is the belief that the corncrake or the landrail becomes a water-rail in winter. In fact, the water-rail is a quite distinct species. The same sort of belief persists about the cuckoo, viz: that it turns into a hawk in winter, and no amount of evidence can persuade staunch believers that it does not. There are many pretty stories about the robin and the wren. From the rhyme which refers to them as God's cock and hen, to the belief that they cover unburied human bodies with moss and withered leaves.

Then there is the belief that the crimson throat of the robin was associated with the crucifixion. Let us look more closely at a few of these beliefs.

There is a widely held belief that young robins kill their parents or *vice versa*. Although this is not so, one can understand how it arose, because the robin is a bird with a very highly developed territorial sense and holds its territory against all comers.

The belief that cock robin and Jenny wren were cock and hen probably arose from the fact that both species are found in the same places, and young robins in their first feathers are easily mistaken for wrens, especially when the young birds are still associating with their parents. In fact, cock and hen robin are both red-breasted and cannot be told apart.

The idea that the cuckoo becomes a hawk in winter must surely be explained by the fact that the cuckoo, which is hawk-like in flight, migrates at about the same time young hawks are dispersing all over the countryside and may be seen occupying ground formerly held by the cuckoo.

Beliefs about the magpie, the raven and the owl are mere superstition, liable to be accepted only by those who still believe that it is unlucky to walk under a ladder or to have the tail feathers of a peacock in the house.

The belief that robins and wrens cover unburied human bodies with moss and leaves is very old and we have it perpetuated to-day in the story, *The Babes in the Wood*. There is a certain basis for the belief—both robin and wren have a pronounced habit of turning over dead leaves in search of insects, spiders and suchlike creatures. One can readily imagine a situation where a robin or a wren was seen leaf-turning where a human being lay lightly covered. This, in turn, could easily give rise to the poet's lines:-

Call for the robin red-breast and the wren,
Since o'er shady groves they hover,
And with leaves and flowers do cover
The friendless bodies of unburied men.

The robin and the wren have attracted other poets and we have, for example, the well-known Scottish rhyme:

The robin cam to the wren's nest
And keekit in and keekit in.

This bears some relation to the facts because robins have been observed feeding the young of other birds in a nest close to their own. Young wrens, too, have a habit of wandering when first fledged and land in all sorts of queer places, including the nests of other birds, and what more likely nest than that of a neighbour robin? Thus the association becomes perpetuated by misinterpretation of observed fact.

EGG THIEVES

Many birds and mammals are fond of eggs. Some eat them on the spot and some carry them off. When Nature's nesting season is over (that is, when all the wild birds have reared their chicks and no longer have eggs) some birds and mammals will turn to the farmyard, knowing perfectly well that hens and ducks often lay outside their appointed places. Crows, magpies and jays are among the notorious egg thieves; though any of them will eat an egg on the spot they are just as likely to spike it with their beak and carry it off to some convenient place where they will drain the egg. Small eggs are carried in the beak and often simply cracked and swallowed whole.

Birds, such as crows, once they discover where farm hens are laying away, will visit the nest daily to eat the eggs and it is for this that farmers dislike them so much. The fact that crows, magpies and jays eat a lot of wild birds' eggs has led to their being blacklisted by law. But, in fact, it has never been shown that this predation has made any difference to the number of birds whose eggs are eaten.

Many gulls become confirmed nest robbers, often stealing from their own kind. But the king of web-footed egg thieves is undoubtedly the Great Skua which is the main predator on the eggs of the eider duck.

Notable mammalian egg thieves are the stoat, rat, hedge-hog, marten and fox.

Stoats frequently store eggs and as many as two dozen poultry eggs have been found in a cache beneath a hen house.

A stoat has also been known to have a cache of eight grouse eggs in a rabbit burrow. The stoat removes eggs by rolling them under its chin along the ground, using its fore-paws to help along and keep direction. The animal can roll grouse and other eggs through deep heather. Because of their egg stealing habits, stoats are ruthlessly destroyed by gamekeepers, which is a great mistake because the stoat's depredations are of absolutely no account.

Rats steal eggs of many kinds, and once they have access to poultry houses can become a serious nuisance. Not only do they eat eggs on the spot, they roll them away and store them as the stoat does, and they move them in exactly the same manner. Stories told of the co-operation of rats in various enterprises, including egg stealing, are mostly of doubtful authenticity.

The hedgehog usually blunders on a nest containing eggs. Once he has done so he will eat any eggs he can break.

The fox is a similar egg stealer. However, it is doubtful if foxes go out with the deliberate intention of looking for birds' nests, but there is no doubt that any egg found will be downed, whether it is fresh, half-incubated, or on the point of hatching. This applies to the eggs of domestic fowls as much as to those of wild birds.

POULTRY

Once upon a time, man treated the domestic fowl as a bird rather than a machine. She was allowed to sit on her own eggs, and hatch and rear her own chicks. Nowadays, her eggs are taken from her, graded and selected, and placed in electric incubators by the thousand. The chicks, when they hatch, know nothing of hens or mothers, or mothering. They are kept warm by artificial heat, fed on artificial foods, and set to work laying eggs from the age of six months.

There are times, however, when nature's way is still allowed to operate. Many people, wishing only to keep a few fowls, still buy a setting of eggs and place them under a broody hen. People who keep bantam fowls still allow the hens to

The broody hen after sitting on her eggs for twenty-one days, now has her family of downy chicks.

hatch their own eggs for replacement stock. Gamekeepers who are rearing large numbers of partridges or pheasants still use bantams for hatching the eggs. Commercially, however, poultry-keeping is now an industry rather than a form of livestock husbandry.

HATCHING OF CHICKS

Millions of chicks of many utility breeds are hatched annually in Great Britain by commercial hatcheries, and the bulk of commercial poultry flocks in the country to-day are supplied as day-old chicks from these places. The day-old chicks travel in draught-proof boxes from the hatcheries to farmers, small-holders and specialist poultrymen. They are then put into brooders, or under lamps, where they remain for six weeks or more, the temperature being reduced gradually as the chicks begin to feather. When the heat has been completely removed, the young birds are placed in arks or other houses to be " grown on ". About a month before they are due to begin laying, they are put into their laying quarters.

Nowadays, it is unusual to see birds on free range throughout the year. This happens more generally on farms. Elsewhere, it is more usual for the birds to be housed throughout the winter. In a great many cases the birds are confined to houses all the time—the intensive system. In other cases, they are put in battery cages where, throughout their laying life, they have barely room to turn round about. Individual poultrymen, who have some thought for birds as well as eggs, try to give them some freedom in good weather and confine them only in winter.

FASHIONS IN POULTRY

There are fashions in poultry as in everything else, and many old breeds, once extremely popular, are now rarely

Modern intensive-rearing cages. In this one there are five floors, just like a block of flats.

A paraffin brooder with curtains to conserve heat. Note the thermometer projecting above the roof for easy reading.

A modern poultry-breeding establishment. Each breeding pen is separately housed and enclosed so that there is no danger of cross-matings. Breeding stock are run on grass. Only fowls for commercial egg production are kept intensively.

seen. In fact, crosses are now far more popular in commercial flocks. Let us look at some of the outstanding breeds which have held their place right up to the present day.

Once widely popular, and still largely used in crosses, are the leghorns, which are of Italian origin. The most common varieties to-day are the black and the white, the brown and the exchequer. They are classed as light breeds, which means that their main function is the laying of eggs and not the production of carcasses for the table. Though a great many people keep pure-bred leghorns, such birds are rare to-day in large commercial flocks. They are not suited for battery work, being brisk, active fowls which thrive on movement.

SEX LINKAGE

Black and white leghorn males, however, are extensively used for crossing with Rhode Island Red females, and both these crosses produce excellent layers. The brown leghorn male is mostly used for crossing with Light Sussex females, and here sex-linking occurs. This means that as soon as the

chicks hatch their sex can be determined by the colour of their down—pullets being brown and the cockerels white. The black leghorn male is sometimes used for crossing with females of barred breeds like the Plymouth Rock, as this, too, produces sex-linked chicks. All the chicks hatch out with black down, but the males have a distinctive light spot on their crowns.

Sex-linked chicks are in great demand to-day. Favourite crosses being Rhode Island Red by Light Sussex, and Brown Leghorn by Light Sussex; the Rhode Island Red by White Wyandotte cross has gone somewhat out of favour. Production of sex-linked chicks means that the hatchers do not require the service of a sexer at hatching time. In all other cases day-old chicks have to be examined by experts before their sex can be determined. This is highly skilled work and the technique of sexing in this way originated in Japan.

NO BEST BREED

As with dogs and other live-stock, people have their

One of the most popular of modern egg-production types is the Rhode Island Red which originated in the U.S.A.

The wyandotte was for long a favourite breed, but is now out of fashion for egg production.

103

Here we have three breeds of fowl which are not widely kept to-day—the strange houdan with its tousled crest; the sleek, flighty Andalusian, and the barred Plymouth Rock which is kept mainly for sex-linking with black Leghorns.

preferences when it comes to poultry breeds and you will hear claims that this or that breed is the best egg producer. In fact, under modern conditions, many breeds have been developed to the highest level and there is no " best breed ". There are good and bad strains in all utility breeds. Some breeds do well in conditions which do not suit others. Management plays a very great part in egg production. A top grade pullet may produce fewer eggs in the wrong hands than a not-so-good pullet in the hands of an expert.

This is not to say that all breeds are equal. Bearing in mind the question of strain, district and management, there are breeds which are pre-eminent in egg-production. The modern in this field are the Light Sussex, the Rhode Island Red, the New Hampshire Red, Leghorns, Anconas, Buff Rocks, and their crosses. There are, however, still excellent high-producing strains of such breeds as the Wyandottes, Plymouth Rocks and Wellsummers, but these are not in such great demand. For really dark brown eggs, the Marans is supreme, and this remarkable French breed is also in great

demand as a table bird because it matures so quickly.

Broadly speaking, we may say that light breeds are kept mainly for egg production, light-heavy crosses as dual-purpose birds, and pure heavies mainly as table birds. This is to be qualified under modern conditions, however, because the modern Light Sussex, once the great table bird, has now reached the top as an egg-producer also and might well be called the main dual-purpose breed of to-day. The good poultryman likes to see his birds reach their full body size before they begin to lay. So he tries to get his light breeds laying at the age of 5½–6 months, his light-heavy crosses at 6–6½ months and his heavy breeds at 7 months of age.

BANTAMS

Most of the popular large breeds of fowl have their miniature counterparts, and these are classified as bantams. They are produced by selective breeding from the big types, so that the bantamised breeds, while they lay much smaller eggs, can produce, under first-class conditions, almost as

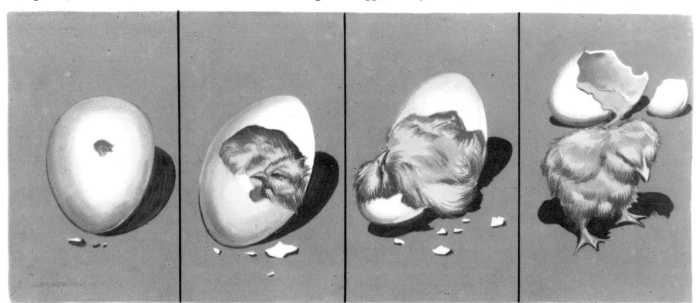

A chick is born. On the left we see the egg being chipped. At hatching time the chick has a little cutting instrument called the egg tooth. On the right the chick has emerged; the egg tooth will soon disappear.

Organised cock fighting is illegal in Great Britain, but mains are still secretly held, especially in the north of England. Cock fighting is a brutal sport, still legal in certain parts of the world, notably Mexico and Latin America.

many eggs in a year. Popular bantamised fowls are the Light Sussex, the Rhode Island Red, the Buff Rocks, and the Leghorns.

There are, however, many bantam breeds of long standing like the old English Game, the Spangled Hamburgs, the Sebrights, Silkies, and the Polish. The modern game bantam is popular in many quarters, but like other true bantams is kept almost entirely for show purposes or as a hobby.

Bantams of all kinds, especially males, tend to be more pugnacious and fearless than their counterparts in the big breeds. A game bantam male is very often the boss bird on the farm—even big roosters giving way to him without argument.

The males of most poultry are naturally pugnacious. This characteristic is so general that on pedigree breeding stations the males are kept apart as much as possible to prevent them injuring each other. In other cases they are dubbed, which means that their combs are trimmed down to prevent damage by other birds or frost, for it is essential that birds kept for breeding should be in first-rate condition. Loss of blood, for whatever reason, does not help this.

FIGHTING COCKS

This fighting instinct being so strong it is not surprising that man (or rather those who like such things), should have exploited it for his amusement. The males of ordinary breeds will fight at any time—indeed the difficulty is often to prevent them from doing so. But man was not content with that: he had to develop distinct breeds specially for fighting and for nothing else. These are the fighting cocks, otherwise known as game fowl. There are many varieties of fighting cock, but in this country nowadays males fight only when they choose to do so. Cock fighting as an organised entertainment is now illegal. In many parts of the world it is still legal, notably in Latin America. A meeting where fighting cocks are matched is called a " Main," and though these are now illegal in Britain, they are still organised, and attended secretly, in several parts of the North of England. Everybody, including the police, knows this goes on, but it is extremely difficult to catch the people responsible, let alone deal with them under the law.

Male and female of the well-known Italian breed, the Ancona. The Ancona is a light breed and an excellent layer, but it is highly nervous unless handled with great care.

Italy has produced many famous breeds of fowl which are still honoured in their own country. Top, we see the well-known black Leghorn, and on the Left the white variety of this universally-famous breed.

105

To the shooting man, and to the countryman generally, a pheasant is just a pheasant; and, in fact, the great majority of pheasants living wild in Europe are either mongrels, or derived from two or three types. There are, however, a great many species of pheasants in the world—some of them among the most brilliantly plumaged of birds.

The types most commonly met with as wild birds, or as birds hand-reared then turned free for the purposes of sport, are the Ring-Necked pheasant (*Phasianus c. torquatus*) and the Caucasian (*Phasianus c. colchicus*), although nowadays they are rarely seen pure in a wild state. Normally, wild birds are a mixture of these two types, with here and there a strain of something else—for example, the melanistic mutant or the silver pheasant. One thing is noticeable in wild birds: practically every wild male has a white ring, or white mark, on his neck; the stamp of the ring-necked pheasant, which is indelibly impressed on every type with which this species is crossed.

Long ago, perhaps more than 3,000 years ago, pheasants were well known and popular in the East—for example in China—and these brilliant birds frequently provided the motif for embroideries and other works of art. The Greeks called the pheasants which lived in the area of the River Phasis " The Birds of Colchis "; in which two names we can see the origin of the species known to-day as *Phasianus c. colchicus*. There were great pheasants living in France in prehistoric times. All our present-day European birds originated in Asia or the Caucasus. In Africa, a species of pheasant has been discovered in the Congo. Before this it was thought that Africa had no pheasants, although it is the home of the guinea fowls and other similar species.

PHEASANT GROUPS

The world's pheasants are divided into several groups—for example those of the genus phasianus, known as true pheasants; those of the genus crossoptilon and the gallopheasants; the junglefowls of the genus gallus (ancestors of domestic poultry); the tragopans and the peafowls.

The true pheasants, the birds of Colchis, are the most familiar and have always been so. A notable feature of this group is that all the forms interbreed freely, producing young which are completely fertile. It is for this reason that it is difficult to keep wild pheasant stocks pure. All the members of the true pheasant group behave very much like each other. In practically all the species the females are indistinguishable, as are the eggs and chicks. The males, however, are distinctive.

In Europe, the Black-necked Pheasants, the birds of Colchis, are of the greatest antiquity. They were introduced early by the Greeks and the Romans and were well established in England a thousand years ago. In fact this type is still known in some places as the old English pheasant. Though still a favourite with European breeders, the black-necks have been much crossed in the last 100 years with ring-necks and Mongolians. It is this readiness to interbreed that has led to the mongrelisation of European pheasants.

Among the black-necks is the Southern Caucasus pheasant, *Phasianus c. cochinus*. In this species the cock has a metallic green head, with throat and neck of metallic green and blue. The neck varies a great deal in colour through shades of green and purple and violet. The mantle is coppery-red glossed with purple. The other Caucasus pheasants are the Northern and the Talisch. The former inhabits the northern side of the Caucasus and the latter the coasts of the Caspian Sea. Farther east, the Talisch is replaced by the Persian pheasant, a sub-species intermediate between the black-neck group and the white-winged group.

Only one of the white-winged pheasants has been intro-

The ring-necked pheasant (Phasianus c. torquatus), *is now the dominant type in the British countryside.*

The Greeks called the pheasants which lived in the area of the River Phasis, the Birds of Colchis.

duced into Europe: the species known as the Prince of Wales pheasant. According to Jean Delacour, birds of this species were imported in 1902, but their identity was soon lost in hybridisation with black-necks and other types. A pure strain was, however, kept in pheasantries until 1914, after which the Prince of Wales disappeared as a type. There are six forms of white-winged pheasant.

The Kirghiz pheasants, which are large birds, inhabit an area of the Kirghiz Steppes from the Aral Sea into Chinese Turkestan. These birds have for long been known as Mongolian pheasants, in spite of the fact that they are not found in Mongolia at all.

The grey-rumped pheasants, a large group, are found in the eastern half of Asia. They differ from the previous types in having light grey rumps. To this group belong the ring-necks, which have been widely introduced into Europe and America. The one most commonly bred in Britain, and the one which has left its stamp on all wild males, is the Chinese ring-necked pheasant, *Phasianus c. torquatus*, while the Formosan type, *Phasianus c. formosanus*, has become well established in America along with the Chinese.

POPULAR PHEASANTS

A popular pheasant in England and France, because of its large size and extreme vitality, is the melanistic mutant. This is a green pheasant, metallic green above, with wings and abdomen of dull black and olive, called *Phasianus colchicus tenebrosus*. This type was at one time thought to be a simple hybrid between *Phasianus c. colchicus* and *Phasianus versicolor versicolor*. That it was a true mutation, however, was definitely established. According to Delacour, " the very dark face of the mutant has become generally established in Europe and America where entirely deep green and blue cocks and black hens are common occurrence. Mutation has reached the end of its course and become stabilised."

The true green pheasants are a distinct group, being made up of *Phasianus v. versicolor*, which inhabits the Island of Kyushu and the Yamaguchi Province; the Pacific green pheasant, *Phasianus v. tanensis* which is found south of Kyushu; and the northern green pheasant which inhabits Hondo and is much lighter in colour than *Phasianus v. versicolor*.

From birds in these groups have been derived the wild pheasants as we know them to-day. Long years of preservation and near domestication have had their effect on birds in many ways—for example, the feral hen pheasant brought up in a rearing field is considered to be a poor mother and a stupid nester, but this is not always so. During the Second World War, pheasants in many parts contrived to keep going when left entirely to themselves. The birds are perfectly hardy and have shown themselves adaptable to a great variety of climates.

THE PEAFOWLS

The peafowls belong to the genus Pavo, and were widely kept as ornamental fowl until recent years. Nowadays, they are far less commonly seen. The peacock has always been popular judging by its prominent appearance in works of art over the last few thousand years. Peacocks were taken to Egypt by the Phœnicians. Once a common ornament of the great country estates, peafowl are nowadays mainly seen in zoological gardens or in small private collections.

One of the best known is the Indian peafowl. These birds were kept by the kings of Egypt and were later reared by the Greeks and Romans for the table. Later on, they became popular in France and England and other parts of Europe. The turkey displaced the peafowl as a table bird in the 16th century, and from then on the peafowl was largely kept as an ornamental bird because of its brilliant plumage.

The Indian peafowl is completely hardy, breeds freely, and is easy to rear. They are not given to wandering as the true pheasants are. Unfortunately they are very fond of flowers and leaves and so can become a nuisance in small gardens. On big estates where they have plenty of room to move about they are not a problem and, being good tempered, are not prone to fighting with each other or with other birds.

The black-winged peafowl is a mutation, known as far back as 1823. The type appeared quite suddenly in England among blue, white and pied peafowls.

There are three Eastern types of green peafowl: the Javanese, the Indo-Chinese, and the Burmese.

The Congo peacock, the only bird of the pheasant family found in Africa, was discovered in 1936. Startling discoveries often have small beginnings, and the story of the Congo peacock's discovery began with a single feather found in the hat of a Congo native in 1913. The existence of the Congo peacock was discovered by Dr. James P. Chapin. The feather was a secondary wing quill and Dr. Chapin was unable to identify it. It was like no feather then known, but it seemed quite clear that it belonged to a bird of the gallinaceous group. From this find, Dr. Chapin pursued his investigations, fortunately discovering a pair of mounted birds in the Congo Museum at Tervueren in Belgium. They had never been placed on exhibition and were assumed to be the young of the ordinary peafowl. This set off a search, and the bird was eventually discovered. The male Congo peacock has a velvety black head with a narrow black crest. The feathers of the upper back and upper breast are black with violet blue borders; the mantle is black and the rump dark bronze green. The overall length of the bird is from 640 to 700 millimetres (twenty-five inches to twenty-seven inches).

SILVER AND GOLD

To the group of gallopheasants belong the Silver pheasants,

The Indian peafowl was once a familiar bird in the grounds of country houses. Nowadays it is rarely seen.

The jungle fowl, which in many ways resembles the modern brown Leghorn, is the ancestor of our modern poultry. The jungle fowls are easily distinguished from the true pheasants.

some of which are quite familiar: the Imperial pheasant, Swinhoe's pheasant, and the Firebacks. Silver pheasants of one kind and another have long been a favourite in aviaries and pheasantries and, when feral, interbreed freely with other types, quickly losing their separate identities.

The genus Chrysolophus contains the most beautiful of all game birds: the Golden and the Lady Amhurst pheasants. These two species are favourites in private collections. They interbreed freely with each other in captivity, producing a fantastic range of types and colours, all of which are fertile. The Lady Amhursts and the golden are also fertile when crossed with other types of pheasant, but fertility is much lower in these cases.

Golden pheasants have been common in Europe since the 18th century. Being hardy, and able to live in small pens, the bird does well in captivity and is extremely popular. Considering this popularity it is surprising that so little is known of the golden pheasant in the wild state. It is abundant in Western Hupeh, living among scrub and bamboo on rocky hillsides, but there is little or no information about its nesting habits or its daily life.

The dark-throated golden pheasant is similar to the common golden type but of a deeper colour. This type is very popular in America, where many are kept in captivity. Many other types of so-called golden pheasant are simply hybrids with Lady Amhursts.

Lady Amhurst's pheasant comes from South-eastern Tibet and South-west China. The hen is similar to the golden hen but she is larger, with darker barring and a green sheen. This green sheen in golden pheasants betrays Amhurst blood. The male Lady Amhurst has a metallic green crown, a crest of crimson feathers, and a ruff of rounded feathers which are white with a blue and black border. He is an extremely handsome bird, popular in all collections.

JUNGLEFOWLS

Junglefowls, of which there are many types, are the ancestors of modern poultry. Some of them, like the Cochin-Chinese red junglefowl and Lafayette's junglefowl, bear a striking resemblance to the modern brown Leghorn male. The junglefowls are so obviously poultry that they are unmistakable. The primitive peoples in Africa, South America, and the islands of the Pacific, have had poultry of one kind or another for a long time, and no one has yet been able to explain how some of these tribes first obtained possession of them. There is evidence that the Chinese had poultry 1400 years before the Christian era. Such fowls were found in the Indus Valley 2500 years B.C. They were established in Europe before the Roman Conquest; then they became common in the Mediterranean and Egypt. Many of our modern breeds of domestic fowl, in fact, originated in the Mediterranean and China.

The Tragopans are large, heavily-built pheasants, sometimes called horned pheasants. In these five species the males have gorgeous plumage, while the females are soberly hued. The males have short crests with two fleshy horns and a great, brilliant throat wattle or lappet. Tragopans range from Kashmir through the Himalayas and Burma to Central China. The five types are: the Western Tragopan, Blyth's Tragopan, the Satyr Tragopan, Cabot's Tragopan, and Temminck's Tragopan.

THE GIN TRAP

The gin trap is the most barbarous instrument ever invented by man for the torture of wild animals, and countless millions of rabbits have died lingering deaths in its jaws. The Americans, with their flair for realism, or perhaps because they are more honest, have for long referred to the gin as the leg-hold trap, which is a very apt description because in nine cases out of ten this trap holds without killing.

In England, to-day, the gin trap is completely illegal and may not be set anywhere to catch any animal for any reason. In Scotland, the position is quite different; there the trap is still legal for the catching of foxes, which is a farcical situation because once it is set it can catch almost anything.

True, it is illegal to set the gin in the open, or to bait it with food as an attraction, but foxes, eagles, buzzards, crows, badgers and otters are still regularly caught in such traps set in the open and baited. It is to be feared that this state of affairs will continue so long as it is legal to use gins for any one creature.

The gin is an illegal instrument in certain Scandanavian countries, and it is noteworthy that it was outlawed in Germany in the days of Adolph Hitler. More noteworthy still is the fact that its use in Germany was subsequently legalised by the victorious Allies.

The humanitarian's objection to the gin trap has always been that it maimed, mutilated and tortured, and seldom, and then only accidentally, killed outright. Foxes have been known to lie for days in a gin trap held by a forepaw; so have badgers and otters. Many a fox and many a badger has chewed off its foot to escape from a gin. Golden eagles frequently have a leg mutilated when they are caught in gins set for hoodie crows. The gin is no respecter of protected birds, or mammals, and it will take whatever comes along, including the foot of a child.

SHARKS

Of all the creatures that live in the sea the shark has probably the most dreaded reputation—a reputation which has been assiduously fostered and added to by storytellers and film-makers over the years.

The impression one is generally given by such accounts is that a man who falls overboard in shark-infested waters is certain to lose a leg at least, and very likely his life. In films one usually sees the splash of the falling body, followed by the sight of a triangular fin cutting through the water, after which one is left to assume that the shark has made a meal of man.

Careful observation of sharks by zoologists bears out this concept only in part.

RARE ATTACKS ON MAN

Though there is no doubt that some sharks can be highly dangerous, attacks on human beings are, in fact, extremely rare. Of about 150 species of shark in the world, only four types might be considered a danger to human beings: the tiger shark, the blue shark, the white shark (sometimes called the man-eater) and the hammer-headed shark.

Despite the fact that there is little solid evidence about any type of shark persistently attacking human beings, the United States considered the development of a shark repellent necessary during World War II, principally for the safety of airmen forced to bail out over the ocean. The shark repellent was in the form of a cake attached to the airman's tunic, and when it dissolved it formed a protective ring round him. The water inside the ring was so distasteful to the sharks that they would avoid the area for several hours.

REASONS FOR ATTACKS

Several factors seem to contribute towards making a shark attack a man. The main one is shortage of food, but individual temperament must play some part because there is no general rule about any species of shark attacking human beings. Some divers will dive among sharks to recover money when the fish are well fed, but will not do so for any money when the fish are hungry.

Nevertheless, modern evidence increasingly suggests that sharks, generally speaking, are nothing like the menace they were once supposed to be.

MONSTERS OF THE DEEP

Though sharks grow to a large size they do not, nowadays, compare with the great prehistoric monsters which had tremendous jaws with up to 100 teeth each about four inches in length. But there are plenty of modern monsters, and one can well understand people being afraid of them.

The biggest of the moderns, and the biggest fish in the sea, is the whale-shark, which may reach a length of seventy-five feet, although lengths of thirty to forty feet are more usual.

Dogfishes, because of their voracity and their numbers, can be very troublesome to fishermen. They hunt in troops.

The blue shark is remarkable for its slender body. It is a migratory species which sometimes visits the south coast of England.

This shark (Lamna cornubica), is much given to attacking whales. With its terrible jaws it tears out great masses of their flesh.

The hammer-headed shark, so-called because of the position of its head in relation to its body, is a dreaded hunter. It is an inhabitant of the Indian Ocean.

A really big whale-shark may weigh up to four or five tons. This gigantic sea animal feeds on such small prey as sardines and squids.

Some people consider that the whale-shark was really the " whale " that swallowed Jonah, but this fish could not have been the one, even had it so wished, because it has very small teeth and its throat is so narrow that it could hardly swallow a man's fist let alone the man himself.

THRESHER

Another big and formidable shark is the species called the thresher. This species reaches a length of twenty feet, and has a tail up to eleven feet long. The tail is used for clubbing prey, and this shark can knock big fish unconscious with the blows. The thresher will even strike at baited hooks, which accounts for the number of times it is foul-hooked.

The thresher has a habit of leaping right out of the water, then lashing with its tail as it falls back, thus churning up

The spiked dogfish (Acanthias vulgaris), *is found in numbers along the south-east coast of England. It has a single spine on its back and in front of the dorsal fins.*

the immediate area and knocking everything within range half-unconscious.

HAMMER-HEAD

The much dreaded and remarkable hammer-headed shark is found in the Indian Ocean. Its head is elongated on either side, into lobes, at the end of which are the eyes. This arrangement makes the shark's head look just like a hammer, but so far nobody has been able to suggest any possible advantage from this development. The hammer-head is a dreaded hunter, being able to kill and eat other formidable creatures, including sting rays.

TIGER

The tiger shark, unlike the tiger, is not a handsome animal. It is one of the ugliest of fish, the only really tigerish thing about it being its ferocity and strength. This is one of the most feared species, although there is no real evidence that it is a confirmed man-eater.

LARGEST SHARK

The basking shark, which is one of the biggest of the clan, can reach a length of more than fifty feet. It is harmless

The small spotted dogfish is one of the commonest species in British waters, particularly along the south coast.

to human beings so far as hunting them is concerned, but it is a menace because of its habit of surfacing under small craft and overturning them in the water. This species turns up regularly in British waters, causing consternation among boating holiday-makers.

Sharks spend much of their time hunting on the bottom of the sea. Many of them prey mainly on fish of their own kind. Dogfish are small sharks, and they are just as ruthless and voracious as their huge relatives.

SAWFISH

A close relative of the sharks is the sawfish, which reaches a length of twenty feet and may weigh up to two tons. The jaws of this fish are extended and fashioned in the form of a double-edged saw. With this tremendous weapon the sawfish rends, tears and disembowels its prey. Sawfish have been known to attack human beings in certain parts of the world, and they will habitually attack whales and sharks.

SOME SMALL MAMMALS

It is not surprising that the smallest mammals, which we refer to roughly as "mice", should be so plentiful, considering that they are for the most part the bread and butter of the hunters. Everybody knows how the lemmings migrate in vast numbers to new territories and how foxes and large owls prey on them. Not so well known is the fact that the small field vole can increase to such an extent, in some years, that it can literally fell young forests as surely as the woodman's axe.

Though so many of the small mammals are mouse-like, they are not all mice. Some of them, like the shrews and the mole, belong to the same family group as the hedgehog. Mice, on the other hand, are rodents, which puts them along with the rats and the squirrels. In everyday language, however, the various species are still comfortably mixed-up. Thus the field vole is often called the short-tailed field-mouse, to distinguish it from the field-mouse with the long tail which is called the wood-mouse. Shrews are often referred to as shrew-mice. Any big mouse is liable to be called a small rat; then you have the water-vole which, as often as not, is called water-rat, although it is not a rat at all.

HOUSE MOUSE

Most people are familiar with the house mouse, so many colour varieties of which are kept in captivity by small boys as pets. The house mouse is not a native of Britain and it cannot live without man. For example, the house mouse of the island of St. Kilda died out when the island was cleared of people.

While the house mouse in town lives mostly in houses, it will live outdoors in the country during the summer months and move into houses for the winter. It is this species which swarms in corn ricks, riddling them with its tunnels and nibbling the ears of corn. It can be truly said that the house mouse lives almost entirely on food provided by man, and, where this is plentiful, they will carry away surplus food and store it.

The male house mice fight each other, and the females fight for possession of mouse-holes. Though usually shy, they can become quite bold when they are not being molested, and will come out in quite bright light even when there are people about. A cat in the house makes them far more wary.

THE WOODMOUSE

The Long-Tailed Field Mouse, or Woodmouse, is a handsome little animal with big ears, pinky feet, and a tail as long as its body. The fur varies in colour through many shades of brown. The underparts are silvery white and clearly lined off from the brown fur of the flanks. On the chest there is very often a bright patch coloured orange or pale red.

Field mice are very common almost everywhere from low ground to the tops of mountains. Though they are very largely nocturnal, many must move about by day, judging by the number killed by kestrels. Owls kill them by night. Indeed the field mouse's enemies are legion—cats, dogs, stoats, weasels, foxes, crows, ravens, buzzards, even moles—yet the field mouse manages to remain one of the commonest of animals.

The field mouse nests frequently in stack-yards but only rarely in a stack of corn. Occasionally one finds its way indoors, but this is exceptional. The nest may be above ground in a warm tussock, or underground at the end of a burrow or system of burrows. The nest is made of grass. Many mice are turned up during autumn ploughing. The field mouse does not hibernate; like the squirrel it is active throughout the winter in suitable weather. It stores food for winter use, quite often in the old nests of the thrush or blackbird. It is very destructive in the garden and will take peas, bulbs, seeds and fruit.

MANY RACES

There are many races of field mice in Great Britain, most of them island varieties, but they are mainly the concern of the specialist zoologists. In the south of England, however, there is a biggish field mouse called the yellow-necked mouse, but even about this one there is some doubt, for it interbreeds freely with other mice and may be no more than a variety.

The tiny Harvest Mouse weighs only a quarter of an ounce. It is becoming rare, but is still most plentiful in the south of England. As its name implies, it frequents cornfields, where it is active by day, climbing the stalks of oats, wheat or barley, round which it curls its tail. It will eat ears of grain on the stalk or on the ground. The nest of the harvest mouse is built about a foot from the ground, woven round stalks of corn or other strong plants, and sometimes built in a bush. Here the young are born. Winter nests are often under corn stacks. But burrows are also used in the open fields, and there the animals store food. In summer, the harvest mouse is sociable and playful, but it is less active in winter.

Here we see the tiny harvest mouse, the woodmouse and the field vole. The harvest mouse has a prehensile tail, the woodmouse a long tail, and the field vole a short tail.

The common shrew and the water shrew are both small, active, and extremely voracious. They have to eat continuously.

VOLES

The Field Vole is very common, and is blunt-faced with a short tail. In some years it reaches plague numbers, when enormous damage is done to young plantations and pastures. At such times you will see the grass yellowing and young trees dying, and usually there is an influx of birds of prey, like short-eared owls, which prey on the voles. When the plague has run its course there is a sudden population crash and the voles die off suddenly. What causes this crash is still imperfectly understood by zoologists.

The Bank Vole is smaller in the body and longer in the tail than the field vole, and is much more mouse-like. It is also far more active and agile. This species is a great jumper and can leap out of a milk bottle or a box nine inches deep. Bank voles are not so common as field voles. This species likes banks covered with ivy or other trailing growth, and under such cover it has its runs. It will use mole runs. It makes its burrows in bankings and here it has its sleeping quarters.

Water-Voles are dark-furred animals, blunter in the face than brown rats, and more robustly built. They are often mistaken for rats and consequently killed. A good specimen of a water-vole will measure fifteen inches from nose to tip of tail, one-third of which is tail.

Water-voles are clannish animals living in small communities. The burrows are often extensive affairs with entrances and exits above and below water. Sometimes the burrows will be found a considerable distance from water. The nest is made of chewed reeds or other water plants and may be in a burrow away from the water. Water-voles have a habit of carrying underground green stalks which are not used for food or bedding. So far no one has been able to explain this habit. Many animals rear two litters in a season, and there is sometimes a third.

THE SHREWS

Shrews are relatives of the moles and eat the same kind of food in the same enormous quantities. In appearance, shrews are mouse-like, but you can tell them by their long, pointed snouts. They are savage little animals, fighting with other shrews, mice and voles. They can kill mice and will eat them. Their life is one continuous search for food, and they will die if deprived of food for a few hours. The shrew has a strong musky smell so that cats, dogs, foxes, stoats, weasels, and other mammals won't eat them. The smell does not, however, prevent such hunters from killing shrews, so the musky smell can hardly be called protective. It may well be, however, that a hunter will kill shrews when it is well fed, and has nothing better to do; but when hunting for food it may avoid shrews because it has no time to waste and already knows that they are useless as food.

The Common Shrew is not a great burrower. It prefers to use the runs of voles and the tunnels made by mice. Its nest, which is of dried grass, will be found under cover of some kind or in a hole in a tree. More than one litter is reared in a season but there is high mortality in autumn. It is almost certain that the shrew's life does not exceed eighteen months.

The Water Shrew is a dark-furred species with a white belly which frequents the same places as the water-vole. It, too, drives burrows into the banks of streams, and these have entrances above and below water. It dives well and finds its food by turning over stones in the stream bed.

The smallest shrew in Britain is the Pygmy, which weighs one-fifth of an ounce or less. It is the only species found in Ireland.

THE MYSTERY OF THE EEL

For a long time it was believed, and in some quarters it is still believed, that eels come from horse hairs.

Probably the belief was strengthened by the fact that nobody could find eel spawn in any stream, river or lake in the country for the simple reason that none was to be found in any of these places. The horse hair belief is pure legend. The truth is remarkable enough in itself.

Sometime in its mature life, possibly between the ages of six and twelve years, the eel is prompted to leave its home lake or pond or canal and make a journey down to the sea; where it has to cross overland it does so, usually at night. Thus eels have been seen crossing fields and commons on their way to the next stream or river. The eels, being slimy, can move through dry grass without discomfort.

When it reaches the sea the eel rests a while, and then begins its long journey to the depths of the Atlantic Ocean where breeding takes place. It was a long time before this breeding place was discovered and the first young eel to be examined by zoologists was caught in 1763. Young eels at this stage are ribbon-like larvae called *leptocephali*, sometimes called glass fishes. They were long considered to be a separate species. The young eels remain in the birth area until they are several inches long and then they set out on their journey to fresh water moving up rivers and into streams, ponds, ditches and lakes. They have become recognisable elvers by the time they reach the rivers and sometimes they move upstream in such numbers that the water is almost black with them. The elvers do not return to the ocean until they in turn are ready to spawn.

Very probably the adult eel dies after spawning.

The Honey Bee

The honey-bee should not be confused with the familiar bumble-bee—the big, fat, furry bees that buzz in fields of clover in summer. The two are distinct in almost every possible way, and not least in appearance. In the small bumble-bee colony there is no permanence; only young, fertilised queens survive the winter, to found a new colony in the spring. In the honey-bee colony, births replace deaths; here we have a great, thriving, bee metropolis which lasts indefinitely.

The honey (or hive) bee probably originated in the Indo-Malayan region of the Far East. Certainly, this is the only part of the world where this type of bee is found in a truly wild state. The honey-bee with which we are familiar (*Apis melliflua*) interbreeds freely with the wild species of India, a fact which suggests close kinship, so that our bee may be considered merely a geographical race. Like the Indian wild bees, our honey-bees establish permanent colonies, and " hive off " to found new colonies from time to time, whereas all our native bees and wasps establish colonies which last only a year.

Though the Orient was the original home of the wild honey-bee, the species is now kept throughout the world for its honey. The wild bees of North America, of the genus Apis, are not natives of that country, being derived from swarms which escaped from the old settlers. Three hundred years ago settlers took bees to North America; before then the country had only bumble-bees. The escaped bees settled in hollow trees (which escaped bees still do), then swarmed to found new colonies, so that the settlers discovered colonies as they moved westward. The bees were most likely to be found in trees close to the prairie edge, where there was an abundance of wild flowers. These bee trees were greatly sought after because of their rich store of honey. At that time the only other sweetening agent was maple sugar, the extraction of which was a laborious business. The little honey provided by the bumble-bees was insignificant, and hardly worth the trouble of seeking it.

It is almost certain that man has kept the honey-bee as a " domestic " insect for more than 4000 years. Thousands of years ago, primitive men were raiding bee nests for their honey, and a cave painting in the south of Spain shows a Stone Age man raiding such a nest, and removing a honey-comb, while he is surrounded by angry bees. So the spread of the honey-bee from the Orient began a very long time ago. When the bees reached America, the Indians called them the white man's flies.

Honey, which is seventy-seven per cent. sugar, is made by the honey-bees from the nectar of flowers; but the honey is not simply nectar. It undergoes a change when it is in the bee's honey-sac, the sugar being split into two simple types called dextrose and levulose. This fresh honey is put by the bees into the comb cells, where it ripens into the honey we know. The cell isn't sealed until about half the water content of the honey has been evaporated. Honey is an excellent human

Typical cells made by the honey bee.

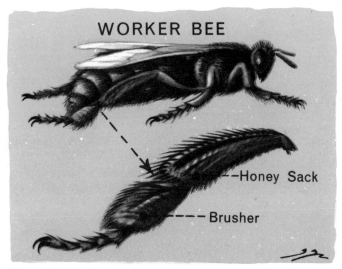

Top: *Worker bee.* Bottom: *Leg of bee showing the pollen basket and brush.*

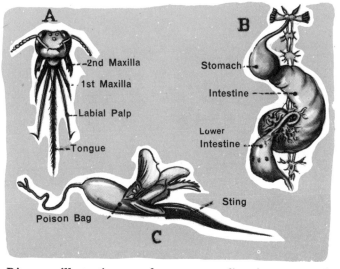

Diagram illustrating mouth apparatus, digestive tract and sting of honey bee.

The nuptial flight of the queen bee. The queen, followed by drones, flies high into the air. Many drones die during this flight and only one mates with the queen.

After her nuptial flight the queen bee returns to the hive. Now her work as an egg-laying machine begins. She may lay over 2,000 eggs per day.

It is the duty of the worker bees to prepare food for the bee grubs. The food is prepared in different ways according to the type, and the stage of development, of the larvae.

food, apart from its sweetening properties, being quickly absorbed in the blood to produce heat and energy.

It has been estimated that a bee would have to make up to 80,000 journeys between the hive and the nectar-producing flowers to make a pound of honey. So the popular conception of the busy bee is a correct one.

Bees are remarkable for their adaptability to habitat—they are dispersed all over the world—and for their ability to produce honey from a wide variety of flowers. Bees in one country may be making honey from flowers unknown to bees in another. The clovers are favourites wherever they grow, and produce a distinct kind of honey. Similarly, heather is a favourite source of nectar in the late summer, and the honey from heather is distinctive in colour and flavour. Honey derived from lime blossoms has a distinctive green colour. The famous buckwheat honey of North America is dark purple in colour and strong in flavour. But, whatever the source of the honey, it fulfils the needs of the bees just the same.

QUEENS AND DRONES

Honey is the food of the bees, and they lay up stores to keep them going through the winter. Bee-keepers make use of these stores, replacing the honey with sugar when the " crop " is removed. The manner in which worker bees feed the larvæ is interesting. When they first hatch out, all the young bees are fed upon the substance known as " royal jelly ". This is secreted from the pharyngeal glands of the workers. This royal jelly is the sole food of those young bees which will become queens; young bees which will become drones or workers are fed, from the fourth day, on a mixture of pollen and honey. This difference in diet is of first importance. An egg from a queen cell, put into a worker cell, will produce a worker; just as an egg from a worker cell, put into a queen cell, will produce a queen. Their diet determines their status.

This is not, however, true of drones. Drones are produced in autumn. What induces the queen to begin laying drone-producing eggs is not really clear, but it may be due partly to seasonal influence, and partly to the stimulus provided by the smell, or shape, or texture, of the cell in which the egg is to be laid. In other words, a drone cell may stimulate the

Illustrated here are: Top left: *eggs of the queen bee;* top centre: *a larva;* top right: *a nymph;* bottom row, left to right: *drone, queen and worker bee.*

queen to lay a drone-producing egg. But the drone's sex is not determined by the food eaten by the larva in the drone cell. It is determined by heredity.

The social organisation of the honey-bee is the highest in the bee world. A colony is made up of the queen, workers and drones. The queen, however, is not a queen in the generally accepted sense; she is, in fact, an egg-laying machine. She does not build comb, or feed the larvæ, or gather honey; she lays eggs. The workers produce the wax for combs, gather the nectar, and feed the young bees. A queen may live for several years if allowed to do so by the bee-keeper.

SWARMING

" Hiving off," or the founding of new colonies, takes place when bees swarm. Swarming—still a lively topic among bee-keepers—is the term used to describe an exodus of bees from a hive, led by a queen. A first swarm is led by the reigning queen, who will take her followers to start a new hive (in practice the bee-keeper catches up the swarm and directs its future as he wishes). The hive, in which many bees remain, is now taken over by a young queen, who makes her marriage flight, then returns to the hive to reign. She remains there, and if another young queen takes off a swarm, that young queen and her followers do not return.

The marriage flight of a queen bee is undertaken so that she can be fertilised by one of the pursuing drones. Once she has been mated, she is fertilised for life, and she will produce eggs for as long as she lives without mating again.

She does, however, control the fertilisation of her eggs. The fertilising material, or sperm, is stored in her sperm sac, and is used apparently as she wishes. If the egg, or eggs, are fertilised, they will produce queens or workers, depending on how the resulting larvæ are fed. If they are not fertilised they will produce drones. This production of young from unfertilised eggs is called parthenogenesis, which means virgin birth, and in some insects it has reached such a stage that males have disappeared altogether, or nearly so.

It has been shown, initially by an investigator called von Frisch, that honey-bees can distinguish certain colours accurately. He established this by laying out pieces of paper, of different colours, in chequer-board fashion, and placing

The entrance to a modern beehive. Guards keep constant watch over the community because bees have many enemies, including wasps, mice, birds and raiding bees.

Swarm leaving an old-style skep. When the colony becomes too numerous, the queen, followed by many of her subjects, abandons her kingdom. Her followers all carry honey with them on the journey.

In the bee society there is no place for unemployed. After the queen's nuptial flight the workers turn on the drones and kill them or drive them from the hive.

Here is a swarm of bees in search of a place to found a new hive. The modern bee-keeper catches up the swarm and places it in a new hive.

Bees divide up the work of collecting pollen and have a regular schedule for different types of flowers. In the hive, different types of pollen are placed in different types of cells.

Bees gathering pollen. When a bee returns to the hive with its basket full of pollen it begins to dance, and in this way the other bees learn where the flowers are.

A. a bee tree. Here a swarm of bees has established itself in a wild state. B. frame hive in foreground, old-fashioned straw skep in background.

over one colour a sugar solution which the bees could not smell. Once they had found the odourless sugar, they kept returning to that colour, even after the sugar supply had been stopped. Alternative explanations of the bees' behaviour were all ruled out by the experiments of subsequent investigators, so that it is now fairly certain that bees can distinguish differences in colour within certain limits. They are blind to red, cannot distinguish between red, black and dark grey, between blue and violet, or between yellow-orange and yellow-green.

TO FIND THEIR WAY

This ability to distinguish colour has advantages for the bees; for example it helps them to find their way, or to find their own hive easily in a group of hives where each is differently coloured. But the recognition of visual landmarks is not the only thing they have to guide them. Light-compass orientation plays a large part, which means that they guide themselves by the direction of the sun. Then there is what has been called " contact odour ".

Bees, like homing pigeons, learn their geography, in the first instance, in the simplest way: by making short trips to begin with. Thus they learn their local geography. Gradually they extend their range until they are familiar with every feature of the landscape for a long way out from their hive.

In bees, one sees the first glimmerings of a kind of intelligence, which is nowadays called plastic behaviour. This is the ability to learn, and to remember. For instance, if a certain flower produces nectar only during a certain part of the day, the bees will learn to visit the locality at the proper time, thus saving themselves fruitless journeys. This has been noted in relation to buckwheat, which secretes nectar early in the morning; and a distinguished apiarist has shown that bees stay away from a field of buckwheat during the afternoon, even although the plants are still giving off a strong, enticing perfume.

INTENSIFIED STUDY

The honey-bee has been the subject of discussion for as long as men have kept bees. The insect made its appearance in literature in ancient times, and the books on bee-lore have become legion. In modern times, the study of the honey-bee has been intensified, and has produced many startling results. Not the least of these is the way in which bees which have found a source of nectar direct other members of the colony to the spot.

Von Frisch was the man who described what is called, among bee-keepers and students of bees, the bee-dance. A bee which has returned with a supply of nectar and pollen from a rich source dances vigorously on the comb, watched by other workers. The pattern of the dance then indicates the distance from the hive, whether near or far. Subsequent posturing gives the location of the source in relation to the sun. These discoveries of von Frisch are generally accepted by bee-keepers and others.

Nowadays, honey-bees are kept in scientifically constructed hives, quite unlike the old straw skeps you may have seen in old drawings. It is a simple matter to watch bees in their hive, because nowadays we have observation hives. You can have one yourself, and can study the whole complex social organisation, and the wonderful behaviour, of the bees for yourself. Bee-keepers are generally enthusiasts, always willing to be helpful and enlighten the newcomer to their ranks.

Whatever the first dogs used by man were like, they were certainly kept to fulfil some necessary function or to do some kind of work. When man became civilised he found a great many other uses for dogs and, in the Christian era, bred dogs especially to fight with each other or to bait bulls or bears. Breeds like the Bull-dog, the Staffordshire Bull Terrier (the old English pit dog), and the Mastiff, were used for such purposes. All these so-called sports have been banned by law, as has cock fighting, which was equally brutal. But whenever civilised man has an opportunity he encourages violence of some sort. Many people still love a dog fight, and in England the ancient sport of badger digging is still legal and has many devotees.

GUN DOGS

During the age of gunpowder, man has evolved many types of working dog for use in sport—breeds mainly concerned with pointing game, flushing game, or retrieving game— certain types being suited to do more than one type of work.

Those concerned mainly with picking up game or following wounded game come under the heading of retrievers, the best known of which to-day are probably the Labrador Retriever and the Golden Retriever. The old Flat-coat and the Curly-coated retrievers are no longer fashionable and indeed were completely eclipsed by the Labrador. Good retrievers should be strong, active dogs with soft mouths and good noses. As an all-round retriever, the Labrador has become supreme, being strong and hardy, with a good nose, an equable temper, and a willingness to face all kinds of cover and to work in any weather.

The Spaniels, which originated in Spain, have always been general-purpose dogs—jacks-of-all-trades, so to speak— being used for working cover, flushing game, retrieving, and tracking wounded. They have, however, gone much out of fashion. The Cocker to-day is for all practical purposes a pet and a show dog. The Springer is still to a great extent a worker, and is the one most commonly used on rough shoots.

The Pointers, which also originated in Spain, and the Setters were used for pointing game before the days of driven grouse and partridges. When the driving of birds became common practice, pointers and setters became largely superfluous, retrievers only being necessary for the pick-up. Pointers, however, are still used for work with falconers, and the German Short-haired variety has become very popular for this work. The breed is still used to a very large extent in Mediterranean countries for quail, pheasant, and partridge.

In this age of driven grouse, partridges and pheasants, pointers are now seldom used by shooting men.

The Labrador retriever is perhaps the most popular gun dog working to-day, and is widely kept as a house dog.

A handsome dog is the collie (right). Very popular as a household pet is the cocker spaniel (left).

The German shepherd dog is often trained as a guard.

The giant Great Dane and the friendly little dachshund.

The St. Bernard seeks out travellers lost in the snow.

Setters, on the other hand (handsome breeds like the English, Irish and Gordon Setters), have gone almost completely out of use. They are much seen in the show-ring, but seldom in the field.

SHEEP DOGS

Wherever man has sheep flocks he uses dogs to work them, and in areas where his sheep are liable to attack by animals like wolves, he uses dogs to guard them. Perhaps the best-known sheep dog is the Border Collie, which has been exported from Britain to many parts of the world, including Australia and New Zealand. This is the breed seen performing at field trials and at exhibitions: not the long-nosed Sable Collie so familiar in the show-ring. There is a smooth-coated variety of the working collie which Scottish shepherds call the bare-skin and, while this is still used, it is not so popular as the long-coated type. The Old English Sheepdog has largely gone out of use.

In Germany, a breed much in use is that which we know as the Alsatian. In Britain, however, the Alsatian is little used for working sheep. Here, it is mainly used as a guard dog, watch dog, and police dog. It is used extensively by the Royal Ulster Constabulary and by the Royal Air Force. It is considered by most people to be the most intelligent of dogs, an assessment which is probably correct.

The Pyrenean mountain dog is an ancient breed which was used in medieval times to protect sheep flocks from bears and wolves. The breed is still used as a guide dog and a pack dog. In mountainous areas of Europe, where wolves are still a menace to flocks, a variety of dogs are used as guards—chosen for strength and courage. While many of these are cross-breds, some are local products.

GUARD DOGS

Guard dogs and watch dogs have always been kept by man. In modern times they are kept mostly by people living in remote areas, or by police. Several breeds have come into favour and gone out again. Nowadays, large breeds like Mastiffs and Great Danes are kept mainly by enthusiasts. The breeds most popular to-day are the Boxer, Alsatian, the Doberman Pinscher, and various crosses. Of these the most commonly used is probably the Alsatian.

The Alsatian for a long time was extremely popular as a guide dog for blind people, but in recent years it has been largely superseded by the Labrador Retriever which is of more certain temper.

The Alsatian is temperamentally better suited to work as a guard dog, a duty for which its great intelligence makes it particularly easy to train.

TERRIERS

Terriers were originally bred, as their name suggests, for going underground, but most of them are to-day kept as pets, showing more readiness to go to town in motor-cars rather than into the ground after foxes.

Britain has produced a variety of outstanding terriers like the Cairn, the Border, the Parson Jack Russell, the Aberdeen, the Skye, the Fox, and the West Highland. Because of the nature of their work, terriers were originally bred as small as possible so that they could follow a fox anywhere. Nowadays, we tend to breed them much bigger so that the modern fox-terrier, for example, is often far too big for such work. The Airedale terrier is so big, indeed, that he could be used as a guard dog.

Many terriers, however, are still used to-day as working

118

The boxer (left), *and the Afghan hound* (right).

The English bulldog and the wire-haired fox terrier.

the world belong to this group. It is still common practice in these areas to cross Huskies with Timber Wolves—the offspring making first-class sled dogs of great strength and courage, suitable for use as Kings, or Lead dogs: the most important dogs in any dog team.

Most sled dogs go under the name of Eskimo dogs, for which husky is another name. Dogs north of the 50th parallel come under this heading, which includes the Malemute, the McKenzie River Dog, the Timber Wolf Dog, the Toganee, the West Greenland Huskies and the Baffin dogs, all of which are extremely hardy and fit to live out in the most rigorous conditions.

HOUNDS

In Great Britain the best-known hounds are the Greyhound, the Foxhound, the Stag Hound, the Otter Hound, the Harrier and the Beagle. Other breeds are kept as pets or for show purposes—for example the Borzoi, the Afghan Hound, and the Saluki. The Irish Wolf Hound and the Scots Deer Hound, are now more or less ornamental breeds.

In industrial areas the Greyhound and Whippet are best known. Though every greyhound owner likes to run his

The Eskimo dogs are strong and tireless, and silent.

dogs and you will find that the working types are kept small. The working fox-terrier, for example, is usually only slightly more than half the height of his show-ring counterpart. Working terriers have to be small, varminty, hardy, and with plenty of courage—the courage to face a big hill vixen underground and bolt her.

Where foxes are hunted with hounds by mounted fox-hunters, a small terrier is always carried to bolt any fox which goes to ground. Otter hunters also make use of terriers to bolt otters which have taken cover where hounds cannot reach them. In the English sport of badger digging, terriers are used to hold the badger (that is to prevent him from digging) until the diggers reach him. Only the staunchest terrier will face a badger, and only a most exceptional terrier can kill one. A great many terriers are literally cut to pieces by badgers underground. It is a pity that we still legally allow people to bring two such brave animals together, to fight and maim each other.

SLED DOGS

In Arctic regions, man has very largely depended on the help of working dogs for transport for himself and his goods. Some of the biggest, strongest and fiercest dogs in

The popular Aberdeen terrier and the giant mastiff, both watch dogs.

Greyhound racing is popular in industrial areas of Britain.

Ladies' pets, the intelligent poodle and the pekinese.

dog after hares, coursing as a sport has gone out of fashion. The majority of greyhounds to-day are used at racing tracks where they run a measured circuit after electric hares. The greyhound is a breed of great antiquity.

The modern English foxhound has probably had more care devoted to its breeding than has any other variety of dog. There are many packs of foxhounds in England, but only a handful in Scotland and Ireland.

Stag hounds have a limited use in Britain, being used by the Devon and Somerset Hunt around Exmoor. This sport has in recent years given rise to much public indignation, and several attempts have been made to have it banned.

The sport of otter hunting is carried out on foot, and otter hounds are not, strictly speaking, a distinct breed to-day.

Harriers are used in the sport of hare hunting, as are beagles and Bassett Hounds.

TOY DOGS

Under the heading of toy dogs come those breeds more familiarly known as lap dogs by uncharitable critics. In this category are breeds like the Pekinese, the Pomeranian, the Miniature Poodle, the Papillon, and the Chihuahua. While some of them are highly intelligent, like the poodle and the pekinese, they are exclusively pets and are usually hopelessly spoiled. Indeed, there is a great tendency to breed some of them to match the colour of milady's boudoir.

MIGRATION

The only certain thing known about migration is that birds migrate. As to why they do so or how they find their way, we are not so much better informed than the one-time Bishop Godwin of Hereford who thought they migrated to the moon.

Many theories have been put forward to explain the migratory urge in birds. One such theory, for long a favourite, was called the Glacial Theory. This held that birds were driven south by the creeping ice cap, then returned as it retreated. For various reasons this theory has been rejected.

Winter food supply may be an important factor, but it cannot explain the whole mystery. It seems reasonable to argue that birds whose food supply is cut off should move south until they reach a place where it becomes available again. But the fact remains that individuals of certain species migrate, where others of the same species stay where they were born all the year round; even individual swallows have been known to stay in the south of England during winter.

Migration in the strict sense must not be confused with "dispersal" or "irruption". Birds which merely disperse over a wide area of the country after a breeding season are not true migrants. Similarly, when bands of crossbills appear suddenly in this country driven by bad weather or by failure of their food supply, it is still not true migration.

True migration is a regular movement, a predictable rhythm; it involves the entire population of a species; it means that a species moves out *en masse* to another part of the world; it means that the breeding and wintering quarters are entirely different.

Migration can be truly spectacular; birds cross continents and vast stretches of water when making their journeys. Our own swallow flies from the north of Scotland to South Africa. Certain terns travel from the Arctic to the Antarctic. The corncrake, which looks such an indifferent flier, travels from the Hebrides to Africa and Palestine.

Many experiments have been conducted to explain why birds migrate and how they find their way. It has been found that increased light and greater activity affect the breeding conditions of birds, and it is known that breeding condition has something to do with the migratory urge, but in fact neither comes near explaining the problem and we are still left with it. Many revealing experiments have been carried out to test the homing abilities of birds in the middle of their actual breeding seasons. Thus swallows, brought over to this country from Germany and released here, returned to their German territory in a few days' time. A great deal has been done with sea birds in this respect, notably by R. M. Lockley. However you approach the mystery of migration, you will have a subject to occupy your mind for the rest of your life. Some day, perhaps, man will at last understand the meaning of this inherent rhythm. In the meantime, all he knows are certain things connected with the actual migration movements.

BIRDS AND THEIR NESTS

We speak of birds as " nesting " in the season when they lay eggs. Therefore the spot on a cliff ledge where a guillemot lays her long, pointed egg, is as much her nest as the intricate structures built by weaver birds or long-tailed tits, even though not one scrap of material is added to the ledge. The nests to be discussed here are the sites where the birds have made alterations or additions to suit their requirements.

The simplest nests are those where the bird makes merely a few alterations to the site chosen. Thus the tiny ringed plover will press out a deep saucer on shingle or sand and be content with that. On shingle she will generally see that the smallest pebbles form the lining of the nest. Oyster-catchers, which nest in similar places, do much the same thing and the habit persists when the bird decides to nest on arable land. There she will merely turn out a depression in the soil which she works smooth with her breast, in the same way as the thrush does with the plaster lining of her nest.

Birds like the lapwing take this a stage further. Choosing a depression in a grassy field or on plough-land, the bird will round and deepen this, and then line it with a few bents roughly criss-crossed or interwoven. The idea of scraping saucer-shaped depressions in the ground and lining them is common to many birds, although the workmanship of the lining varies. The snipe, which nests in wet pastures and boggy places, lines her nest with bents and dry grasses; the woodcock lines her chosen depression with old leaves and bracken; the curlew makes a consider-able nest either in a hollow or in a clump of vegetation. Birds like the pheasant and partridge also make scrapes, and line them, but in addition they cover the eggs during their absences when the clutch is being built up.

NESTS OLD AND NEW

Some birds use the old nests of other species. Thus you will find the tawny or long-eared owls rearing families in the old nests of crow, magpie, or sparrow-hawk. You will find kestrels doing exactly the same thing. When merlins decide to nest in trees, instead of on the ground, they use the old nest of a hoodie crow, while on the ground they are satisfied with a mere scrape. The raven and the buzzard build considerable nests of sticks and twigs on rocky ledges (the buzzard will do so in trees), but the peregrine falcon builds no nest of her own—she will use the old nest of the raven, or be content with laying her eggs in a scrape on a rocky ledge. The golden eagle, on the other hand, carries great quantities of nesting material to her chosen crag and there builds a considerable nest which often reaches such a size that a man can curl up comfortably in it.

Owls and kestrels choose sites other than ready-made

Storks do not nest in the British Isles, but are familiar in many parts of the Continent where they nest in close association with man, notably on houses where many people provide them with nesting platforms.

The goldfinch, like the other members of the finch family, is a seed-eater, and often to be found among seeding thistles. At one time it was very popular as a cage bird, but the law now prohibits the taking of wild goldfinches.

The red-necked grebe, like other grebes, is a bird of fresh-water lochs. Its nest is a heap of water weeds and decaying vegetation which the birds build up until it appears above the surface of the shallows.

The golden eagle, which nests in the highlands and islands of Scotland, is the largest British breeding bird of prey. It is specially protected by law, but despite this many birds are still shot, trapped or poisoned.

121

The great reed warbler builds its nest in swamps and marshes in Southern and Central Europe and in Western Asia. This species is a frequent victim of the cuckoo.

The great Indian hornbill is nearly five feet long and is the largest of the family, which includes hoopoes and kingfishers. The bird is found in Southern India and Malaya.

The common heron usually nests in tall trees. Its range extends over Europe to Asia and Africa. Though mainly a fish-eater, the bird takes a great variety of other food.

nests. The barn owls may desert loft or ruin for a hollow tree; the tawny may nest at the mouth of a rabbit burrow or in a hollow tree, while the long-eared owl may nest on the ground. Similarly, a kestrel finds a rocky ledge or ruined building as suitable as the warmly-lined nest of a crow.

Among birds which do build nests you will generally find that the bigger the bird the less artistic the nest. This has nothing whatever to do with the strength or durability of the nest and, in fact, bulky, ragged nests can stand up to the storms of several winters—for example the nests of crows, magpies, herons, ravens and eagles. Though many of the big birds do not go in for artistic niceties, many of them do line their nests. The eagle, for instance, uses woodrush or heather. The carrion crow likes a warm lining of sheep's wool; the raven will do the same, while the rook and the magpie are content with taking in some soil and roots.

NESTS IN CAVITIES

Birds which nest in tunnels and similar sites, may excavate the tunnels or take over ready-made sites. The sand martin, a member of the swallow family, will drive tunnels two feet long in sand banks and build a warm nest lined with feathers at the end. The kingfisher, another burrow nester, will line her nest with fish bones.

Some sea birds are burrowers, as for example the petrels, or the Manx shearwater, an oceanic bird which, in the western isles of Scotland, nests on cliff tops and mountain tops. Woodpeckers drill holes in the trunks of trees, and thereafter excavate a considerable cavity, the eggs being laid in a nest of sawdust. The starling, which is fond of cavities in walls or holes in trees, quite often evicts woodpeckers and takes over the site. More usually,

The flamingo's nest is cone-shaped, made of mud and fine gravel which the birds gather with their curved beaks. Male and female take turns at sitting on the eggs.

There are about fourteen species of penguin, all of which are found in the Southern hemisphere. The king penguins illustrated here live in the cold regions of the Antarctic.

The common swallow is a migrant which winters in South Africa and arrives in Britain in the spring. Swallows will rear two broods in a season.

starlings choose natural holes in trees or suitable cavities in buildings, stuffing them untidily with straw and feathers.

Tits like holes in trees or walls and will come readily to man-made nesting boxes. But if the entrance hole to the box is made too large, house sparrows will take over. House sparrows, like starlings, like holes in trees or suitable sites in buildings which they will stuff with a mixture of straw, dried grasses, and feathers.

Swallows and house martins are good plasterers, using well puddled material which they stick on to the timber, stone, or bricks of walls. House martins usually build in the eaves of houses, leaving an entrance at the top of the nest. Swallows mix a great deal of straw with their plaster and they place the nest on top of a beam or cement it to the face of it.

Ducks and geese line their nests with down. Swans build substantial nests on or near water. Grebes will build either among reeds or ashore, covering the eggs during their absences with decaying vegetable matter which not only conceals them but keeps them warm. Coots and waterhens build substantial, cup-shaped nests among reeds, rushes or flags, but the waterhen quite frequently builds some distance from water. Small birds like reed warblers, hang their deep nests among tall reeds.

INTRICATE NESTS

Generally speaking, the birds we refer to loosely as songbirds fashion the most intricate nests. The chaffinch, for example, builds an extremely neat, regular, mossy, cup-shaped nest in bush or conifer or against the trunk of a mature hardwood tree. Blackbirds, mistle thrushes, and song thrushes build deep, substantial nests in bushes or trees, and the song thrush adds a plaster

The toucan, with its eight-inch, orange-coloured beak, pecks out its nesting hole in the trunk of a tree. The species is mainly found in the great forests of Brazil.

The common nuthatch is found in Europe and Western Asia. In Britain, its distribution is local and it is not found in Scotland. It nests in holes in trees.

The oven bird derives its name from the peculiar shape of its nest, which closely resembles a primitive miniature baking oven. Some species build their nests in trees, others on the ground.

The great spotted woodpecker of Europe and Asia is the species most widely distributed in Britain. Like all woodpeckers, its claws are well adapted for climbing and its beak for drilling the trunks of trees.

Humming birds, of which there are many species, are usually brilliantly coloured and often no larger than bees. Like bees, they visit flowers to extract nectar.

The common cuckoo is a large bird often confused with the sparrowhawk. It has a distinctive call note. The cuckoo lays her eggs in the nest of other birds.

The tailor birds are noted for their habits of sewing two or more leaves together to hold their nests. The nest of the weaver bird is composed of hair, cotton-down and fine grass. The tailor bird belongs to the family of the warblers, many of which are notable nest builders.

Cape Weaver bird. Weaver birds are very like finches. Some species build their nests so close together that they look like some strange fruit on the trees. Nests vary in shape from species to species, some, like this one, being flask-shaped. All are finely woven.

The weaver finches are found in several parts of the world, notably Africa, India and Australasia. They derive their name from their style of nest building. The nest is usually described as retort-shaped. The sociable weaver bird (Philetairus socius), seen here, nests in colonies. The bird collects a great umbrella-shaped mass of sticks and grass and then bores out its nest from underneath. Three hundred such nesting burrows have been found in one mass or, literally, under one roof.

The Baltimore Oriole belongs to the family Icteridae. They are confined to the American continent and derive their name from the long, pendant nests which they build like flasks in the branches of trees. The nests are made of strong, thread-like vegetable fibres.

The cock pheasant is usually polygamous, but in cases where he has only one mate he will sometimes take a turn at sitting on the eggs. The cock illustrated is the old dark-necked type (Phasianus c. colchicus), which is now seldom seen as a wild-bred bird.

lining. The warblers build fragile but warm nests under cover—the willow warbler, for example, makes a small, domed nest, warmly padded with feathers. The common wren builds a spherical nest, often in ivy or among the roots of fallen trees, which has a neat little entrance.

Birds which nest in bushes and other low cover, generally aim at cup-shaped nests, although the long-tailed tit is an exception to this, building a feather-lined ball of moss and lichens with a small entrance hole on the side.

Bush nests like those of the linnet, dunnock, chaffinch, the garden warbler, greenfinch, and the whitethroat, are all cup-shaped. So are those close to the ground, like that of the yellow hammer and the reed bunting, robins, skylarks and nightingales. Ground nesters also build cup-shaped nests, but the robin retains this type whether it is nesting above ground, on the ground, or in kettles or jacket pockets. The spotted fly-catcher, which nests in ivy-covered walls or against trees, also favours the cup shape. In fact this is the commonest type of nest, variations being in size, location, and intricacy.

The dipper is one bird which varies its style occasionally. When the nest is built against a rock face or on a ledge, it is a great ball with a hole in the side. When it nests in a fissure in masonry it will merely add a lining or build a cup at the end.

Thus we see that from the tiny humming bird to the great golden eagle or the swans, most birds make a nest of some kind. Some are weavers, some are pleaters, some plasterers; while some are wood borers or earth borers; others take over ready-made sites; yet others are extreme specialists like the weaver bird and the tailor bird and, of course, there is the cuckoo which doesn't build at all.

DOMESTIC CATS

All our domestic cats, despite variations brought about by selective breeding, have come from the same original stock.

The Kaffir cat, or bush cat, of Africa, and the jungle cat of North-East Africa, are important members of this family tree, but the wild cat has also played its part, and many of the big, tiger-marked specimens in northern countries owe a great deal to wild-cat blood somewhere in their ancestry.

Run-of-the-mill household cats come in all shapes, sizes and colours, breed freely, and produce offspring of unpredictable markings. To this group belong the well-known alley cats, farm cats, house cats, factory cats, and poaching cats. Pure-bred varieties, once crossed with these, soon lose all their special characteristics and their identity of colour, shape or markings. For a generation or two the specialised stamp may be traced in offspring, but it wears thin in succeeding generations and presently disappears altogether.

The domestic cat is one of the few animals kept by man which is still largely able to fend for itself, and it is for this reason that so many cats are still kept as killers of vermin: for example mice and rats. Most farm cats, apart from the milk they receive, will manage to feed themselves and their offspring on prey caught by themselves, at least for long or

Despite variations in types, colours and sizes, all domestic cats have the same family tree.

shorter periods. Many a farm cat, taking to a life in the woods, can survive indefinitely, even in winter-time, unless it falls victim to fox, dog, or man.

CAT AS HUNTER

Apart from their vermin-killing abilities, cats are extensively kept entirely as pets, and many cat owners attempt to restrain the animals' natural instincts, but it is extremely difficult to dissuade a cat from catching mice, voles, shrews, rats, or birds. Because so many people keep cats as pets and do not have them neutered, endless litters of unwanted kittens are born, many of whom suffer painful deaths. A great many are simply turned loose to die or be taken care of by anyone who finds them. The caterwauling of cats in the night, which so many people find annoying, is due entirely to the fact that the majority of pet cats are left sexually entire. The neutering of all domestic cats not wanted specially for breeding, would solve not only cat population problems: it would cure the sleeplessness of neighbours.

Because of lack of selective breeding on the one hand, and highly selective breeding on the other, we have a small group of select cats and a large group of just-cats. It is

Here is a beautiful long-haired specimen from Angora.

The Siamese is handsome and intelligent.

The true wild cat (Felis sylvestris) *is a large powerful animal, with a thick bushy tail.*

The paw that kills is used as readily in play. The most playful cats can be the deadliest hunters.

quite clear from this state of affairs that man did not devote to the cat anything like the time in selective breeding he gave to the dog.

COMMON CATS

In the just-cats group, you will find greys of all shades with tiger-striping in greater or lesser degree. You will find pure whites, although true albinos are rare (white cats with pink eyes). Melanism is common, however, so there are plenty of black cats, and this colour has led to a great amount of cat superstition. You will also find smoky-coloured cats, blue cats, tawny cats, cats of varying shades of orange, cats with varying amounts of white, and tortoise-shell cats. Tortoise-shell cats are usually females, but toms of this kind do occur. Some white cats are deaf; others have hearing as acute as that of any other type. Orange cats may be either toms or tabbies. Apart from colour, the texture and length of coat varies, and a long coat usually indicates an admixture of Persian blood somewhere. The long-hairs, in their turn, go through all the colour ranges. These domestic cats, alley

cats, or ordinary cats, whatever you like to call them, are often very handsome and when well-cared-for can compare with the best of the select breeds in coat, carriage, eye-colour and anything else you may care to look for.

Among the special breeds, the long-haired types (Persian and Angora) were for a long time extremely popular. They come in all colours of coat and eyes. Persians have for long had a reputation for " cattiness " and some of them do tend to be unpredictable. They are cats which should be kept strictly as pets in good homes where they will receive care and plenty of grooming. At farms and such places they soon become dishevelled, their coats matted and knotted with burrs and mud.

Abyssinian cats are a very hardy breed, rich ruddy brown in colour, pencilled with black or dark brown. Cats showing double or treble pencilling are much sought after. The body is unmarked and the belly and the insides of the forelegs are lighter than the rest of the body which should be orange-brown in colour. Abyssinians are quite like the Siamese breeds but do not have the blue eyes.

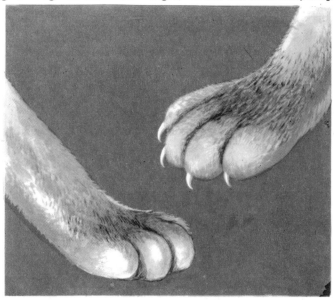

Illustration shows cats' paws—one with claw retracted and one with claw unsheathed.

Cats are devoted mothers, and teach their kittens to hunt mice, voles, and other small mammals.

One of the handsome breeds and once widely kept is the Persian, which is often of uncertain temper. On the left, we see the blue Persian and on the right, the white. In the centre is an ordinary cat for comparison.

AN ARISTOCRAT

The Siamese is fast becoming one of the most popular of the select breeds. It is a handsome, svelte, panthering animal with sky-blue eyes changing to ruby-red in certain lights. In many ways it is more dog-like than cat-like. An aristocrat by any standards, the Siamese is intelligent and affectionate although it does tend to be a one-person cat. The breed comes in three " point " phases: blue-point, chocolate-point, and seal-point. Though many specimens are cross-eyed and some have a kink near the end of the tail, neither of these is a standard requirement. Kittens are born almost white in colour but with dark-shaded points. The body colour darkens gradually as they grow older and the kittens assume full adult dress around the age of nine months. The Siamese has a loud, distinctive voice and it is not the kind of voice that one can ignore for any length of time. Because of this many people tend to shy from the breed.

Closely related to the Siamese is the Burmese, but its body

The bright, alert, intelligent face of a seal-pointed Siamese. Note the bright blue eyes which are a feature of this breed. Siamese cats are in many ways more dog-like than cat-like in behaviour. Most of them prefer water to milk. Some become good hunters, many are not. The Siamese is one breed which will not permit itself to be ignored. It requires affection and if shut off from the person it likes, it will squeal insistently as no other cat can.

is more chocolate coloured. The pointing of the Burmese resembles that of the Siamese and the eyes are yellow instead of blue.

RARER TYPES

There are other types, less widely kept, like the Russian blue and the Hairless Siamese. A once-popular breed was the Manx cat, a short-bodied breed with long hind legs and little or no tail. This combination gave the cat a definite lynx-like appearance. Manx cats were bred in many colours, but many so-called Manxmen were shams because more than one unscrupulous breeder docked ordinary, long-tailed kittens and passed them off as the real thing.

So far, no one has succeeded in domesticating the pure-bred wild cat, although its blood runs in many strains of domestic cats. Quarter-bred cats can, however, be quickly won over. Half-breeds take a little longer but, with patience, they, too, will come round in the end. Once they have settled down, they become as affectionate and demonstrative as the Siamese, which is often the way with the " wildest " animals once they have lost their fear of man.

A common type of domestic cat is the orange tom, and there are many handsome specimens of this type.

SOCIAL WASPS

The wasps familiar to most people in this country are the social wasps of the house of Vespa, the well-known yellow-jackets with the painful stings, who help themselves to our fruit in the garden, and invade houses in autumn in search of jams and jellies and suchlike sweet things.

The most familiar species are the Common wasp (*Vespa vulgaris*), and the German wasp (*Vespa germanica*), which are equally abundant. These two make their paper nests underground. The tree wasp, or Norwegian wasp, nests in trees and bushes; the Cuckoo wasp is a parasite and lives on *Vespa rufa* which nests underground but doesn't enter houses. Then, of course, there is the Hornet, the giant wasp which nests in hollow trees and is easily recognised by its great size, its brown markings, and deep yellow coloration. The hornet is confined almost entirely to the south of England.

The nests of the social wasps are annual affairs, started off by a fertilised queen after she emerges from hibernation, and deserted in the autumn when the workers die and the young queens, already mated, retire for the winter. The large wasps seen on the wing in early spring are young, fertile queens which have survived the winter.

As soon as they are active, they set about the business of starting a new colony. The site most often chosen is a deserted mouse-hole, and to this the queen carries the first mouthfuls of pulp, made from sound but weathered wood gathered from fence posts and suchlike objects. To the roof of the cavity the queen wasp fixes her paper anchor in the form of a disc. From this disc the nest will be hung. It is important to realise that the nest is built from the roof downwards. When the first floor of cells has been completed it is covered with several layers of wasp paper so that it becomes like an umbrella. From this, paper pillars are hung and to these the next floor is attached. And so building progresses until the nest is roughly spherical in shape, consists of many floors, and is completely enclosed by layers of paper.

Once she has the colony under way, the queen allows the workers to tend the grubs and confines herself to the business of egg-laying.

The queen wasp builds her paper cells from wood pulp.

In the early stages the queen naturally has to do all the work herself. As soon as she has a number of cells ready, she begins egg-laying, and when the first workers emerge they take over the building. They are subsequently assisted by further generations of worker wasps produced from eggs laid by the queen. The larvæ in the cells are fed on insect food which may be either fresh or decayed. When the larvæ receive food from the worker wasps they produce from their mouths a sweet saliva which the workers accept in exchange, and quite often wasps develop the habit of taking saliva without providing food in return. Adult wasps themselves need food which is rich in sugar, so they like such energy-producing foods as fruit, nectar and honey. When they are feeding larvæ, they receive this food in the form of saliva so that there is really an exchange which ensures that the larvæ are kept growing and the adults kept active.

The brood cells, as you will have realised, are " upside down ", being closed at the top and open at the bottom. Despite this, the young larvæ do not fall out, as they are glued down to the sides of the cells. When the larvæ are ready to pupate, each spins for itself a cocoon and closes the mouth of its cell. Some four to six weeks pass before wasps emerge by biting their way out of the cells. This new brood immediately sets to work building further cells and feeding other broods already in existence. The queen, from the time the first workers emerge, devotes all her time to egg-laying.

Near the end of the summer, larger cells (called royal cells) are built for the production of young queens. It is at this time that males are also produced. The eggs laid in the queen cells are exactly the same as those laid in the worker cells but queens, as in the case of honey-bees, are produced simply by better feeding. In short, the amount of food given to the larva determines whether it will be a queen or a worker. The male wasps are always produced from unfertilised eggs laid by the queen. Male wasps have no sting.

128

In exchange for food supplied to the larvae, the wasps receive sugary saliva from them.

there is no activity and larvæ still in cells are either left to die there or are thrown out. Thus, in the course of a single season, many generations of wasps are born and die, and a great citadel, laboriously built, becomes deserted and is left to fall into ruins, perhaps even providing a winter home for a field-mouse.

The tree wasp, whose spherical paper citadel may be seen suspended from the branch of a tree, lives a similar life to the ground-nesting species and the nest is built in exactly the same way.

A normal winter is the best safeguard for hibernating queens because then they stay asleep until spring, instead of coming out too early and being nipped by a subsequent wintry spell. While the queen wasp is asleep cold doesn't affect her, but once she has moved out and become active, she is vulnerable. One of the main enemies of the ground-nesting social wasp is the badger, who is very fond of wasp grubs. A badger will tear out nest after nest when the colonies are at their height and the great hole which he tears in a bank, besides the scattered paper and stones, betrays where he has been at work. Brock is seemingly little annoyed by stings; in fact, his thick coat and thick hide allow a great protection. In addition he does his work at night when the wasps are least active and is therefore not unduly troubled by them buzzing around his ears.

When the young queens of the year have been mated, the colony begins to disintegrate. The queens themselves prepare for hibernation, while the workers gradually drift away to become nuisances about houses, shops and such places. Many remain about the nest for longer periods, but eventually

PUPPIES

No-one should have a puppy who is going to lose interest in it after a few weeks and leave it to organise its own life in its own way. A puppy has to be properly fed, properly cared for, and taught obedience. Teaching a puppy to be obedient is one of the simplest things in the world, but it has to be done in a disciplined manner.

Each lesson has to be carefully taught, and there are several things you must never do. The puppy should not be scolded because he cannot understand what you are trying to do, or he is not responding as quickly as you like. Never shout at the puppy or lose your temper, and never carry on with a lesson after the puppy has lost interest.

Usually the first lesson the puppy has to learn is to sit when told, and the way to do this is as follows: take the puppy into the garden on a leash (you can stay indoors with him if you want to) and once you have got his attention, press your hand gently on his rump until he is seated, accompanying the pressing with the word " sit ".

The word will mean nothing to him, of course; it is quite likely he will rise up immediately you take your hand away, so you must do the thing a second time and a third and a twentieth time, if need be. Each time you press him down you should say clearly the word " sit ". Soon you will be able to stand up while the puppy remains seated.

Once he has done this you should walk him around the garden for a bit, then stop and try him again. You will have to go through it all again, but you will probably find that this time he will stay seated after the second or third telling. He is now beginning to get the idea. At this time you should fuss him and tell him what a clever dog he is; then get him to do the thing all over again.

Once he has learnt to do this you should never change the word nor movement.

On the second or third day while you are telling him to sit you can either raise your hand at the same time or snap your fingers, or stamp your feet, so that by and by he associates these movements with your command. In this way you will find before long that he will sit without the word of command being used, but merely at the sight of your raised hand or the snap of your fingers, or the stamp of your foot. There is no teaching in this part at all; the puppy is taught with the word. He merely learns to associate the movement with the word and thereafter will sit to the movement alone.

When the puppy has learnt to sit, you should now teach him the signal for rising. The simplest way to do this is to tug gently on the leash, at the same time making a clicking sound with your tongue. If he is slow to understand, lift him to his feet and go through the motions again. He will soon know what you are wanting and from then on the sound will be his instruction to rise and follow you.

This command has nothing whatever to do with teaching the puppy to walk to heel. It gives him permission to rise and follow you, nothing more. You now have to teach him how to walk once you have called him up.

When you are walking the puppy around between sitting lessons, keep him on a short cord at your heel. Do the same when you take him for a walk. From the moment you leave the house, never allow him to rush off at the outset; he will run on by your permission later.

When he is walking well at your heel, let the cord trail slack so that he has yards to spare. He will soon discover it and he will probably go ahead. At this point stop dead, pull him back firmly but gently, put him in his proper place and say the word " heel ". Do this every time he moves in front of you. If you persevere with this you will soon have him walking to heel without any cord at all.

WADING BIRDS

The birds referred to as waders are almost all of a type easily recognised as such at a glance. But recognising them as waders is one thing—identifying individual species is quite another. It is in the matter of species recognition that great difficulties often arise.

Broadly speaking, the group may be described as birds which walk and run, sometimes wade, and frequent marshes or seashore at some time or other. All have longish legs and some have very long legs; some have short beaks, others have long beaks, and some have curved beaks. Mostly they are accomplished fliers, with quick wing action, and carry

The maribou stork inhabits much of tropical Africa. In general habits it resembles the white stork, but it is a much bigger bird; it is an eater of carrion and offal.

The roseate spoonbill, which is a native of South America, is a water bird like its European relative. It has the same spatulate beak, from which it derives its name, and the same long legs, typical of waders.

their legs extended beneath the tail in flight. Much confusion arises in certain species because the summer and winter plumages are quite distinct, and it requires a great deal of field experience to become expert in plumage phases. Some waders are gregarious during the breeding season ; others are not. Most of them do, however, tend to flock outside the breeding season, and migration is carried out mostly at night.

Waders belong to the great order of the Charadriiformes. There is, however, another group of birds, also long-legged and long-billed which frequent marshes and which do wade. This is the Order of the Ciconiformes which includes the herons, storks, ibises, spoonbills, flamingos and others.

CURLEWS

One of the most familiar of British waders is the Curlew, easily recognised by its large size, brown plumage and long-curved bill. The only bird with which it can possibly be confused is the Whimbrel, a migrant which breeds in Orkney, Shetland, the Outer Isles and Inverness-shire. The common curlew is widely distributed where there is suitable nesting ground—for example hill pastures, grassy moors and peat mosses. The common curlew is about two feet long, with a bill varying in length from four inches to six inches. The whimbrel is a much smaller bird, about fifteen inches long, with a bill of three and a half inches.

SOUTHWARD MOVEMENTS

The common curlews which nest in Britain make a south-ward movement during July and August, but so far only one bird ringed in Britain has been recovered abroad. The whimbrel, on the other hand, winters in Africa and the shores of the Indian ocean. The curlew nests in April and May. The eggs take about twenty-nine days to hatch, and the chicks

The white ibis of the Nile has long been considered a sacred bird. It frequents marshes and mud flats and breeds colonially in reed beds or among bushes and trees. The bird's general shape is that of the common curlew.

The little egret is a small, white heron with black bill, black legs and yellow feet. In summer, adults have a long, drooping crest and a cloak of feathers falling from the shoulders.

In his breeding plumage the male ruff is unmistakable because of his great ruff and ear tufts; the female is called the reeve. Ruffs breed on tundra and marshes.

are able to run about as soon as their down is dry. Both parents care for the family for some weeks afterwards.

Perhaps even more familiar than the curlew is the Lapwing, Plover or Peewit, which frequents not only hill districts and moors, but lowland pastures, arable fields, and commons. In early spring the peewits make their nest in scrapes which they line with a few bents. A favourite site on which the birds will work, is the hoof-mark of a horse or bullock. The usual clutch is four eggs, but the peewit will go on to lay again if her first eggs are taken. Many birds will, in fact, produce a third clutch of eggs. Because of their liking for arable fields, a great many lapwings lose their early clutches when the ground is being worked by harrows.

The lapwing is a widely distributed species being found over most of the North European region. Its migrations have been much studied, and birds ringed as chicks in the British Isles have been recovered mostly in France and Spain and occasionally in parts of the Mediterranean coast. Birds ringed in other parts of Europe, from Italy to the

Baltic, have appeared in Britain as winter visitors.

BIRDS OF MOOR AND MOUNTAIN

The Golden Plover, a speckled black and gold bird about eleven inches long, frequents upland moors in Britain and is found in Holland, Denmark, Norway and Germany. The golden plover of America is notable for its spectacular migrations, North American birds flying right down to South America in the winter. The Grey Plover, which breeds in the tundra of Siberia and other parts of the Arctic, is a winter visitor to the British Isles, where a few pairs have also been recorded during the summer.

A very familiar wader found mostly on shingly river flats, or on the coast, is the Oystercatcher, conspicuous in its pied plumage, with beak and legs of red. In recent years this species has shown an increasing tendency to nest in arable fields in certain parts of the country. It is noisy, and readily draws attention to itself when its nesting territory is invaded. Frequently found beside the oystercatcher on the coast is

The crocodile bird is so-called because of its association with crocodiles, from whose jaws it extracts its insect food. That it does not entirely trust the crocodile can be deduced from its habit of jumping clear when the crocodile moves its jaws.

The feet of birds give a good indication of their manner of life. Ducks have webbed feet for swimming; coots and water-hens have lobed feet for running over ooze. The jacana walks over water weeds with the greatest of ease.

131

The shoebill derives its name from its beak.

The common heron is an early nester and builds in trees.

The hammer-head is sometimes called the umber bird.

The crane is a large, stately bird resembling the heron.

the small, handsome bird called the Ringed Plover, which also nests on coastal sand flats. It is a very small bird just over seven inches long, with legs of orange-yellow, a black and white collar, and a black and white face. These markings make the bird almost invisible when it is standing still on shingle.

A member of the family, which breaks with the usual tradition, is the Dotterel, which in Britain prefers nesting on mountain tops between 3000 and 4000 feet. This species breeds in Norway, Sweden, Finland, and North Russia as well as in certain mountain ranges of Germany and the Balkans. After the breeding season it migrates to North Africa, Arabia and Persia.

The dotterel, at nesting time, reverses the usual trend in birds, for in this case the male sits on the eggs, and he is mainly responsible for looking after the chicks when they hatch.

DRUMMING AND RODING

A very common and familiar wader, which draws attention to itself by its habit of drumming, is the snipe. Most people who walk in the country have learned to recognise this sound and to identify it with the small bird which flies at great speeds and circles high above their heads. The drumming of the snipe is not vocal; it is instrumental—being produced by the vibration of the outer tail feathers which the bird extends almost at right angles during the drumming flight.

Not so familiar to the casual rambler is the roding of the woodcock. The woodcock, as its name suggests, is a wader which mainly frequents woodlands or thickets. In spring, the male has a special flight during which he circles above the wood at dusk, uttering a croaking sound, followed by a chirp, at regular intervals. Unlike the snipe's drumming the woodcock's croaking is vocal. Quite regularly the woodcock will rode for a short period in the morning just before sunrise. This species has been recorded carrying its young. While there is still a great deal of controversy about this habit, it can be taken as an established fact for many experienced observers have confirmed it beyond doubt.

The Cream-coloured Courser, an Ethiopian and North African species which turns up occasionally in Britain, is about nine inches long, and was a familiar bird to the troops who fought Rommel in the desert during the Second World War. It is a buff-coloured, plover-like bird, with a bold white band, edged with black, running from its eye to the back of its neck. The undersides of its wings are black.

An unusually shaped wader, more like a large brown swallow than anything else, is the Pratincole. It is no more than a rare vagrant to the British Isles, but breeds in the south of Spain, in the Mediterranean, Egypt and South Russia. It breeds on the muddy flats of estuaries and is a familiar bird in the Marismas of Southern Spain. It is about ten inches long.

BEST-KNOWN BIRD

Of the group which includes the herons, egrets and storks, the best known in Britain is the Common Heron, which is to be found in any part with suitable fishing waters and nesting sites. Normally this species nests in tall trees, but in certain parts of the country as, for example, in the Hebrides, it will nest on the ground or among rocks. Their nests, when first built, are small; but they increase in size over the years because the heron, like the rook, returns to the same place each season and adds to the old nests.

Herons breed early, some birds laying in February, although most of them do not do so until March. The usual clutch is from three to five eggs, and the pair may begin to incubate at any time during the laying period. Some do so with the first egg, some with the second, while others wait until the clutch is complete. The young are fed by both parents in the nest; they seize the parent's bill from the side and take regurgitated food. When the young birds are older their parents may simply disgorge food on to the nest and allow them to pick it up for themselves. The young birds leave the nest when they are between seven and eight weeks old. Despite this lengthy nesting period, some herons manage to rear a second brood.

The food of the heron is mainly fish of some kind, but small mammals are frequently taken. Voles, mice, shrews, baby rabbits, and frogs are favourite items. It is not an uncommon thing to find a heron paying regular visits to a pond where frogs are spawning.

The Purple Heron, which is a smaller bird than the common heron, breeds in North-West Africa, Portugal, and Spain, right through to Persia. To the British Isles it is a rare vagrant. The Great White Heron, which is about the same size as the common species, usually nests in reed beds although it has also been found in trees. Its distribution is practically world-wide, although it is only a rare vagrant to

Britain. The Little Egret, which has pure white plumage, is very much smaller, being about twenty-two inches in total length, half of which is made up of beak, neck and tail. It is an extremely rare visitor to the British Isles, but is found in many parts of Europe as well as Africa and Asia.

NIGHT BIRD

The Night Heron, which breeds in Southern Spain, the Mediterranean, Ethiopia and the Orient, is about two feet in length. It has now nested for some years in the Zoological Gardens in Edinburgh. It is a compact, cobby bird, with a short neck and short legs, black head and mantle, and grey wings and tail. In the wild state this species is crepuscular in habit, roosting in thick cover all day and flying to its feeding grounds at dusk. When breeding, however, it hunts regularly by day. The call of the night heron closely resembles that of the raven.

Flamingos are pink birds which suddenly blossom into scarlet when they take flight. They have extraordinarily long legs and neck, with down-curved bill. They fly with their neck and legs fully extended and are unmistakable in the air or on the ground. They are gregarious birds and flocks sometimes number several thousands. They breed in the

Birds of the winter tide-line, the oystercatcher and curlew.

The white stork nests in trees and on buildings.

The night heron is a native of Southern Europe.

The black-winged stilt has very long, pink legs.

The flamingo has long legs and a long neck.

shallow waters of lagoons or the edges of lakes. In Spain, they nest in the Marismas. Flamingos are only rare vagrants to Britain, being found from Spain to Ethiopia and East Africa, from Ceylon northwards to Lake Baikal, and in Florida southwards into South America. The nest is a heap of mud, conical in shape, which is scooped up by the birds until the top projects a few inches above water-level. In a shallow depression on top of this heap, the eggs are laid.

STORKS BLACK AND WHITE

It is a curious thing that while the White Stork breeds in Spain, France, Holland, Germany, Denmark, Sweden, the Baltic States and Russia, it should be no more than a rare vagrant to the British Isles. In Europe it is familiar because of its close association with human habitations in the breeding season. Besides nesting on houses, it is to be found in marshy country and wooded districts far from populated areas. This large white bird, over three feet in length, is distinctive in its white plumage with black flight feathers and long red beak and legs. Birds which nest far from human habitation tend

to be shy and wary, but those which nest on buildings become extremely tame, almost as domesticated as dove-cote pigeons. In certain parts of Spain the nest may be only a few feet above the ground, but high buildings are a common site in Denmark and Germany. The birds take readily to artificial nesting sites provided by man. Nests used year after year sometimes become very bulky. Young storks are fed by both parents by regurgitation. Food is principally frogs, newts, slow-worms, snakes, fish, worms and insects, but sometimes the stork will devour the young and eggs of small birds as well as a variety of small mammals.

In size, shape and general characteristics, the Black Stork resembles the white, but in plumage it is completely different, being entirely black except for the breast and underside. The plumage of the black stork has a brilliant green and purple sheen. This species breeds in Spain, Portugal, Germany, and the Baltic States. It is not a sociable breeder and usually nests in dense forests or caves. To Britain, the black stork is a very rare vagrant, under thirty specimens ever having been recorded.

POLLUTION AND POISONING

In this age of progress, much of our progress appears to be based on poison. Poison on the farm, poison on the garden, poison on the orchard, until one begins to wonder what our forebears did to save their crops and their fruit and their vegetables. In recent years, poisoning has taken a serious turn because of the now-general practice of dressing corn at sowing time. Millions of birds in Britain have died as a result of this and poisoning reached such serious proportions that the Ministry of Agriculture found it necessary to ban certain types from 1961; notably the deadly heptachlor, aldrin and dieldrin.

To use a poisoned or stupefying bait to kill mammals is now illegal in this country; the spraying of poison on trees, or the dressing of seed with toxins is not. The man who kills a buzzard with rabbit bait doped with strychnine has committed an offence and can be prosecuted accordingly. The man who kills hundreds of song birds and perhaps many partridges and wood pigeons with an approved seed dressing has committed no offence at all. To say that in one case the

poisoning was deliberate and in the other accidental, is merely dodging the problem.

No one would deny the need for controlling the numbers of the brown rat, and the traditional way has been by using poisons of many kinds. In recent years certain poisons used for rats proved most effective, and it has been claimed for them that they were harmless to other forms of life. There is plenty of evidence, however, that such birds as barn owls often died at farms as a result of killing rats dying from certain forms of poisoning. It is another indication of the main drawback of poisons, viz: that after they are put down, they cannot be controlled. You cannot kill just what you want to kill; the effect is liable to be cumulative.

Modern man also poisons the water, and one of the great tragedies and scandals of the 20th century is the wholesale pollution of our rivers by chemicals and industrial effluence. Pollution not only causes the destruction of fish stocks, it destroys the whole wild-life complex of the river. No problem is more urgent than the problem of river pollution.

THE LIFE OF THE BEAVER

Often, when observing the behaviour of animals very different from ourselves, our own feeling of intellectual superiority is shaken. This increases when we study the prodigious worker of the northern forests, the beaver.

A long Indian canoe, passing in a cloud of spray, heads upstream. But, suddenly an obstacle prevents further progress: a broad barrier of trunks and branches stretches across the bend in the river, and the water froths and bursts through at numerous break-through points. In the woods are heaps of twigs, scattered trunks of trees felled and cleaned, piles of stones and mud all ready for use, all witness to the intense activity of the builders. Dark shapes glide through the water just under the surface and head silently for the depths when alarmed by the noise of human footsteps. The animals are the beavers, the prodigious engineers of the forests and rivers. Alerted by their sentinels hidden among the trees, they have stopped work and now hurry away to take refuge in their inaccessible underwater dens.

Let us try to approach as silently as any wild animal of the woods and get close enough to one of these extraordinary animals to observe it going about its business.

The beaver is just over three feet long and covered in thick, dark, shining fur. It has a blunt face and its mouth is armed with formidable incisor teeth, the kind of teeth possessed by the whole rodent family. The hind feet are webbed and the beast has a curious tail, short and broad like a spatula.

In the water, the beaver moves swiftly and surely, his body elongated like a torpedo, his muzzle on the surface and his flat tail stretched out behind as a rudder. He can stay submerged for long periods of time. His coat is completely waterproof. He is, in fact, highly adapted for the kind of life he leads.

Over many thousands of years he has moved ever farther northwards so that now he is found almost exclusively in North America and occasionally in Northern Europe. His

Adult beaver with her young.

The beaver has always lived in wild forests.

With its formidably strong incisor teeth, the beaver has no difficulty in felling trees, even of considerable size.

Ruthless hunters began the decimation of the beaver population.

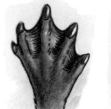

Illustration of the beaver's teeth and webbed feet.

Warned of danger, the beaver dives to safety.

The lynx is an enemy of the beaver.

enemies are the large carnivores and man. The beaver has turned to good effect, in wonderful ways, the means of defence which nature has given him. He can build dens like fortresses; regulate the flow and force of rivers; and live on the toughest kind of vegetarian diet. The beavers form themselves into little colonies, highly organised, so that each individual becomes part of a well-oiled machine.

THE UNDERWATER DEN

The banks of the pool beside which the canoeists have stopped appears to be completely deserted, but the men know that below the ground, near the water, the beaver tribe lies concealed, waiting for the danger to pass before leaving their deep dens. If we open one of these refuges and examine its structure we will see first of all an entrance tunnel, between four and five feet below the surface of the water at a depth where water doesn't freeze even in the hardest winter. This tunnel rises gradually as it penetrates deeply into the bank. Two parts of the tunnel are flooded but immediately above water-level it widens into a kind of terrace and finally there is the den. This den, or lodge, is a low, wide room, very clean, the floor of which is covered with wood chips. The roof is formed of earth and pressed mud, sometimes domed with wood. Sometimes this first chamber communicates with a second at a higher level, the second being furnished with an opening towards fresh air. The beaver uses this when a sudden spring flood inundates the lower chamber.

At the mouth of the tunnel there is usually a heap of poplar and birch branches held there by a big trunk. This is the store and winter food reserve of the beaver who, between spells of sleeping, swims out to bring back to the den some pieces of wood for himself and his family. Wood, especially that of young poplars, maples and birches, constitutes the beavers' principal food, along with certain herbs in summer-time. Protected by the water which hides the entrance to his house, the beaver lives through the long northern winter. When the ice breaks up, crashing and grinding, and the river level rises, swollen by the melting snows, the beaver knows that spring has arrived and then begins for him a busy period during which he displays his wonderful capacities as a builder.

THE BEAVER AS ENGINEER

In order that the beaver's home may be secure against enemies, he has to ensure that the entrance to it will be below water-level at all seasons. It is essential, therefore, that the level of the river or lake should be kept constant, whether

The ingenuity of the beaver is remarkable, and here we see them transporting material for the construction of their dam.

during periods of flood or drought. This involves damming the river. The beavers in squads work along the river banks. While some are nibbling at the bases of young birches, using their strong incisor teeth like chisels, others are busy constructing the wall of the dam. The animals working in the forest are as skilful as any woodsman— nibbling at the tree in such a way that it will be sure to fall into or near the water. Suddenly there is a shower of branches followed by a loud splash, and a birch tree is in the water. Immediately it is stripped of its bark until it is as smooth as a ship's mast. It is then cut into suitable lengths. Logs dressed some distance from the water are rolled there by co-operative effort and heaved in; when, with the aid of the current, they are manœuvred into the position where they are required. Here other squads are already at work; using big stones and mud, they build and plaster and wedge, accumulating material until the dyke stretches from bank to bank. Many outlets are left so that the impetus of floods is reduced.

In this way spectacular dams are built up which may be twelve feet in height and a quarter of a mile in length. From an engineering point of view, the dams cannot be faulted. When timber is felled far from the water, the beavers excavate long channels which serve to transport lengths of wood to the scene of operations. Once the dams have been constructed, the animals open and close the vents as required—exactly as hydraulic engineers do. Seeing beavers at work in this way, with such obvious division of labour, one cannot help thinking of an organised plan to which every animal of the community works.

FAMILY LIFE

If we observe beavers carefully, we will soon be struck by the close family bonds and the care taken of the young by

Mother strips bark for her young.   *Beaver eating bark of the poplar.*

The upper entrance is used during open weather, the lower tunnel in winter.

A completed dam. In this picture you can see the overflow outlet.

SECTIONAL VIEW OF BEAVER'S DAM

OUTLET→   RAISED LEVEL

NORMAL LEVEL

DAM OF MUD, STONES AND BRANCHES

LODGE OR CHAMBER WITH UNDERWATER ENTRANCES

Diagram of a completed beaver dam. The dam maintains the water level so that the den is left dry.

At one time, hunting in the huge forests could be practised freely. The crack of a rifle in the brooding silence meant a beaver lying dead somewhere in the snow.

The beaver will live and breed readily in captivity. Its skin is precious and was once so much sought after that the animal was in danger of extinction.

Catching beavers was once a full-time occupation with trappers. The fur being valuable, the animal was hunted incessantly and special traps were designed for catching beavers even when they were swimming about underwater. Man, therefore, was the greatest enemy.

A family of beavers in captivity. All thrive well if properly looked after. The young ones are most affectionate and the mother looks after her family with the greatest of care. Beavers make delightful pets if taken young.

spanks them soundly, making them cry loudly in protest.

If captured, young beavers become most affectionate towards those who have the care of them, as the man called Grey Owl showed in his stories of Canadian beavers. In captivity, beavers take their food with obvious relish, and will roll about on the ground with every manifestation of pleasure. As they grow up, however, they become increasingly dangerous, and are completely domesticated only with great difficulty and by people who give much thought to the psychology of the animals. In captivity, some of them often begin to lose condition which may be due to some kind of instinctive longing for the rivers and forests which are their real home.

The family ties are strong and obvious. When the young beavers are strong enough to follow their parents, the mother will take them on forays into the forest during which she will cut wood or carry supplies to the den while they follow her, watching. By parental teaching, the young learn a great deal about the facts of life and the nature of their enemies. Beavers are mostly protected now, both in Europe and North America, but at one time they were trapped extensively and hunted by special dogs.

HUNTING THE BEAVER

The beaver possesses one of the warmest of skins, and as a result he is much sought after by fur trappers. Ruthless

the adults. During their life span of ten years or so, beavers retain their strong family ties and the females are most attentive to their young. Young beavers whimper like newly-born children, can be as mischievous and playful as children, and as a result have often to be scolded by the mother who

Animal skins deteriorate quickly if not cured. Here we see a tub of beaver skins containing a solution of alum. The skins were put into this tub immediately after stripping.

apart. There is, however, a difference in habit. The European beaver does not indulge in the great engineering projects for which its New World cousin is so notable. The European species does not dam rivers, but it has been suggested that this is due to persecution and that where unmolested, it too, will build dams like the other species.

In the beavers we have a clear example of how man in his greed can decimate a wild animal population by ruthless exploitation without thought of to-morrow. Only by energetic government efforts was the North American beaver saved from extermination.

An old-style market. Here the beaver trappers sold the skins after tanning them in rudimentary fashion.

A brutal leg-hold trap set in the snow. The agony of a beaver caught in this trap may last for many days.

hunting in the past reduced the population of beavers in the Old and New Worlds to danger level. In both places conservation is now the rule, and the species is no longer in danger of extermination. Hunting, where it does take place, is carried on under strict regulations.

The old-time trappers were forest experts who spent many months at a time going round their trap lines. Despite the animal's cunning and retiring habits, and despite his ability to stay in his lodge for whole days at a time, he was no match for man in the long run, and the species became very rare.

There are two species of beaver: the Canadian, which is probably the best known because it has been most written about in fact and fiction; and the European beaver, about which little is known. The latter, once widely distributed in Europe, is now rare—being confined to Eastern Europe and a few isolated localities in France and Germany. The two species appear identical so that only an expert can tell them

EGG-COLLECTING

Before scientific ornithology reached the heights it has attained to-day, much valuable knowledge was contributed to the subject by oologists or, in more popular language, egg-collectors. The old-style egg-collector, in many cases, played an important part in standardising the description of eggs, egg weights and clutch sizes; but, then as now, a great many people collected eggs for no other reason than mere acquisitiveness. At the present time, except in very exceptional circumstances, egg collecting is quite unjustifiable and a complete waste of time. It is quite wrong for anyone (teacher or parent) to tell a young person that there is no harm in it.

It is a bad habit which ought to be discouraged. While it is true that in this country the law allows certain eggs to be taken and that common birds are not greatly affected by reasonable collecting, the whole business is pointless and often leads to serious breaches of the law, i.e. when the collector turns to the eggs of rare and protected birds. The worst egg collectors are those who pursue and harry rare birds for no reason other than their rarity, and it is a sad reflection on a civilised country like ours that the osprey can only nest in Scotland when it is supervised by watchers twenty-four hours a day.

THE GREBE FAMILY

Grebes and divers, for so long placed together in a single group, have now been separated into two distinct orders, because it is extremely doubtful if they are in any way related, although, superficially, they closely resemble each other.

The Great Crested Grebe is widely distributed over Britain on suitable inland waters. Although absent from many areas in Scotland, it is to be found in some numbers in the Tay area. In this grebe, the adult has a prominent frill on the side of its face during the breeding season. This frill is lost in autumn. But, even in winter plumage, its former presence is betrayed by the chestnut and black markings on the side of the head.

During the nesting season, this species frequents reservoirs and large ponds where there is plenty of reed cover. In this the nest is usually anchored. Where cover is scarce the nest may be placed out of the water altogether. It is composed largely of dead vegetation, which is raked over the eggs when the bird is absent. This practice performs the double function of keeping the eggs warm and concealing them from view. The usual number of eggs is three or four, but five are not uncommon and bigger clutches have been recorded.

Nesting time is largely determined by the availability of cover and, where this is slow to develop, the birds may come on to lay late. May to July is the normal period, but the birds sometimes breed as late as August or September. Both sexes share the task of incubating, and when the young hatch they are at first looked after by both parents. But the male's interest soon wears off. The young are independent of their parents at about two and a half months of age.

WINTER VISITORS

The Red-necked Grebe, which has pale grey cheeks and chestnut-coloured neck, is a winter visitor to the British Isles —mainly to the east coast. Abroad, it breeds in Denmark, Germany and Sweden, into Finland and Russia, and as far as western Siberia, as well as in southern Europe. The wintering area is the Mediterranean region into Asia Minor.

Like the great crested grebe, the red-neck nests on fresh-water lochs and lagoons where there is plenty of aquatic vegetation, or in flooded areas. The nest is a typical heap of water weeds anchored in shallow water. The breeding season is May and June. The red-neck feeds on small fresh-water fish and frogs, besides a great variety of insects.

SMALLEST OF THE FAMILY

The Little Grebe, sometimes called the dabchick, is resident in the British Isles, as well as being a winter visitor. It is widely distributed as a breeding species but becomes scarce in the north of Scotland. Many British breeding birds move out to estuaries and tidal waters in the autumn, returning to their breeding quarters in March. There is no evidence that any of these birds move abroad.

The little grebe nests on small ponds and the margins of lochs, in beds of rushes or flags. It likes a site with branches hanging low over the water, forming a screen. The nest is built of water weeds, built up just above the surface of the water, and the incubating bird covers her nest before going off to feed. The nesting season extends from April into July, and sometimes as late as September. Two broods are the rule and sometimes a third is attempted.

The little grebe, as its name implies, is the smallest as well as being the commonest of the grebes, and it is the only European species which has no head ornaments at any season. It is a dumpy bird, dark brown in summer with chestnut cheeks, throat and neck. The base of its beak is bright yellowish green. In winter plumage the bird is paler in colour and the chestnut of the throat, neck and cheeks disappears, becoming buff fading to white.

In the breeding season, the bird is often betrayed by its familiar trilling call. It skulks far more than any other grebes in dense reed beds, and is seldom seen on water by day. It doesn't often come to land, nor does it normally perch ashore or on the nest. It stands erect. When frightened, it will dive and stay submerged for long periods with only its head showing on the surface of the water.

The red-necked grebe (Podiceps griseigena), has a black crown, small, black ear-tufts, and chestnut-coloured neck.

The little grebe (Podiceps ruficollis), is also known as the dabchick. It is the smallest grebe.

Parrots

Despite the splendour of their plumage, their vivacity, their accomplished mimicry, and the affection they display towards their owners, characteristics which make these delightful birds

" In the small cage, a grey parrot tried to prop up his companion which, having suffered an injury to its claws, was crouched down uttering lamentable cries. It was almost dusk and a last ray of sun came through the bars—the injured parrot stretched her head towards that light and for an instant seemed to recover strength; but then she drew back her little head and drooped it on a wing. Thus desolately she awaited death, while her mate tried to open her beak to feed her. When the agony came to her he did not move from her for an instant and, after her death, shut himself up in an obstinate silence. Two days later, he too, died."

It was more or less in these words that a naturalist told the story of a pair of parrots which he had captured and kept for some time in a cage. Though this quotation savours very strongly of anthropomorphism, it is nevertheless a clear indication of the intimate relationship often established between caged parrots, although it would be extremely dangerous and unwise to read too much of human emotion into their actions.

Parrots belong to the order of climbers, and you will notice that their toes are arranged two in front and two behind, unlike those of perching birds where the arrangement is three in front and one behind.

Parrots have long been associated with sailors and old ladies, and the associations are not difficult to understand. Since their homes are far beyond Europe, it was inevitable that sailors should become the main importers in the early days, and considerable importers even in modern times. In the second association, it is not surprising that old ladies living alone might prefer a parrot to a dog or a cat because, after all, the bird could be trained to mimic the human voice and in that way be more of a companion.

No one really knows when parrots were first domesticated, but there is no doubt that they have been held in high esteem since very ancient times. Affectionate (in the main), excellent mimics, and endowed with a considerable memory, they are still popular to-day in drawing-rooms and zoological gardens. Not the least of their attractions is their brilliant plumage.

Despite the bird's powers of mimicry, it would be a gross mistake to believe that any parrot understands the meaning of the words or phrases it uses. This belief is very tempting when one hears a parrot making an appropriate remark in a given set of circumstances. When you hear this it is as well to remember that very often the bird learned the word or phrase in association with the circumstances, and so the two become associated in the bird's " mind ". When a parrot, seeing a door open, cries out, " Shut the door," it is simply using words it has heard frequently in this exact context. The parrot would just as readily cry " Open the door " when the door had to be shut, if it had been taught in this way. For the parrot, the words themselves mean nothing.

Parrots have thick, strongly hooked beaks which are very

widely popular, their importation into the United Kingdom has been prohibited because of the disease called psittacosis associated with them.

The cockatoo is easily recognisable at first glance by the crest of erect feathers on his head. Here we see the great sulphur-crested cockatoo (Kakatoe galerita), the Spanish flag cockatoo (Kakatoe leadbeateri), and the roseate cockatoo (Eolophus roseicapillus).

powerful and designed for crushing seeds. They have also strong climbing feet with extremely short shanks. The wings have ten flight feathers, and the tail ten rudder feathers. Some species fly very well, others clumsily. Their voices are strong and strident, well suited to mimicking the pitch of the human voice—unlike the budgerigars which tend to chirp their words.

Parrots nest usually in the cavities of trees or rocks, although some species build on the ground. They come mainly from America, the Moluccas, and Australia. They are found, but not nearly so commonly, in Polynesia, Africa and New Zealand. Their life is almost entirely arboreal and when parrots unite into parties to raid plantations the devastation wrought by them can be great.

Modern research has shown that there are at least 500 different species of parrots in the world. These are divided into groups—the parakeets, cockatoos, typical parrots, lorys, etc.

PARAKEETS AND COCKATOOS

The parakeets are birds of small dimensions, the most common being the Carolina parakeet which is a New World species hailing from the Americas. From Australia comes the Small Waved Parrot, greenish yellow in colour, embellished with black stripes. It is one of the commonest of all parrots. It is sociable, affectionate and clean. In this species the female constructs the nest. The usual clutch is from four to eight round, white eggs.

Cockatoos are familiar birds in zoological gardens and are recognised at once by the crest of upright feathers on the head. They are also commonly found in aviaries and are most amusing because of their antics. In size they compare with a dove. The best-known cockatoos are those of Timor and Samoa. The Spanish Flag Cockatoo of Australia is a very beautiful bird much sought after. Normally its crest lies flat and is opened only when the bird is excited, or when it sights something unusual. When the crest is opened it reveals the colours of the Spanish flag, from which the species takes its name.

The Rosy Cockatoo, a favourite species in zoological gardens, lives in Australia, where it prefers mountain areas. Like the other species it feeds on fruit and grain and has a strong preference for green maize. Though not as accomplished speakers as the grey parrots, many cockatoos become excellent mimics.

With the cockatoos can be linked the Microglossum which hails from New Guinea. Its fierce aspect, produced by its bare, rosy face and uniformly black-grey body, contrasts sharply with its docile character.

The Amazon, or true parrot, which is common in all regions from Brazil to Venezuela, is an excellent mimic and individual birds have been recorded as being able to articulate 250 separate words or sounds. The Amazon, contrary to what its name might suggest, is most docile and in captivity loves nothing better than to sit for hours at a time on someone's shoulder pecking at any stranger who happens to come near. In the wild state it feeds on oily seeds and fruit. In captivity it is extremely adaptable in the way of food. It is affectionate, accomplished, with a good memory, and well-taught speci-

The Amazon parrot with the blue forehead is one of the true parrots or Psittaci; *it is a first-class mimic, and has been known to produce about 250 different sounds.*

mens will fetch their masters' slippers or paper as readily as any dog, and wish him good morning and good night.

A naturalist has told how one of these Amazon parrots, on the day after its mistress died, asked, " where's mistress ? " It continued uttering this cry for a week and its sad words were uttered in tones of lament. After a week the bird died of grief. In this account there is again a strong flavour of anthropomorphism, but again one has to bear in mind that this species develops strong attachments and might well pine away when deprived of its normal company.

Two other beautiful parrots, about the size of turtle-doves, are the *Conurus auricapillus jandaia* and the *Guaruba*, both of which come from the Amazon. Very beautiful also is the Collar parrot, a species which readily gives voice, but which is only rarely able to pronounce words. This species feeds on palm fruit and nests in holes in trees where it lays four white eggs.

The *Myopsita monaco*, which is the size of a dove, live in Brazil, Uruguay and Argentina, and is a nuisance in the maize fields, which it raids frequently. It constructs roomy nests in trees. The *Ara macao*, which lives in Mexico and Central America, and the *Ara araruna* of the Amazon Valley, are two big parrots. They will measure a yard in overall length from tip of beak to tip of tail. With their strong beaks they can crack the hardest nuts. The tail feathers of these birds were once used by Indian chiefs and priests to decorate their headgear.

In the forests of Equatorial Africa lives the *Psittacus erithacus* and the parrot of the Verster. You will notice that the first-named of these two species bears the name associated with the disease mentioned earlier. It is a good mimic of the human voice. The second species, although it is not nearly such an accomplished mimic, is greatly prized because of its brightly coloured plumage.

Seen in their natural setting, in tropical or sub-tropical forests, parrots of all species are extremely beautiful. All of us, perhaps, would like to possess a parrot that would repeat our words, but nowadays it is difficult to satisfy this wish because of the strict regulations regarding the import of parrots.

Monaca parrots from the Argentine. The plumage on their backs is dark green; their tails and thighs are lighter green. They construct their nests in holes and trees.

THE HIPPOPOTAMUS

Lords of the great rivers of Africa, the Hippopotami look like legendary monsters, descendants of the great prehistoric ungulates. Giants in stature, they have been driven to a largely aquatic life because of progressively increasing body-weight.

" River horse " is the imaginative name for this African animal: a name which may have been given to him by the first man to see him jumping out of the waters of the Nile and plodding up the bank, his mighty body making him look like one of the legendary horses of Neptune. In fact, there is nothing more unlike the elegant horse than this massive beast, with his monstrously great head and squat barrel body, carried about on four short, solid legs which are not in any way suited for quick movement.

Only reluctantly does the hippopotamus indulge in the doubtful pleasure of galloping about on dry land. At the most his run will be a short one, made usually under pressure of imminent danger. Then, with a great breaking of reeds and shattering of shrubs he will thunder over the ground with only one aim—that of reaching the safe waters of the river. Once there he becomes a different animal altogether. There we can see that his big body, so cumbersome on land, now becomes agile. In the water he is at home, swimming with back and head above the surface or submerging himself until only his big nostrils show above the water. His eyes and nostrils are placed on the upper part of his head so that this great animal, even when his whole body is submerged, is able to breathe and look around him.

Apart from man, the hippopotamus has no important enemies. His great bulk, the enormous thickness of his hide, which is impervious to the teeth of the greatest carnivores, together with his own formidable teeth, render him practically immune from attack.

In spite of his squat build, the hippopotamus reaches enormous weights—in the region of three or four tons, most of which is made up by his hide, which is extremely thick and as hard as armour plate.

ENTIRELY VEGETARIAN

When the hippopotamus opens his jaws in a cavernous yawn, you can see his strong eye-teeth and the great molars, each as big as a fist. The hippopotamus has the biggest mouth in the whole kingdom of land mammals and takes second place only to the whale. His mouth is, indeed, a terrifying spectacle, and when open it looks more dangerous than it really is. The hippopotamus is entirely vegetarian, and he can quickly devastate great stretches of riverside growth. For this reason he is already something of a problem in certain parts of Africa.

At one time the hippopotamus was found all over Africa, as well as in parts of Europe and Asia. Some years ago, the skeletons of some forty hippopotami were found in a bog in Southern Germany. To-day, as the result of great changes in climate, and of the hunting to which they have been subjected throughout the ages, hippopotami are found only along the river courses, and on the banks of the lakes of Equatorial Africa. Even the Nile, which was once populated right to its mouth by numerous herds of these animals, is now almost completely cleared of them except for the upper reaches.

The great hippopotamus (Hippopotamus amphibius), *of Equatorial Africa, is a predominantly aquatic animal which feeds on water plants.*

It seems to us impossible that primitive people, armed with only spears, could confront these armoured monsters with any hope of success. But they did it, and even succeeded in killing them, striking at those points where the skin is less thick or spearing the animals in their wide open jaws. The animal is hunted by natives and Europeans for its flesh, which is said to be delicious, for its fat which is as useful as the fat of the pig, and for its hide which can be made into strong belts and whips, and is much sought after. The beast's eye-teeth, which are extremely long, provide excellent ivory. Protection is now afforded to the hippopotamus in certain parts of Africa but this, in turn, has given rise to a new problem because the animal is building up its numbers so well that it has become a danger to its own habitat.

ONE OF SWINE FAMILY

Zoologically, the hippopotamus is a typical mammal belonging to the ungulates or hoofed animals, and more strictly to the swine family. Thus the gigantic river horse is in reality more closely related to the pigs, which are non-ruminants. The group to which pig and hippopotamus belong is called artiodactyls, which means that they walk on only two of their four existing toes, in contrast to the horse which uses only one toe which we refer to as its hoof. Another feature which distinguishes the hippopotamus and the pig from other ungulates, is the roundness of the points of the molar teeth, in addition to the presence of strong lower canines. Similar to the tusks of the hippopotamus are those of the wild boar which are visible also when the mouth is closed. Nevertheless, there could be no possibility of anyone confusing the hippopotamus with the pig. The thickness of the beast's hide brings it into the group of pachyderms (thick-

Hippopotami remain in the water for hours at a time, lying submerged with only eyes and nostrils showing above the surface.

skinned). This massive armour is sparsely haired (the presence of hair is a characteristic of mammals; even the whale has a few), the scarceness of hair probably being due to the long aquatic life of the species. The hippopotamus's tail is short and thick and ends in a tuft of thick black bristles.

HABITAT

Hippopotami live for the most part in small herds among the reeds and scrub along the banks of African rivers, in zones which are usually off the beaten track for human beings and where the animals can find shade and coolness during the torrid hours of the day. Their tough hide does not make them completely invulnerable to attack from vigorous tropical parasites, some of which manage to penetrate into the folds of skin to bite and draw blood. To escape such parasites as well as to protect himself from the heat, the hippopotamus spends much time deeply submerged in mud banks and wallows, remaining immobile for many hours.

In Africa, especially in Liberia, there is the pygmy hippopotamus which is identical in appearance to the great hippopotamus, but much lighter in weight. The pygmy hippopotamus rarely exceeds half a ton.

Thus they acquire a protective coating of mud in the same way as pigs do to protect themselves from sun-scald.

When the hippopotami rise from the mud, the cracking of the crust can be heard and it seems as though the disintegrating surface were releasing imprisoned, red-jawed monsters. The mud coating helps the hippopotamus in another way: by keeping his hide damp. Otherwise it would become dried in the sun and cracks in the skin would afford too easy access to insects. The insects which lodge on his skin are sought after by small birds which perch on his back and seek them out with their beaks.

SEASONAL MOVEMENT

The hippopotamus lives entirely on aquatic vegetation, such as water-logged bushes which grow along the river banks. To find this kind of food the herds go up river during the rainy season. They retrace their steps during the succeeding dry period. The beasts move in slow stages with the ponderous step which is characteristic and which they do not lose even when fighting among themselves. During fights the animals attack each other with their formidable teeth.

The females give birth to one young only at a time. The normal lifespan of the hippopotamus is difficult to calculate in the wild state, but the long life of captive animals suggests that it is certainly thirty years, and perhaps forty or more.

In some parts of Western Africa, there is found a hippopotamus which is similar in all respects to the one described but which is of much smaller dimensions. It doesn't weigh more than half a ton and stands about three feet tall. This species has a tremendous appetite and in captivity, despite its small size, will consume over sixty pounds of herbs and other vegetation each day.

The hippopotamus, as has been said, is not a dangerous animal, and professional hunters even say that to kill it with a couple of pellets properly aimed at the middle of the forehead is child's play. But it is far safer to assume that hippopotami can be dangerous; this applies with equal force to bears. People who are killed by bears are generally those who have convinced themselves they know all about them. Not uncommonly hunters and keepers have been killed by hippopotami because they were sure that the beasts were not dangerous.

SWANS

The tame or semi-tame swan with which we are familiar in this country and which breeds on canals and ornamental waters, is widely distributed in Europe as a truly wild bird, nesting in Denmark, Sweden, parts of North Germany, Poland and Russia. In addition, it nests in Asia Minor, Persia, and east to Mongolia and Siberia. These wild birds migrate to the eastern Mediterranean region, into Asia, and occasionally as far as India.

The swan was once thought to have been introduced into Britain, but the modern opinion is that it is truly indigenous. Originally, its range was probably confined to East Anglia and the Thames area. This wild stock was gradually brought to a semi-domesticated condition by pinioning captives. From the thirteenth- to the eighteenth-centuries all swans in England were the property of the Crown and swans were kept only under licence. Swan-keeping was controlled by very strict rules and all qualified owners had their own licence marks. Marking consisted of notching the bill in some way or making distinctive slits or holes in the webs of the feet. This custom died out in the eighteenth-century and most British swans have, although still semi-tame, reverted to a feral state. The swannery at Abbotsbury in Dorset is the largest in Britain. The birds at Abbotsbury are full-winged and free, although they live a largely artificial life and are extremely tame. The swan was never a royal bird in Scotland.

MUTES WILD AND DOMESTIC

Mute swans in the wild state breed usually in reed beds or on swampy islands. In the semi-domesticated state the birds will nest almost anywhere near water. The nest is a large heap of water weeds, sticks, reeds, rushes, and vegetable matter, conical in shape and bulky. Both sexes carry

material for building but actual construction is carried out by the female.

Eggs usually number five to seven, but bigger clutches have been recorded. Very large clutches usually indicate that two unmated females have been laying together. While most of the incubating is done by the female, the male will relieve her when she goes off to feed during the night. Young swans at birth are not white and in their juvenile plumage are a dirty brown colour. The family is tended by both parents, the female usually leading.

The mute swan has an orange-red bill, black at the tip and with a prominent black basal knob. This swan habitually swims with neck curved, bill pointing down over the breast, and the wings arched over the back. It is normally a silent bird but under certain conditions can snort and hiss. The cygnets have a feeble piping cry.

At nesting time, the mute swan can be most pugnacious and the cob will face even man when he considers his nest is threatened. He doesn't hesitate to display aggressively before an intruding dog and is fit to drive away all but the most persistent. It has been said that a blow from a swan's wing can break a man's arm, but this is most unlikely.

WHOOPER OF THE NORTH

The Whooper swan is of similar size to the mute, the overall length being five feet, with a body of two and a half feet. It breeds in northern Norway, and Sweden, north Finland and Russia, and as far east as Japan. In winter, the birds migrate over Europe to Spain and the Mediterranean, North Africa, and as far east as the Crimea and the Caucasus.

In the British Isles a few pairs of whooper swans breed—all of them in Scotland. To other parts of Britain the birds are winter visitors. Numbers in winter vary according to the

Mute swan and Bewick swan. The mute swan is five feet in length and the Bewick is four feet.

The whooper swan nests in the far north, but visits Britain in winter. It has bred in Scotland.

a herd is passing overhead the music sounds like that of foxhounds. This is the call heard during the southward migration when the great white birds, with long necks extended, fly in the trailing V-lines or chevrons so characteristic of the geese.

A smaller swan than either mute or whooper is the species called Bewick's, which measures about four feet from beak to tail with a body of two feet. To the British Isles it is a winter visitor only. Abroad, it breeds in parts of Russia, such as Novaya Zemlya, and along the Siberian coast.

Like the whooper, the Bewick's swan has a yellow beak tipped with black, but the yellow area is differently shaped and does not project into the black as in the case of the whooper. Bewick's is also shorter necked than the whooper, and of generally stockier build.

On water, Bewick's swan utters what has been described as a babble of musical sounds. In flight its call is softer and lower pitched than that of the whooper.

The Black swans come from Australia and Tasmania, but specimens are to be found in zoological gardens in Europe, where they are artificially maintained as ornamental fowl.

severity of the weather. The bulk of wintering whooper swans frequent Scotland and the extreme north of England; farther south, numbers dwindle rapidly.

Whoopers feed almost entirely on vegetable matter, though they do take worms and a variety of aquatic insects.

In the breeding season the whooper frequents islands and the drier areas of swamps. The nest is built of moss and marsh plants mixed with mud for stiffening. The same nest may be used year after year, so that it assumes a great size, and such mounds remain as landmarks for many years after the birds have ceased to use them. The breeding season is in May and June depending on altitude and latitude. Like young mute swans, the cygnets of the whooper are grey. When they leave the nest they are looked after and fed by both parents.

In the whooper, the beak is yellow at the base and black at the tip, and there is no basal knob. This distinguishes it at once from the mute swan. In addition, the whooper habitually swims with its long neck held straight and its posture is quite different from that of the mute.

The call of the whooper is a loud bugle-call, and when

The black swan, which comes from Australia and Tasmania, is to be seen in certain zoological gardens in Europe.

QUESTIONS AND ANSWERS

What is myxomatosis?

This disease is caused by the myxoma virus, which in South America is the main controlling factor in the coney population of that country. When first introduced into Europe, myxomatosis killed 98 per cent. of rabbits which became infected. The disease was used in Australia in an attempt to solve the problem of the rabbit scourge there, but it did not kill them all. The virus is not now killing such a high percentage of rabbits because it is becoming attenuated; that is to say, losing its full power.

Are rabbits controlled in other ways?

Yes. One of Nature's ways of reducing the birth rate in rabbits is by the phenomenon of reabsorption. This means that a percentage of every litter conceived by a doe, or even the entire litter, is reabsorbed into the mother's body instead of being born.

What is refection?

In rabbits and hares (the *lagomorphs*), we find the phenomenon of refection. This means that when food passes through the bowel and is voided in the form of droppings, it is re-swallowed and passed through the body again.

The final type of dropping produced by a rabbit or a hare is quite distinct from the other "first time through" pellet. Refection may well be likened to chewing the cud in cattle, although it works in quite a different way. Although the habit has only recently been rediscovered, it was obviously known to the Ancients who referred to rabbits chewing the cud.

When did the rabbit come to Britain?

The rabbit was introduced into England with William the Conqueror and in due course, like William, completely conquered England.

The native feline of Britain is the Wild Cat, now confined entirely to the Highlands of Scotland: the last stronghold to which it has been driven by human pressure. Between the First and Second World Wars the number of wild cats in Scotland diminished greatly, but from the 40's to the present time the animal has been increasing in numbers and extending its range. Unlike Poland, Scotland does not protect the wild cat by law.

It is unfortunate for this cat that it is so easily trapped. The situation therefore arises in Scotland that a man may trap a score without ever seeing one alive and free. Wild cats are most frequently seen when fox-hunters are out with terriers in the spring, going round fox dens. Then, wild cats are quite often found by the dogs and hunted over rocks and scree. The wild cat will always try to escape without a fight, but, if cornered, is a terrible fighting machine fit to inflict severe injuries before it is killed.

The true Scottish wild cat is a wide-skulled, big-bodied, animal with short, ringed tail, blunt at the end. Its teeth, claws and limbs are far more powerful than those of the domestic tabby. Nevertheless, wild cats will sometimes interbreed with domestic cats—usually a wild tom mating with a domestic female—but this hasn't had the effect of causing degeneration of the wild cat: rather has it led to an improvement of size in the domestic breed. It has, indeed, been said that the stature and prowess of domestic cats in Europe improves as one goes northwards, due to the increasing intermixture of wild-cat blood. As a result of interbreeding, it is possible to find, in Scotland, cats living wild which are not true wild cats.

In Scotland, the wild cat breeds twice a year, kits being born in the spring and late summer. When very young, the kits might well be mistaken for kittens of the domestic cat, but they are spitfires from the moment their eyes open and the true wild cat is considered completely untamable. Wild cats kept for many years in captivity have remained as intractable as they were when kits. Half-bred specimens, on the other hand, can be completely tamed in a few weeks.

The wild cat hunts the same ground as the mountain fox and takes very much the same kind of food, which means that it will kill anything it can catch and hold. Prey items recorded are grouse, ptarmigan, mountain hare, rabbit, squirrel, and roe deer fawns. It is likely, however, that much of the wild cat's food will be small mammals like voles, field mice, and baby rabbits.

The Lynx, which is a bob-tailed, big-fisted, tuft-eared cat, has long been extinct in Britain. It is now also scarce in Europe, where its depredations on livestock incurred the enmity of man, and it hasn't shown itself as able as the wild cat to stand up to persistent persecution.

The Spanish lynx was a smaller species whose caterwauling used to be familiar in the mountains of Spain.

The Caracal, or desert lynx, is found in many parts of Africa outside the tropical forests. The Canadian lynx is probably the best known to-day, and has been most studied. It is about three-and-a-half feet in length, and is well adapted for hunting in snow. Its big feet enable it to bound over the snowdrifts when it is hunting snow-shoe rabbits or small deer. This lynx is a specialist predator on the snow-shoe rabbit and its numbers fluctuate in relation to the numbers of snow-shoes. The snow-shoe population fluctuates in cycles and lynx numbers rise or fall correspondingly.

The other North American lynx is the Bob-cat, which occurs in the Southern United States. It fares better than the big lynx in face of human competition. Bob-cats are much smaller in size, and manage to live on much smaller prey.

The Puma (in North America referred to as the mountain lion, cougar, or panther) is a New-World cat which is found in Canada, the United States, and parts of South America. This cat can live at great altitudes and its tracks have been found in Ecuador at over 14,000 feet.

As in the case of most of the big cats, many blood-curdling stories have been related about the ferocity of the puma but, in fact, although such stories are still widely believed, modern research tends to discount them. Like the wolf, the puma makes a habit of frequenting camp sites, and otherwise investigating human activities, but this is largely a matter of curiosity. The puma is, in fact, notable for the benign interest it appears to take in man. This is not to say that such a big cat cannot be dangerous. When cornered or wounded, or held at bay by dogs, the puma will naturally fight back, and can be extremely fierce.

In North America, pumas are predators on deer, wild sheep, and small game. In certain parts this cat probably plays an important role in controlling the numbers of deer.

MAINTAINING NATURE'S BALANCE

The Kaibab Plateau in Arizona provides a most significant example of this. Aldo Leopold has shown that at the beginning of the twentieth-century a stable population of 4000

The black leopard, or black panther, with its prey.

deer lived on this plateau of 127,000 acres. There were also pumas, wolves, and coyotes living at their expense. Between 1907 and 1939, 816 pumas were destroyed, wolves were completely exterminated and over 7000 coyotes killed. As a result of this slaughter of predators, the deer numbers increased from 4000 to 100,000 in a period of nineteen years. This led to such over-grazing of the habitat that food shortage then began to decimate the deer. The numbers fell from 100,000 in 1924, to 10,000 in 1939. From this it can be seen that there is often a delicate equilibrium between predators and prey and the vegetation of any area, which man can upset by thoughtless intervention. Similar population relationships have been noted between lions and antelopes in the Congo.

JAGUAR

Besides the puma, South America has another big cat: the Jaguar. The jaguar is spotted like the leopard and is about leopard size. As in the case of the leopard, black jaguars turn up from time to time. Like the leopard, again, the jaguar is a forest cat, although it also haunts swamplands near rivers. Despite many hair-raising stories to the contrary, the beast is not usually a menace to man, although it will attack his domestic livestock whenever opportunity offers. It preys largely on the sloth and capybara (the pig-like aquatic rodent), but it is also an important predator on smaller mammals. As in the case of the puma, the jaguar would appear to be an important controller of certain animal populations.

Cats are generally looked upon as animals which dislike water, but all cats can swim and the jaguar, like the tiger, is an excellent swimmer. It doesn't hesitate to take a ducking when in pursuit of fish, although its usual practice, when fishing, is to crouch on a tree or rock overhanging the water and scoop fish out with a nimble paw. As a matter of fact, there have been reports that the jaguar will dangle its tail in the water to attract fish, but while this may well be true there is little scientific evidence so far to support it.

SMALLER CATS

South America has two smaller cats. The Jaguarondi is a tawny or grey, otter-like creature showing two colour phases. The other cat is the Ocelot, which ranges from

The serval is a cat-like animal, found in Africa.

Lioness with cubs in her den.

South America to Mexico. It has a grey or buff coat, well spotted, and its skin is well known to the fur trade where it is used for making coats and collars.

Colour phases in the smaller cats are common. The jaguarondi, already mentioned, comes in red or grey. The Serval is usually tawny with spots and stripes of black. Its other colour phase is tawny with tiny spots, and cats with these markings are called servalines. The Tiger-cat of Africa may be red or grey. The same phases occur in the Golden cat of South-East Asia.

Several of the smaller cats, for example, the jungle cat and the Kaffir cat of Africa, and the wild cat of Scotland, have been involved in producing the domestic cat, but nobody really knows how this has come about.

The big cats of the Old World, because of human pressure and encroaching civilisation, are faced with an ever-intensifying struggle for mere survival, and it is quite likely that most of them will eventually become extinct except in national parks or other sanctuaries set aside by man.

LION

The Lion used to be much more widely distributed in Africa than it is to-day and its future is now bound up with that of national parks. The lions of the Cape and Barbary, which were merely geographical races of the typical lion, have disappeared altogether. Outside protected areas, lion numbers are decreasing, although danger point has not yet been reached. The man who goes to Africa to see a lion need not be disappointed—unlike he who travels to Scotland to see a wild cat, who almost certainly will be.

Lions live usually in family parties (called a pride) commonly made up of a lion, two lionesses and cubs, and such groups can readily be seen from the road in Africa's national parks. Common prey animals are the zebra and antelopes, but pigs and other game are killed as opportunity offers. Probably these great cats hold what the modern zoologist calls a " niche " which is important for the population equilibrium of the plains and scrublands where they live. Lions never could be the cause of exterminating the species on which they prey—that has been left to man in his reckless destruction.

Lions in the wild state are not normally a menace to man, unless wounded or otherwise roused. In zoos they are usually amenable and thrive readily, and in zoos they have been successfully crossed with tigers, producing offspring known as Tigons and Ligers. In the latter the lion is the male parent and the tigress the mother; in the former the tiger is the male parent and the lioness the mother. A noticeable feature of captive lions is the extent to which the mane develops. In the wild, this is not usually so pronounced, as movement among scrub and in thickets tends to keep the hair plucked down. On the other hand, there is a great deal of variation among wild lions in mane development—some being almost maneless.

The roar of the lion is so well-known by repute that people who have never heard one roar will speak of " roaring like a lion ". The animal has highly-developed vocal chords, a feature it shares with the tiger, but which in the puma is relatively poorly developed. Adult lions will measure up to nine feet in length and weigh perhaps 500 pounds. They used to be well distributed in Southern Europe and Asia, but they have been almost entirely exterminated in these areas.

In modern times, the late Jim Corbett probably contributed more to the understanding of tiger behaviour than any other man, hunter or zoologist. His books on the man-eating tigers of India are deservedly famous. Corbett, who was in many ways a remarkable man, had a great liking and respect for tigers and has shown that the man-eater is always an animal incapacitated by injury, more often than not the result of a bullet wound. This is something which cannot be too strongly stressed, because there is a widespread belief that the big cats, including the tiger, hunt man as a matter of course. This is not so—indeed the number of wild animals in the wild which will deliberately attack human beings is very small indeed. As a really dramatic introduction to tigers in general and man-eaters in particular, the books by Corbett are essential reading. The tiger is about the same size and weight as the lion but its " tiger-striping " is unique and distinctive. Because of its orange, black-striped coat, William Blake described it as:

" Tyger! Tyger! burning bright
In the forests of the night "

But while its markings might be called cryptic by day, in forests penetrated by sunlight, at night " all cats are grey "

To-day, tigers are still found in India, Assam, Malaya, and Siberia. The Siberian tiger is a pale, thick-furred animal, hunting the snow-line, and after the First World War it was on the verge of extinction. It was saved for posterity largely by the efforts of the Russian government, and its place now seems secure.

Tigers anywhere will prey on man's domestic live-stock if available. Generally speaking, they live on wild ungulates: for example, pigs, deer, antelope, wild sheep, and ibex, besides smaller game. Old age or sickness may turn one into a man-eater, but it should always be borne in mind that any man-eater killed by Corbett was found to have been wounded by a bullet or by porcupine quills, at some time in its life.

LEOPARD

The Leopard, sometimes called the panther (in melanistic specimens Black Panther is the term used), is found in Asia and Africa and is perhaps still commoner than either lion or tiger. Some become man-eaters for the same reason as tigers do, and individual leopards have been credited with killing up to 200 people. The bulk of leopards, however, prey on pigs, deer, monkeys, and such-like, and their "niche" appears to be to exercise pressure on the numbers of baboons and wild pigs. Though measuring seven feet or more in length, leopards are lightweights compared with lions and tigers, scaling about 140 pounds against 500 pounds for the bigger cats. Like the others, they are enormously strong and can drag heavy prey among rocks or into trees well out of reach of such camp followers and scavengers as jackals or hyenas. Compared with the lion or tiger, the leopard is usually much more difficult to hunt down.

Colour in leopards varies considerably, as does the texture of the pelt. As you would expect, the best and thickest pelts come from the cold areas of Asia, while the melanistic variety, called the black panther, is to be found in the wettest jungles—for example Assam and Java. The so-called Snow Leopard, or Ounce, which is really not a true leopard, lives above the tree-line in Central Asia and Tibet at a height of 13,000 feet. It preys largely on small mammals, up to the size of the mountain sheep and the ibex.

CHEETAH

The Cheetah, or hunting leopard of India, was once a common species in Asia and Africa but is now scarce. Though an obvious cat, the cheetah has non-retractile claws and is dog-like in many ways, so that for a time it was not considered to be a cat at all. Structurally, however, it is entirely cat and among the felines it remains.

This animal is considered to be the fastest land mammal. Over a short distance it can reach a speed of seventy miles per hour; after a quarter of a mile its pace begins to fall off rapidly, so that it can easily be run down by a man on horseback or in a motor vehicle. But it is faster over a quarter of a mile than any greyhound, and has long been used in sport to hunt fast, hoofed animals like the black buck. In many ways, hunting with cheetahs was akin to falconry, for the animal was transported hooded into the field, then unhooded and slipped when the quarry was within range and sight. Cheetahs tame readily and are easily handled in captivity. Though relatively harmless, and almost completely defenceless, the cheetah was ruthlessly hunted down because of its predations on sheep and goats.

The tiger is the biggest cat in the world.

The reindeer, called in North America the caribou, is familiar to millions of people who have never seen it because of its association with Santa Claus and Christmas. As every child knows, Father Christmas's sleigh is drawn by a team of reindeer, heralding their approach by the jingle of bells. It is no accident that the reindeer, rather than some other species, has become associated with Santa Claus, because it is the deer of the snowy wastes of the Arctic tundra, fit to survive in a habitat where most other deer would perish quickly. In addition, it has a long association with man, especially in North Europe, as a domestic and semi-domestic animal. Therefore, everything was in its favour as Santa Claus's choice.

Reindeer are found to-day in Scandinavia and in the Arctic regions of North America and Russia. At one time, possibly only about nine centuries ago, the reindeer inhabited the Scottish Highlands where it was hunted for its meat, and, in the opinion of Fraser Darling, it was uncontrolled hunting which led to its extermination. In recent years, a small herd of Scandinavian reindeer has been established at Rothiemurchus in Inverness-shire under the charge of Mikel Utsi, who is himself a Scandinavian herd owner and an expert on this species.

In the early days of the reintroduction to the Cairngorms, the reindeer herd made little progress, partly as the result of accident or disease and partly owing to attacks by tabanid flies. The herd is, however, now slowly increasing and, having been allowed access to the higher hills, appears to be thriving. One of the reasons for the reintroduction of the reindeer to Scotland was that it feeds largely on a lichen, called reindeer moss; it was thought that if the animal confined itself to this kind of food in Scotland it would not be a competitor of deer or sheep on hill grazings. While it is true that the herd feeds largely on this lichen in Scotland,

Reindeer are able to live at great heights, even in the worst weather, and they live on so-called reindeer moss.

animals have been observed grazing herbage also eaten by deer and sheep, so that the most that can be said is that results are still inconclusive.

BOTH SEXES ANTLERED

In reindeer, contrary to the general rule in this family, both sexes have antlers. In bull reindeer, these often become of great size, numbering up to forty points. A bull reindeer will stand four feet seven inches at the shoulder, which is considerably taller than the average red deer stag of the Highlands. The body colour varies greatly from very dark brown, through all intermediate shades to grey. The calves at birth are unspotted and chestnut in colour, so the baby reindeer cannot possibly be confused with the young of the native species of deer.

In Lapland, the reindeer is mainly a domestic animal, and sometimes the domestic herds reach enormous numbers. The animals are used mainly for transport and meat and are branded with the special mark of their owner as are cattle in America. In Northern Scandinavia, however, there are still herds of truly wild reindeer as there are in North America.

The caribou of Canada, which is simply a race of the European reindeer, has long been noted for its spectacular migrations, when great herds move *en masse* from one range to another. During this migration, the animals are often wantonly shot for their meat. It is notable that during the migration of the caribou, the wolves move with them and live off them, pulling down weak members and stragglers at every opportunity. But predation by wolves has always gone on without making any impact on the numbers of caribou. Only man can cause significant reductions by his actions.

The North American reindeer has provided one significant piece of evidence in the study of population dynamics, which deserves mention here.

EXPERIMENT IN INTRODUCTION

In the year 1911, the U.S. government, with the idea of providing a continuing source of fresh meat to the natives, turned loose twenty-one cows and one bull reindeer on St. Paul Island. The introduction was successful and in the spring of 1912, seventeen calves were born. For forty years afterwards the herd was kept under almost constant observation and counted regularly. The numbers were not influenced by pressure of hunting, which was slight, and there was absolutely no attack by predators of any kind, so far as could be observed. There was no outbreak of disease. The history of the herd was as follows:

By 1921 it numbered 284 animals. Ten years later the number was 472. By 1938 it had reached the figure of 2046. Thereafter a rapid decline set in, the herd dropping in strength to 120 in 1948, sixty in 1949 and only eight in 1950. From this it would seem that the reindeer ate themselves out of existence. In other words, the cause of the decline was over-population of the range, which in turn would be partly due to the absence of predators. The lichens on which the reindeer fed required time to recover from grazing; this time was not allowed to the plants, so the winter supply of food was inadequate and the reindeer almost disappeared.

PREDATORS

Under natural conditions, of course, the reindeer had its important predators, notably the wolf, already mentioned. In addition, it is likely that the wolverine, which is the giant weasel of North America, may attack calves and young animals, for its strength and ferocity greatly exceed its size. In this connection, Thomas Pennent wrote, in 1784, that the wolverine " will climb a tree and throw from the bough a species of moss which elks and reindeer are very fond of, and when these animals come beneath to feed on it, will fall on them and destroy them ". While the idea of a wolverine gathering moss to attract a reindeer is unlikely, and nakedly anthropomorphic, there is no reason to doubt the wolverine's ability to kill a calf. It is equally certain that any flesh-eater big enough to kill a reindeer, for instance a bear, will do so when opportunity affords.

The Lapps take great care of their reindeer and here we see a transport animal being checked over before a journey.

MIGRATIONS

Much study has been given to the migratory movements of reindeer in America. These observers, notably Clarke, Hoare and Muirie, have shown that herds live on the barrens in summer and begin to move south towards the timber-land some time in July. There is a temporary return to the north again in August or September. During the worst of the winter, herds move about in their winter zones, making regular movements from place to place. Between February and early May the animals return to the barrens again for the summer. The same routes seem to be followed year after year so that the trails become quite visible on the ground and from the air. During such movement, mass drownings sometimes occur, as in the case of lemmings, and Clarke reported one case where over five hundred animals died in this way. Mating takes place during the autumn migration southwards, the young being born the following year during the spring migration.

From America has also come some information about the rich quality of reindeer milk, so highly prized by the Lapps in North Europe. Reindeer milk is similar to that of seals and whales, having a very high fat and protein content, and it may be that this composition has something to do with survival in young reindeer.

The milk of the reindeer is, of course, used by Lapp herdsmen, who also say that the venison is of a better quality than that of the red deer. Much of the venison from Scandinavia is now exported to Germany. There is also a considerable trade in reindeer hides between the two countries, so that in North Europe at any rate, the reindeer is an animal of considerable economic importance to be compared with the cattle herds of Britain. It is unlikely to become so in Britain itself.

DISPLAY

Blackcock, which is the male of the black grouse, is notable for its display, known as lekking. This occurs in the spring. The ground on which the display takes place is called a lek and is usually hillocky. The blackcocks fly to the lek early in the morning, long before daylight, to posture and challenge and fight. They also display in the afternoon. Each blackcock has his display on the lek where he croons and crows, with lyre tail spread. When the birds are running at each other in challenge, or jumping, the display often looks like some strange figure dance. Sometimes a blackcock will be found displaying alone and sometimes birds will visit the lek in winter.

The cock pheasant, another game bird, does not have this kind of communal display. When he has displayed to a hen he walks round slowly with the wing tilted and his long tail fanned out. When the hens are nesting he has a display in which he stands on tiptoe with his chest puffed out, flapping his wings and crowing lustily. This can be heard before sun-set until the edge of dusk. It can also be heard early in the morning.

Quite distinct from either of these, but just as easy to observe is the display flight of the woodcock, called roding. At dusk the bird flies above the trees on a definite circuit, croaking and chirping. The flight is fast and the wing beats slow, almost owl-like. The same circuit is flown each night; early in the morning just before sunrise the bird repeats the performance, but the flight is of much shorter duration.

Anyone who walks in the country must be familiar with the drumming of the snipe. The displaying bird flies in wide circles, usually at some height. At regular intervals it swoops in flight and it is then that the drumming sound is produced. For a long time it was thought that the drumming sound was vocal. It has been clearly established that it is instrumental, being produced by the wind passing through the two outer tail feathers which are held out at right angles, almost like lesser wings.

THE ANT-EATERS

Ant-Eaters belong to the order of mammals called edentati. One of the characteristics of this group is that they are toothless. Length varies in different species from under eighteen inches to over six feet. This, of course, includes the tail which, generally speaking, is just a little shorter than the trunk. The trunk is strong, compressed at the sides and entirely covered with hair which in some species is very long and hard and in others short and soft. The legs are strong, the forelegs being often stronger than the hind ones. The toes, numbering from one to four, are furnished with extremely strong nails which are useful to the animal for procuring food, in climbing trees, and for defending itself. The head is almost indistinguishable from the neck and tapers into a long narrow muzzle at the end of which is the very small mouth. Ant-eaters have curious tongues which are of extraordinary length; they are covered with a thick sticky saliva on which insects remain stuck until swallowed. In the bigger species of ant-eater, the tongue may be close on two feet in length.

Ant-eaters live in the hot regions of South and Central America, in the forest zones. For the most part they lead a strictly nocturnal life, remaining well hidden in their dens during the day. There are species which live on the ground, and others which are mostly arboreal. The movements of all ant-eaters, and their intelligence, are very limited. Their senses of smelling and hearing are, however, very well developed.

The biggest of the ant-eaters is the Giant Ant-Eater (*Myrmecophaga tridactyla*), sometimes called the bear ant-eater, or Yurumi. It often reaches a length of more than six feet. Entirely covered with long, rough hair of dark ash-grey colour, it is a strange-looking animal because of the structure of its head and muzzle, which are very long and narrow. The eyes are small. The limbs end with three toes furnished with nails more than two inches in length, and curved in such a way as to prevent the animal from walking on the soles of its feet. This species is common in the hot, dry, wooded zones of South America. Here it moves slowly and awkwardly on the ground during the hours of darkness. During the day it sleeps among bushes.

HUNTS BY SMELL

The giant ant-eater finds its food by smell. In this way it has little trouble discovering ants and termites, whether in the open or hidden among rotten timber. With its powerful nails the ant-eater tears into the ants' nests or demolishes the most solid termitary. The sticky tongue is insinuated into every crack and crevice, gathering the insects, which are swallowed rapidly and in great quantities. Only the strongest mammals of the forest dare to attack him and they don't always have the best of it. Outside the breeding season the giant ant-eater lives a solitary life. The female gives birth to a single young which lives for many months on her back, clinging to her hair.

Similar in many ways to the giant ant-eater is the Tamandua (*Tamandua tetradactyla*). It is much smaller than the giant ant-eater, being about three feet in length, including the tail. This species prefers to live in trees. The tamandua has a characteristic odour, strong and unpleasant, which is said to be a defence mechanism because it repels would-be attackers. Though more nimble than the ant-eaters, the tamandua is no more intelligent. It lives in South and Central America.

The *Cyclopes didactylus* is the smallest representative of the family, being under eighteen inches in overall length. It lives in South America in regions covered with dense vegetation, leading an almost exclusively nocturnal and arboreal life. It climbs with the greatest of ease, helped by its strongly prehensile tail. During the day it stays among the thickest leafy branches, sleeping upside down, clinging on with all four feet. Its head and muzzle are not as long and thin as those of the ant-eater and the tamandua. Its coat is also different, being short, very soft, and reddish brown in colour.

The giant ant-eater, found throughout South America.

The four-toed tamandua, a typical representative of the family.

WOLVES

Wolf legends abound in Europe, and people's fear of this large mammal is very real. Yet all modern evidence tends to discredit the idea that wolves, under normal circumstances, will attack man.

One has, of course, to be sure what one means by " attack ". If, for instance, a wolf is approached when in a trap, or when wounded, it would be surprising if the beast did not make an effort to defend itself. But this would not be a deliberate attack by a free animal exercising choice. It would be the natural action of an animal fighting for survival. It would, in fact, be a " counter-attack ". Behaviour of this kind has nothing in common with the idea of a wolf or wolves deliberately stalking human beings with the intention of attacking them.

Once, when the author was discussing the whole idea of wild animals attacking man, he was told by a Pole, who had considerable experience of wolves in Poland and Russia, that he had never known wolves to attack travellers although he had seen them and heard them following a sleigh. The explanation of this is probably very simple. The wolf, being an animal of considerable mental prowess, soon becomes aware that, where men have camped, titbits may be found afterwards. In short, the wolf becomes a camp-follower, not because he wants to eat men, but because he wants to eat what they leave behind.

Similarly, wolves have learned in Europe, Asia, and North America that domestic livestock can be found near human habitation and so, in extreme weather, they will raid farm-lands to kill—not man but his livestock. All stories of great bands of wolves raiding remote villages, and running riot in the streets, can be treated with the greatest suspicion.

Modern research has shown that the wolf pack is generally a family unit of dog, bitch and puppies with, perhaps, one or two hangers-on. The great wolf packs of history, of

The American wolf (Canis occidentalis), *which is found all over the whole of North America and most of Mexico. There are many types of this wolf, including the timber wolf.*

fifty or a hundred beasts organised like an army with commanders and lieutenants, are mostly the stuff of legend.

Stories of the wolf's cunning, on the other hand, stand up very well to investigation by modern methods. Individual wolves have become quite notorious, not only for their depredations, but for their cunning in avoiding traps and poison baits. Once a wolf has become trap-wary, and learns the killing power of a modern rifle, he constitutes a serious problem to man.

There is no reason to believe that Ernest Thompson Seton's account of the Currumpaw Wolf was exaggerated; rather does it indicate how much we still have to learn about the workings of the animal mind.

Professor Osmond P. Breeland of the University of Texas tells the story of a wolf called Three-Toes, which was alleged to have destroyed stock worth between 25,000 and 50,000 dollars in his lifetime. Three-Toes did this despite the fact that every man's hand was against him.

RANGE AND DISTRIBUTION

Wolves hunt over a vast range, but investigation has shown that they do not wander aimlessly. They have their fixed territory, vast though it may be, and they work their ground by definite routes. This is not immediately obvious because a beast which kills at dusk may have travelled forty miles before sunrise. Nevertheless, he makes his circuit by favourite routes, returning eventually to his starting point, from which he will begin his excursions over again in due course.

To-day, wolves are neither as plentiful nor as widely distributed as they were even a hundred years ago. They have gone altogether from Britain, and are scarce in Western and South-Western Europe. Russia and the mountains of Eastern Europe are their Old World strongholds to-day. In America, they have been exterminated in many States. They have been deliberately cleared out of all America's

The little coyote of the American plains is a small animal, well-known for its vocal displays at night. Its prey range is about the same as that of the European fox.

national parks, an act about which the United States Field Staff is having second thoughts.

The best work on the wolf this century has probably been done in America and Russia.

In the United States of America, the war against the wolf really began when cattle ranchers and sheepmen raised the hue and cry against him. The wolves which preyed on the buffalo herds were there to harry domestic livestock once the white man had exterminated the buffalo. So, over most of the country, the wolf had to go. But America and Canada still have their wolves, and in these countries their habits and movements have been carefully studied in recent years by skilled observers. It is quite clear, indeed, that America intends to keep this interesting member of her fauna.

In the Mount McKinley area, the Americans maintain a definite number of wolves as deliberate policy. There the wolf has his place in the ecological pattern, helping to maintain at a safe level the numbers of other creatures such as deer and wild sheep. Money and labour spent on killing excess deer and sheep can be saved when wolves do the work.

Modern research on the wolf has shown that dog and bitch share the work of rearing the family. The dog wolf, like the dog fox, provides all the food for his mate in the early stages. It has also been established that single, unmated wolves will sometimes carry food to a den containing cubs —in other words there seems to be some kind of kinship among the wolves in a given area. Game killed by wolves is normally much bigger than that taken by foxes or coyotes, animals like deer and caribou being usual. They do, however, kill rabbits and hares and will take prey much smaller than that when larger game is scarce. Contrary to popular belief, wolves are not a menace to the continued existence of such species as deer; they are, in fact, beneficial in reducing excess population on the range, thus benefiting the deer themselves.

Wolf cubs closely resemble fox cubs in their behaviour. They play just as much about the den mouth when they are very young, and are just as much given to hiding things which they like. In the same way, again as young foxes do, they often carry a favourite plaything about with them. Wolf cubs taken young enough can be tamed, but are likely to prove difficult as adults. Some remain manageable but others become morose and aloof. Probably man produced his

The Abyssinian wolf is a wild dog which closely resembles the fox. It feeds mainly on small mammals.

original dogs by breeding only from those specimens which remained tame and manageable. Man still uses the wolf to-day in the breeding of Arctic sled dogs. Such out-crossing produces animals of great physique and endurance.

There are many species of wolf in the world but the animals still found in Germany and Spain, Eastern Europe and Russia, are kin to those that once roamed over Britain. The common wolf is like a big Alsatian dog and a good specimen will weigh over 130 pounds and measure fully six feet in length. There are wolves bigger than that, great muscular beasts, built for speed and endurance with no fat on them. Colour varies through many shades of grey, yellow and brown and some specimens are near black.

There is little in the literature of Britain about wolves that is reliable; they disappeared before the years of the great inquiring naturalists. It would seem that the people of those far-off days were so afraid of the wolf that they thought only of avoiding or killing him and made little effort to study him. Fact and legend have come down to us in an inseparable mixture and the picture we get is of a cruel, sinister beast, often an evil beast with supernatural powers, and a menace to man and his stock. Modern man is more familiar with werewolves than with wolves. Legend has had a long start over fact, but present-day research is slowly discovering the truth.

Where there are no wolves people laugh at the wolf. Walt Disney, for example, has made a stage villain out of him so that children laugh at his antics, knowing perfectly well that half a dozen little piglets are going to make a fool of him in the end. Cry " wolf " to-day and toddlers titter; they know that Little Red Riding Hood always escapes. Probably Little Red Riding Hood always did escape; more probably she was never menaced.

In England, the wolf was exterminated by Royal decree, helped by the bounties offered for each scalp, and he had gone by the dawn of the sixteenth-century. The beast created considerable havoc in the shrinking countryside of England, and total war against him began early.

Scotland kept her wolves for 250 years longer than England, but the records of the last Scottish wolf are not very reliable, showing as they do that he died in about a dozen different places. There can be no absolutely unassailable record concerning the last wolf in Scotland, but certainly he had disappeared by the middle of the eighteenth-century, the year seems to have been 1743. The distinction of killing the last wolf was probably claimed by a number of people, but the best account, the one that ought to be the right one even if it is not, concerns Macqueen, Deerstalker on the Findhorn, and more people should know the story of him.

Said the Macqueen to the laird: " As I came through the slochk by east the hill there, I foregathered wi' the beast. My long dog there turned him. I buckled wi' him and syne whuttled his craig, and brought awa' his countenance for fear he might come alive again, for they are precarious creatures."

It is a wonderful story; one of the great understatements of history. The man just set about the wolf and cut its throat. Just like that. . . .

Ireland kept her wolves for longer than Scotland, and that despite the six pounds a head offered by Cromwell for every bitch wolf killed. It almost seems that the Irish refrained from killing wolves to show Cromwell they were not interested in his money. Whatever the reason, it was 1770 before the last wolf made his final bow on the Irish stage.

snakes

" And I will put enmity between thee and the woman, and between thy seed and her seed; it shall bruise thy head, and thou shalt bruise his heel."

Thus, the words of the Lord in the solemn verses of the Old Testament, in which the snake was condemned as a devil and a deceiver, cursed for all time because it was alleged to have tempted the woman in the Garden of Eden.

As a result of this biblical denunciation, snakes in general have had a very rough time of it at the hands of man right down to modern times. It is still a fact that most people go out of their way to bruise the poor serpent's head—often when the serpent is not particularly concerned with wounding anybody in the heel. Snake-killing, often the killing of harmless snakes, is almost a ritual throughout Europe, and the average person's reaction on sight of a snake is to find a stick or stone to smash its head in. This is unfortunate, because there is nothing in the snake either diabolical or cunning. Man persists in seeing the work of an active, malignant intelligence where there is only uncorrupted instinct and behaviour.

Like all reptiles, snakes are cold-blooded animals which regulate their own internal temperature according to that of their surroundings. One result of this is that they curl up in warm sunshine and seek cover during cold spells when they become torpid. In other words, they hibernate.

PREFER FLIGHT TO FIGHT

The main objection to snakes is that they are venomous, even although this does not apply to all of them. Relatively few species are really dangerous and, in fact, most snakes always prefer flight to fight when they are attacked. In Europe, the only poisonous snakes are the vipers.

The Common Viper, which is viviparous (that is, it produces living young) has a triangular head with the V-sign on top, a slim neck and a dark zigzag pattern along its back. Though this viper may be found anywhere, it prefers arid or mountainous areas. Mainly nocturnal in habits, it feeds on small animals like mice or frogs. Generally it spends the day in some sort of cover, or you may find it in bracken or heather, or by turning over large stones on the banks of a river. In the winter it seeks underground retreats and then, as occasionally in summer, you may find a number of vipers tangled together. The winter tangle may have something to do with reciprocal heat concentration.

Akin to the common viper is the Marsh Viper, which is a little bigger than the common asp, and *Vipera Ammodytus* which has a little horn on its nose after the fashion of a rhinoceros.

The simplest way to catch any viper is to use a forked stick with which to pin the snake's head to the ground; thereafter it can be milked of its poison by offering something, other than a part of yourself, on which to bite. Once it has been milked of its poison it can be safely handled. You will probably notice first of all the forked tongue, which is a tactile organ constantly flicked out and in. If you prise the mouth open gently you will observe that the jaws can be opened until they are almost in line with each other. This is because the jaws are not articulated. In the palate you will notice two long, curved teeth (if they haven't been broken by biting) and these are the poison fangs. The poison is conveyed from a small vesicle, along grooves in the poison fangs, which introduce it into any wound made by them. When the viper bites, a small muscle compresses the bladder or poison vesicle and so its contents are forced into the grooves of the teeth. This method of introducing poison into a wound might well be called hypodermic injection.

Though the poison of the common viper can be lethal to

The anaconda from the rivers of Brazil is perhaps the world's biggest snake. Because it can close its nostrils like the seal, it is able to stay underwater for long periods.

Vipers are the most common poisonous snakes in Italy. The viper has long poison fangs. Above is a diagram of a poison fang in the striking and inactive positions.

The cobra of the Indian jungle is one of the most deadly of all snakes. Its poison acts rapidly and is always lethal. Note the characteristic hood of the cobra.

The rattlesnake is a native of the deserts of the United States and Mexico. The rattle is produced by the horny rings on the end of its tail.

man, as it is to other warm-blooded animals, death from snake bite is largely a matter of geography or attention. In the northern part of its range the snake's bite is rarely serious, and in Britain deaths are almost unheard of. This doesn't alter the fact that dogs and sheep die of viper bite, and a sickly person who was bitten and received no attention whatever might well die. But such neglect is almost inconceivable. The writer has been twice bitten by vipers in Southern Europe and, apart from feeling ill and headachy for a day or two, was not seriously upset.

Fortunately, the viper is the one and only really dangerous snake in Europe, but in the tropics we find other species which are much more dangerous. High on the list of really lethal snakes is the Cobra, which lives in the forests of India. It is recognised by its puffed-out neck and hood, and by its curious markings which look like spectacles. Death follows quickly on the bite of the cobra, and it seems to be the case that in India cobras kill more people than do man-eating tigers. One of the cobra's natural enemies is the mongoose, and in this connection the story called " Rikki-Tikki-Tavi ", by Rudyard Kipling, is well worth reading.

TERRIBLE REPUTATION

In the hot areas of North America there is the Rattlesnake, which has a terrible reputation, although, in fact, it might well be described as something of a gentleman because it gives warning of impending attack. Quite frequently, in the deserts of Mexico and the United States of America, a traveller will suddenly hear this warning rattle followed by the sight of the glistening head of the snake as it prepares to strike. The sound is produced by the horny rings on the tail. When the snake is angered, the rings knock against one another, causing the rattling or tinkling sound, but it would be a great mistake to assume that rattlesnakes go out of their way to attack human beings. The snake rattles

when angered or alarmed, and its so-called attack is really its defence against an imagined attack on itself.

Not all snakes are armed with poison glands either for defence or securing prey. In some species a constriction of the prey is the rule. This is the method used by Pythons. *Python Reticulatus*, the species found in India, is a strangler. So is the Boa Constrictor, which is about the same size and lives in the forests of America. Either may reach a length of seven or eight yards with correspondingly thick muscular body. The pythons will lie in wait in the branches of a tree for hours at a time, pouncing on their prey from above and strangling it in a matter of minutes, depending on its size. Because of the nature of their jaws and the elasticity of their bodies, these snakes are able to swallow very large prey whole—often up to the size of sheep or young deer. After such a meal the snake, with body now bulging, may remain motionless for weeks during which the meal is digested.

We must not, however, forget the harmless snakes like the common grass snake and smooth snake, or the little snake-like lizard called the slow-worm. Not only are these species harmless: they are useful.

The skins of many snakes are used for making shoes and handbags; from others, modern medicine obtains anti-venin, a serum now being used successfully on victims of snake bite. This serum is now widely available in certain countries. Where it is not available, one has to have recourse to the old ways—that is, to incise the wound and tourniquet above it, thus slowing down or arresting the flow of poison through the system.

Snakes have many enemies. The mongoose is the great snake killer in India. In Britain the hedgehog has been recorded killing adders and grass snakes. The secretary bird is a great killer of snakes, even the mole has been recorded killing small snakes, probably caught in mistake for earth-worms. But the greatest enemies of snakes are other snakes.

QUESTIONS AND ANSWERS

Which British animals hibernate?

Bats, hedgehogs, dormice, snakes, frogs and toads. Squirrels do not hibernate nor do badgers, though both are often said to do so.

Do insects hibernate?

Some insects do; in the fully adult state, for example, the queen wasp and butterflies like the small tortoiseshell, the Peacock and the Red Admiral.

HARES AND RABBITS

Hares and rabbits form a group which in many ways is distinct from the true rodents. The difference in their teeth is notable. Rabbits and hares have small incisors behind the main incisors so that they were referred to as the double-toothed rodents, or *Duplicidentata*. Nowadays, zoologists are coming round more and more to the view that there is no true relationship between rodents on the one hand and rabbits and hares on the other.

Formerly, the European rabbit was confined to the Iberian Peninsula and perhaps North Africa; but the Romans, blamed for so many things during the expansion of their empire, almost certainly brought the rabbit to the rest of Europe. In Norman times, the rabbit was brought to England and reared in warrens, but since then it has spread, sometimes unaided, sometimes by human action, to almost every part of Britain, including mountains, sea coasts and islands.

Until the disease known as myxomatosis decimated the European rabbit population, the beast was a major agricultural and forestry pest, even although it was largely prized as an item of food, or for its pelt by the felt hat manufacturers. Before myxomatosis, the rabbit was, in fact, treated as a crop to be harvested, and this partly explains why the animals, so defenceless and easily accessible, managed to maintain high numbers for so long. Now that Rabbit Clearance Areas have been set up in this country, it is obligatory for occupiers of land to destroy rabbits and an offence to preserve them.

The introduction of the rabbit to Australia by misguided settlers provides yet another example of the dangers of introducing exotic species to any country. In Australia, the rabbit found a suitable climate, plenty of food, and practically no enemies capable of significant predation. As a result, its breeding became explosive until a stage was reached where the rabbit became the public enemy number one. Myxomatosis did make a spectacular reduction in the number of Australian rabbits but the problem has not been solved.

In this country, myxomatosis destroyed something like 98 per cent. of the rabbits in the first wave. In later outbreaks, the disease was noticeably less virulent, so that the rabbit is tending to re-establish itself in many areas. Recurrent outbreaks of myxomatosis are leaving an increasing percentage of rabbits unaffected. Some may have immunity to the disease.

BURROWING ANIMALS

Before myxomatosis, European rabbits were habitually burrowing animals, but since the disease it has been noted that a very high percentage of them have become confirmed outliers. There were always outliers, of course, but this habit seems to have become a rule rather than an exception. Only where certain densities are reached, does the burrowing and colonial habit seem to become normal again.

With its prolonged breeding season and high fecundity, the rabbit hefts itself easily, even when the stock has been hard pruned back. Disease was not unknown before myxomatosis, because periodically there were outbreaks of what was called rabbit scab. This disease had a certain check on numbers. More important as a check is nature's reduction of the birth-rate by way of the phenomenon of resorption, where the developing young are resorbed into the mother's body instead of being born.

Though not in the same class as rodents, rabbits can and do gnaw quite successfully when their normal terrestrial food supply is sealed off by snow. Then they will turn to the bark of trees and the leading shoots of saplings protruding above the snow. Though much more earthbound than rodents, rabbits can and do swim when they have to, and under great pressure may even manage to climb trees. They have the additional advantage of being able to lie up for days on end

The European wild rabbit is a pest to agricultural forestry and large sums are spent each year netting ground against rabbits. Poachers use a long net to catch rabbits.

The mountain hare, in winter dress, tries to elude the talons of the golden eagle which is the main predator on this species. The mountain hare is also known as the Alpine hare.

in their burrows during hard weather, and this ability is probably connected with the other rabbitine phenomenon of refection which means that the animal re-swallows its droppings. In other words, food which has been once passed through the bowel is eaten again, a habit which gave rise to the belief that rabbits chewed the cud. Refection takes place in a definite rhythm, and recent research has indicated that the habit is common to all wild rabbits. The process of reingestion is easily observed in tame rabbits.

YOUNG RABBITS AND HARES

When ready to give birth to young, the doe rabbit drives a short burrow, which is referred to as a stop, and makes her nest at the end of it. The nest is composed largely of wool plucked from her own body. Young rabbits are born blind and naked, are nursed by the doe in the stop, and are ready to fend for themselves at the age of one month or thereabouts. Sometimes the doe gives birth to her young in a side pocket of the main burrow system.

Unlike the young of the European rabbit, the leverets of

The Angora is a domesticated rabbit kept as a pet and for the production of wool. It is a very large type. It is not as popular as it used to be.

the brown hare are born above ground (occasionally a doe rabbit will make her nest above ground in thick cover), in a small forme. At birth they are completely furred and their eyes are open. Soon afterwards the leverets move, or are moved, to separate formes some little distance apart, and there each is visited by the doe hare to be suckled. This spreading out of the helpless family probably has considerable survival value, because a predator like the fox then has to find each leveret by separate search, which is not easy. The leverets are soon able to run about and quickly develop a speed which, even at an early age, allows them to outrun most pursuers.

MAD MARCH HARES

The main mating season of the brown hare is early spring when the animal becomes the " mad March hare " but, as a matter of fact, breeding often begins long before March and may continue until October. February leverets are not at all uncommon, and hares in Scotland have been found with newly born young at the end of September. Spring is, however, the time of the gatherings when several hares may be

The European wild rabbit (Oryctolagus cuniculus L.), *was brought to England by the Normans who kept it in warrens; subsequently it spread to all parts of the British Isles and became a pest.*

seen in the same field kicking, jumping, and boxing. The jack hare does not take any part in the rearing of his family.

Brown hares are extremely fast, and at their best when running uphill. If a hare has any start at all, it takes a really first-class greyhound to catch it. When running, the hare brings the hind feet past the forefeet and thus prints his direction of travel in reverse. This you will see quite easily when there is snow on the ground.

The mountain hare, sometimes called the Varying hare, the Alpine hare, or the Arctic hare, lives at higher altitudes than the brown, and ranges farther northwards. Where the ranges of the two overlap, interbreeding sometimes takes place. Unlike the brown hare of the low ground, the mountain hare frequently lies up under cover—for example, under rocks or in peat holes. During severe weather, white hares shift ground and may be seen doing so in considerable numbers. In certain years their numbers increase considerably and then they are rounded up in droves, driven and slaughtered.

An important predator on the mountain hare is the golden eagle.

In North America, right up to the limit of the tree line, lives the Snow-shoe rabbit which changes its coat to white in winter. This species has great, hairy hind feet which enables it to skim swiftly over the snowdrifts. Its numbers are subject to spectacular fluctuation, and it has been noted that corresponding fluctuations take place in the numbers of the animals which prey upon it, the wolf, fox, lynx, and marten. Because of these spectacular fluctuations, North Americans speak of " rabbit years " and " years of no rabbits ".

Since both hares and rabbits are useful food items, man has inevitably made great efforts to breed them and domesticate them. There are now a great many varieties of domestic rabbits in a great variety of colours, some having been developed mainly for carcass meat and others for skins for the fur and felt trade.

The Angora has been developed into a great woolly creature which can be stripped like a sheep. But the rabbit kept by small boys in hutches, however tame and whatever its colour, remains a rabbit, and if it escapes and survives will eventually interbreed freely with its wild relatives.

MONKEYS

While it seems certain that man and monkey are divergent lines from some remote common ancestor, there is no question of man having evolved from any existing species of ape. One has only to look at monkeys to realise the extent of their manual abilities, and their quick adaptability to new situations, characteristics which place them at a much higher level than any other mammal. These capabilities are often highly developed in the anthropoids—that is to say, in the animals which in stature and physical aspect most closely resemble man. These large apes we shall discuss elsewhere. Here we shall discuss only certain smaller species of monkeys which are to be found more or less everywhere in the tropical zone.

Scientifically, monkeys are divided into two main groups

The capuchin monkey (Cebus capucinus) *derives its name from the strange arrangement of the hair on its head.*

The shrieking monkey from the forests of the River Amazon.

From the forests of the River Amazon come the leonine or mida monkeys, so-called because of their tawny mane.

A never-failing attraction in any zoological garden is the monkey house, and almost certainly part of that attraction is due to the fact that visitors see in the monkeys caricatures of human beings. Whether we like it or not, the similarity is striking; not least in the matter of aping. When we speak of one person aping another, what we are really describing is simply mimicry or copying, which is a pronounced characteristic of monkeys in general.

Monkeys are quick, volatile, keenly perceptive, with a pronounced flair for mimicking the gestures of man—apart from an inherent ability to perform many man-like acts. Mentally, monkeys are second only to man in development, but a great many misconceptions exist regarding the relationship between the two species of higher mammal.

One of the smallest species of the monkey is the marmoset (Callithrix jacchus), *which comes from the forests of Brazil.*

The rhesus monkey, a common species of macaque from India.

The white-nosed monkey of which there are several species.

—the Platyrrhines and the Catarrhines. Like man and the anthropoids, they belong to the order of the primates.

The Platyrrhine monkeys of South America have broad noses with laterally-opened nostrils. These tailed monkeys have thirty-six teeth, as compared with thirty-two teeth in man and other monkeys.

A good example of the tailed monkey is the Pithecia, which stands about eighteen inches tall and has a tail roughly as long as itself. This monkey has a thick black coat and a striking beard of the same colour. The pithecia pays a great deal of attention to the grooming of his beard, spending much time combing and smoothing it. The long tail is not prehensile, which means that he cannot use it like a hand for grasping, so it is no help to him in climbing trees. Pithecia is a timid, retiring animal who prefers a solitary life or living in very small groups. Only the highest trees attract him. This monkey, both in the wild and in captivity, uses his hand as a cup when drinking water.

A close relation of pithecia is the Capuchin Cebus, which also lives in the equatorial zone of America. A smaller animal than pithecia, it lives in small families and is almost always found in trees, which it leaves reluctantly and rarely. This species is familiar to many people because many are imported into Europe.

Closely resembling these two species is the Shrieking monkey, which is aptly named because it advertises its presence during the night by its deafening shouts. Living in big parties as they do, and making a habit of co-operative shrieking, they appear to be scolding incessantly and furiously.

The smallest monkey in the group of primates is the Marmoset, a native of the forests of Brazil and Guiana. The marmoset is a pretty little creature, docile and easily domesticated, which resembles a squirrel in size and coat.

Not much bigger than the marmoset is the Mida, or Leonine, monkey which lives in the Brazilian forests. The name leonine monkey is often used for this species because of the tawny mane which covers its head and shoulders, giving it the appearance of a small lion. Like the marmoset, the leonine monkey is easily domesticated.

DOG-LIKE HEADS

To the Catarrhine group belong the Asiatic or African

Ursine Colobus monkey, an arboreal monkey from Africa.

Colobinae are long-tailed monkeys from Africa and Asia.

The baboon (Papio papio), *from Equatorial Africa, is easily tamed and is a favourite in zoological gardens.*

The Canicephaloid family of the Catarrhine group is so-called because of the dog-like face. Here we see the mandrill.

monkeys which are bigger than the species just mentioned. In this group we find the long-noses: those species with muzzles suggestive of the dogs.

Baboons are big monkeys with dog-like heads, and are found in Africa, Arabia, and India.

The Mandrill, which has a startling blue and red muzzle, has often been described as repugnant of aspect. But this is a purely human opinion which would not be shared by other mandrills. Mandrills live in parties, frequenting the ground more than trees, and are dangerous because of their great strength, quick tempers, and aggressive natures. Still more ugly by human standards, and more ferocious even than the mandrill, is its near relative the Drill.

Another of the dog-headed tribe, just as strong and sturdy, is the Baboon, which has an olive-green coat and a long tail, thus differing from the mandrill. The baboon lives in the forests of Abyssinia and Central Africa. In Abyssinia there is another dog-face, habitually named the Hamadryad after the nymphs of the trees so well known in Greek mythology. The hamadryad is a large, strong, active monkey standing more than three feet tall, with a grey coat and exceptionally long powerful teeth.

One of the commonest Abyssinian monkeys is the hamadryad. This species was sacred to the Ancient Egyptians.

Smaller than the dog-faces, and far more attractive to human beings, is the group to which the Macaque belong. This monkey is represented both in Africa and India and is well known to everybody. The macaque is the attractive little monkey so common in zoological gardens. In the wild state it lives in very large herds. It is an extremely agile monkey, leaping and swinging from branch to branch and performing bewildering aerial acrobatics which almost make one dizzy to watch. Though a fruit-eater, it will, if living near the sea, feed on molluscs and crustaceans. Being a highly intelligent monkey, it is a favourite in circuses.

Another monkey of the macaque group is the Rhesus, which lives in India and South China. This is the species which has been invaluable to man in the field of medicine. It has been used in experimental work, and research, more than any other species, so a great deal is known about it. Adults are brown, tinged with grey, and scale from ten to twenty pounds in weight. The Rhesus has bright red, naked buttocks. This was the species most often found accompanying the once-familiar organ-grinders.

Another well-known monkey in this group is the Bertuccia of North-East Africa which is a lively, attractive creature and the only monkey which has been successfully transplanted into Europe. This is the monkey which lives on the Rock of Gibraltar.

The Entellus monkey, which belongs to another group in the Catarrhines, is a strange-looking animal with a beard, and eyebrows which protrude like a cowl. It is a native of India, where it is considered sacred, and is fed by the people. Its status as a sacred animal may have something to do with its monkish aspect.

We do not normally consider monkeys as fur-bearers, but there is such a group: the monkeys of the Colobus type which live in Abyssinia and have reddish black coats. Of these the most notable is the Guereza, an incredibly agile monkey which leads an arboreal life and which is adorned with a white, shining, silky mane and an elegant tassel above its tail. Fortunately for monkeys in general (with the exception of the species just mentioned), man has found little use for them economically or in the field of sport, so that they are ignored by most hunters. As a result they live a comparatively carefree life in the trees, where they are safe from most ground predators.

THE GORILLA

No sooner had the white man confirmed the existence of the great ape which we know as the gorilla than he began the process of misrepresentation and invention which made this name a synonym for horror throughout the world.

Any great man-like creature which was not a man had to be a monster with monstrous characteristics, and the gorilla suffered from sensationalism and invention in a way that few animals have suffered. It became saddled with a reputation for implacable ferocity which only modern research has proved to be a myth. It can be said with truth that the gorilla has suffered far more at the hands of man, both physically and in reputation, than any individual human being has ever suffered at the hands of a gorilla.

The gorilla is one of the great apes belonging to the same family as the chimpanzee and the orang-utan. The family of the great apes, in turn, belongs to the hominoid group, the other family in the group being composed of human beings,

Gorilla climbing to its sleeping quarters in a tree. The family constructs a crude platform of twigs as a bed.

Though an extremely fierce animal, the gorilla prefers to keep itself out of human sight, and thus not seek trouble.

living and extinct. The gorilla is the biggest species in the family of the great apes. An adult male gorilla is as tall as a policeman and scales three times or more his weight, reaching some 600 pounds. Usually, the gorilla walks on all fours—that is to say with the knuckles of his hands touching the ground, but he can walk erect for a few paces at a time.

TWO TYPES RECOGNISED

Zoologists recognise two types of gorilla: the Lowland type, which lives in West Africa, and the so-called Mountain gorilla which is found in East Africa west of Lake Kivu and Lake Edward. The habits of the two species differ considerably. The lowland type lives in virgin forests where the undergrowth is dense and almost impenetrable; while the mountain type lives in volcanic country with forests.

Just a little over 100 years ago the existence of the gorilla was definitely established outside Africa when an American

missionary sent a skull to Boston. Since then it has been the subject of much misrepresentation and invention and its very existence is now threatened by the advance of civilisation in Africa. Only the strictest and most sympathetic type of conservation will ensure its continued survival.

STRONG BUT SHY

The gorilla in the wild state feeds on berries, leaves, and other kinds of vegetable matter. Though an extremely powerful animal, it prefers to keep itself out of sight rather than obtrude itself upon the notice of human beings, although

Young gorillas are highly intelligent. They do not readily adapt themselves to captivity and require much affection shown them.

162

A tribe of gorillas foraging. The animals are entirely vegetarian.

The gorilla inhabits the forests of the Cameroons and the Congo.

The gorilla falls victim to the ingenuity of man.

it will make demonstrations when too closely pressed. In its family life, polygamy is the rule and adult males often fight fiercely with each other, inflicting considerable wounds. The scars are frequently seen in old males which have been shot by hunters.

Unlike the chimpanzee, the gorilla does not adapt itself readily to captivity, although modern techniques are leading to more successful rearing of young animals. Work so far done suggests that they are less intelligent than chimpanzees —at least where mechanical ability is concerned. They do appear, however, to have memories comparable to chimpanzees.

Young gorillas are neither so boisterous nor so destructive as other young anthropoids and are not such ready imitators. When captive, they require a great deal of affection to thrive, just like human children.

In the wild state, gorillas are less arboreal than other apes although they do sleep in trees, where they build rough platforms on which to spend the night. The great size of the animals has probably brought about their more terrestrial way of life.

ALBINISM

Species for all practical purposes have specific characteristics which lend themselves to near-exact description. Thus twenty artists painting a dunnock, will paint a bird that everybody will recognise as a dunnock. But species, even those that we know well, are not immutable and this is especially so in the case of colour and markings.

Albinism (the complete absence of pigmentation resulting in a white individual with pink eyes) has cropped up in a multitude of species from elephants to man, and is a genetic characteristic. So, it is never really lost and it is always liable to crop up in the offspring of apparently normal individuals. These we call sports.

Albinism is commoner in some species than in others. Albino rabbits, moles, voles, jackdaws, blackbirds and deer have been recorded. But in no species does the albino type become the standard unless by human interference. White mice, white rats and white rabbits have been bred by man as pets, or for other purposes. The white ferret is simply a domesticated polecat of the albino type.

In blackbirds, white is a relatively frequent colour and albino blackbirds are not rare. Blackbirds with white markings, for example, white head or white shoulders, white wings or simply white spots, occur quite regularly. In the case of a mated pair where the cock blackbird had white shoulders, one of the chicks in the nest was a pure albino, complete with pink eyes.

Jackdaws sometimes show white feathers and albinos have been recorded in this species. Rooks and crows also produce individuals with white markings from time to time. A pure albino dunnock turned up in Glasgow in 1957.

Albino foxes have been recorded, but they are extremely rare in Britain. An albino fox would not be readily overlooked; in the dark it would stand out even more plainly than the badger's face.

SOME BRITISH DEER

Deer are cloven-hoofed mammals with the same complex stomach as cattle, and like cattle they chew the cud. Because of this, deer and cattle are known as Ruminants. But deer are quite different in the matter of horns. In cattle, the horns are really made of horn and are permanent. In deer, the antlers are made of bone, and they are cast and re-grown each year.

Generally speaking, only male deer have antlers, although a notable exception is the reindeer, which in Canada is called the caribou. In this species both sexes are antlered. Horned females are very rare in most other species of deer, although they do occur rather more frequently among roe.

Antlers grow yearly from knobs on the skull called *Pedicles*. New antlers are usually complete from four to five months after the casting of the old ones. During the growing stage, before the bone has hardened, they are covered with skin and hair which is supplied by a fine network of blood vessels. This covering is called *Velvet*. When the antlers are fully grown, the blood vessels shrivel up; the velvet then rots and is rubbed off by the deer. When the velvet has stripped completely the antlers are said to be *Clean*.

There are various names for male and female deer, but there is an accepted name for them in each species which does not vary. For example: the red deer male is called a Stag, the roe deer male a Buck, and the male moose and reindeer a Bull. In the females we speak of red deer Hinds, roe Does, and moose and reindeer Cows. Similarly, the young have their special names, the offspring of the moose being called a Calf, that of the red deer a Calf, while the young of the roe deer are known as Kids or Fawns.

The mating season of deer is called the "rut", but the rut does not take place at the same time in all species. When the males come into breeding condition and begin to challenge or fight other males, they are said to "take the rut". In species where the male takes more than one mate, he is said to be polygamous, while in others, where he takes only one mate, he is said to be monogamous. The red deer comes into the first class, the roe deer into the second.

RED DEER

Red deer stags stand about four feet at the shoulder while hinds measure about three feet six inches. In this species the male is polygamous. He takes the rut in September and

The red deer hind gives birth to her single calf in early June. The calf is spotted at birth, but the spots disappear in the autumn when the animal is growing its winter coat.

The red deer stag casts his old antlers in March or April and during the summer grows his new ones, which are fully grown by September. Once he cleans the velvet, he is ready to take the rut.

The roe deer (Capreolus capreolus thotti), is much smaller than the red deer, standing from 2 feet 1 inch to 2 feet 5 inches at the shoulder. The usual number of points carried by a mature buck is six.

The red deer is an extremely mobile animal and will move daily from the low ground to the high tops, depending on the weather. In winter, when the hills are blanketed with snow, the deer come low, feeding in the valleys in the evening and early morning, and lying on sunny ridges during the day. Though actually forest animals, the red deer of Scotland have adapted themselves to living on the open hill, but they will seek forest cover when it is available, especially during hard weather. Stags are especially prone to breaking into forest, particularly when they are growing their new antlers. Woodland stags are generally heavier than hill stags of the same age.

October, and gathers as many hinds as he can. For the remainder of the year the sexes live mostly in separate groups. Calves are born in early June, and are spotted with white at birth. These spots disappear during their first autumn. Single calves are usual. Red deer are social animals. The society is founded on the female and is said to be a Matriarchy; in other words, the red deer hind is the real leader of the herd. The stag may lord it over the hinds during the rut; he may bellow and make the hills rumble with his thunder, but he does not lead.

Wild red deer are among the wariest of animals. They have exceptional sight and hearing and a sense of smell which is extraordinary. They rely mostly on their sense of smell. Usually their movements are governed by the wind which carries scent to them. They shift ground regularly and readily. During heavy snow they come down to the low ground; during hot weather they go high for the fine grazing and to escape the flies. Their summering and wintering grounds may be many miles apart.

A Master Stag is a mature beast in possession of hinds. But few masters manage to hold their harem throughout the period of the rut. They are kept continually on the move by younger stags trying to cut in on their hinds, so that they have little time to eat or sleep. As males thus lose condition quickly, they are eventually ousted by younger beasts. This means that the same group of hinds may be taken over by a succession of stags in the course of the rut.

For some days after birth the calves of the red deer are hidden by their mothers who come to them only to nurse them. Not until they are strong on their legs are calves allowed to follow the hinds. This is a very wise precaution and allows the hind freedom of movement during her calf's helpless days. In Great Britain, red deer, which are not game in law, may be treated as either game or vermin depending on where they live. On Exmoor they are hunted by the Devon and Somerset Staghounds, but in the Highlands of Scotland they are stalked with a rifle, which is perhaps the most humane way of killing deer. Red deer in Britain now have a close season.

ROE DEER

Roe are woodland deer, but in certain parts of Scotland you will find them on the open hill where, for many months of the year, they lead the spartan life of the red deer.

This species is very much smaller than the red deer, a fully grown buck standing from two feet one inch to two feet five inches at the shoulder. Does are smaller than this. A big buck may turn the scale at sixty pounds, so he is a lightweight compared with the red deer stag of eighteen stones or more.

During the rut a master stag may hold his hinds for a week or more, but he soon becomes run out and it is then he retires to a quiet place, leaving his harem to a younger beast. During his retirement the master stag often has with him a small stag, who acts as his watch-dog during the recuperative period.

Except during the rutting season, red deer tend to separate by sex into herds. Whatever the composition of the group, the real leader is an old hind; this applies when the hind group is held by a master stag during the rut. Every deer-stalker knows that when he is approaching a herd during the stalking season, he has to watch the leading hind of the group rather than the stag, who is the quarry.

Unlike the red deer, the roe buck takes the rut in July August. He does not roar or wallow like the red stag. His vocal demonstration consists of barking like a dog. During this period the bucks chase the does in rings, treading out well-marked circuits. These are often referred to as the Fairy Rings of the Roe Deer. The animals usually frequent these rings very early in the morning, after which they retire to cover to lie up for the day, though in quiet places you will find the bucks afoot and active at any time.

Roe deer fawns are born usually from the last week in May into June, but there are records of births far outside this period, notably in April and August. Fawns are spotted at birth but these spots disappear in the autumn. A fawn

The rifle is the only proper weapon for killing a stag and it must be of a calibre to kill him clean where he stands. The shotgun is a brutal weapon to use against deer, and small calibre rifles should never be used because they prick and wound and cause slow, painful death to the stag.

born in May will lose his spots in August, but one born in July will be spotted until October.

In roe deer there is the phenomenon called delayed implantation. This means that development of the young deer does not begin immediately; though mating takes place in July or August, the fertilised ova do not become implanted in the uterine wall until late in December. If mating takes place earlier than normal, implantation takes place earlier; if mating is later, say in October, implantation is correspondingly later. The period of actual development of the young remains constant.

Mature roe bucks usually carry three points on each antler. The antlers rarely exceed nine inches in length and are usually fully grown and clean by April. They are shed in November. Horned does occur from time to time and are not necessarily barren. Does of this kind have been seen nursing fawns.

Being shy, secretive animals, roe are not often seen except by those who look for them, consequently their numbers in any given area are usually underestimated. They are most active from dusk to dawn and, except in very quiet places, spend most of the day in cover. They eat a variety of food from grass to fungi. They browse a great deal on twigs and leaves of trees; they like bramble leaves especially, and are very fond of mushrooms.

The roe buck, despite his small size, is a powerful animal, fit to handle any fox, or any single dog of moderate size. Individual bucks, running with doe and fawns will take an active part in their defence, and probably there is still a great deal to be discovered regarding the roe deer's behaviour in this respect.

SIBERIAN ROE

A number of roe of this species have become feral in England, after escaping from Woburn Park. They are larger than the European roe, with bigger antlers, and they show a little tail which the European species does not. The home ground of the Siberian Roe is Asia.

THE BROWN RAT

The Brown Rat has been one of the most successful invaders in all history. It came in ships from the Middle East and successfully occupied most of Europe, so that for centuries people have been familiar with this animal. Robert Browning, in his poem " The Pied Piper of Hamelin ", gave it something like literary status, and the poem is still the source of many apt quotations on the subject of rats.

When any bird or mammal becomes resident in a country where it is not native, one of two things usually happens: the species either dies out, or it becomes a pest. In Australia we have the example of the rabbit, which soon outnumbered the people, and the stoat and weasel which died off soon after introduction. The rat has been as successful as the rabbit. Both are aliens and pests.

Apart from being a pest of agriculture, and destructive to a great many of man's other interests, the rat brought disease to Europe—notably cholera, more often called the plague. In the Middle Ages this disease ravaged many parts of Europe and was responsible for decimating the population of England, although the actual species involved in the Black Death was the Black Rat, which arrived earlier than the Brown.

The brown rat is one of the most adaptable of mammals and can live in cities, towns and villages, in farms, warehouses and ships, on islands and on the shore, everywhere, in fact, except the tops of mountains. Because of the brown rat's vigorous colonising, the black species was pushed out of most of the countryside and is now relatively scarce in Britain.

Though the brown rat is often called the Sewer Rat and, indeed, swarms in the sewers of London, this description is far too narrow. In the country, those brown rats which live

The brown rat was brought from the East in ships, not by design, but by accident. A big specimen of this species will measure 18 inches from tip of nose to tip of tail, and will weigh over one-and-a-half pounds. Rats in excess of this size and weight have been recorded.

in barns and other farm buildings in winter, move out into the fields in summer, taking up residence in the burrows of rabbits and water voles, in walls, hedgerows and banks. In such places they breed and, during the summer, rats old and young do a great deal of damage to the nests of small birds. Partridges, for example, are frequently the victims of rats living in hedgerow burrows. The rat is the worst enemy of the game preserver.

PROLIFIC BREEDERS

Rats are prolific breeders, and you will find females with young in every month of the year. But the females do not breed continuously throughout the year. Each has her resting period, but since all females do not have their resting period at the same time you can always find a number with young. One terrier (helped by a pick and spade) dug out a family of eleven in mid-winter after a badger had already tried to excavate the nest.

Though rats are beyond any question extremely resourceful and intelligent, they are also creatures of habit. For example, if a rat gets into the habit of moving round a well-known obstacle, it will continue to move round for some time after the obstacle has been removed. This is something you can try yourself, for example, in a barn or stable. If you put down food for the rats, and place a few obstacles in their path, they will soon work out a route to the food. When you remove the obstacles you will observe them using these routes for some time after their removal.

Many stories are told of the rat's resourcefulness, one of these being connected with the removal of eggs from a poultry house. The story goes that one rat lies on its back clasping the egg to its belly, while the second rat lays hold of the first one's tail and drags it away. It has been vouched for, but is for many reasons wholly unconvincing.

A rat's courage is also beyond question. A cornered rat or a wounded rat will face terrier or fox, and it will readily face man if it is cornered and has no hole to run to. It will indeed face a man in the open if it has no way of escape.

DESTRUCTIVE POWERS

Rats destroy food at all stages of growth and storage and do vast damage each year. They will also kill anything they can catch and hold such as small birds and small rabbits. They also raid birds' nests and can even manage to remove eggs from under a sitting fowl.

Among the rat's main enemies, apart from man, are the weasel and the fox, the stoat, eagle and buzzard, most cats and dogs, many owls and some hawks. Birds such as kestrels and owls take only small rats. The eagle, on the other hand, will take them any size at all.

One of the best illustrations of the menace of the rat comes from the island of North Rona, an Atlantic island off the north-west coast of Scotland. On that remote island the people died of famine because rats had eaten their entire store of winter food. After that the rats themselves perished because they could not survive without the people.

THE CROCODILE FAMILY

Crocodiles, although they spend so much of their lives in the water, are not amphibians like the frogs, newts and salamanders. They are true reptiles, like snakes and lizards.

Almost everyone can recognise a crocodile at a glance, because this reptile has featured so often in films of many kinds, and because its photograph has appeared in so many magazines, periodicals and books. Croc. is a familiar abbreviation of the name. Most of us have seen, at some time, the familiar film shot of crocodiles hurrying into a tropical river when disturbed by man, or when a man falls into the water. We are left to assume that the crocodile drags the man into the murky depths and devours him.

FULLY DEVELOPED AT HATCHING

Like the amphibians, the crocodile is cold-blooded, and

Crocodiles are carnivorous, and some attack human beings.

has a similar heart circulation. But there is one great difference between them. The crocodile has no tadpole stage. He is born a complete crocodile. The adult crocodile lays eggs from which hatch young crocodiles exactly like their parents in everything except size.

On the other hand, the eggs of the amphibians hatch into tadpoles which live entirely in water until the time when they are ready to become proper adults.

CANNOT BREATHE UNDER WATER

Young crocodiles would drown quickly if they were held under water. They cannot breathe through their skins as frogs do.

There are crocodiles in the Old World and the New. America has one species of crocodile and one alligator. China, too, has a species of alligator, and these two make up the total alligator species of the world. There are crocodiles of various types found in many parts of the world, including Africa, India, Mexico, Central and South America.

The crocodilians called Caymans are found in the New World and are, in fact, alligators. The Gavials, which are found in India, are distinguished by their long, thin snouts. The alligator's snout is broad and rounded. The crocodile's is pointed and the whole head is narrower. In addition, two teeth can be seen on either side of the crocodile's lower jaw when its mouth is closed.

SIZE OFTEN EXAGGERATED

No present-day crocodile ever reaches the size of the extinct members of the family. Reports of crocodiles over thirty feet in length have to be treated with great caution. The biggest crocodile ever measured by a scientist was twenty-two feet four inches in length. Most are very much smaller than that.

The gavial, the fish-eating crocodile of India, is usually under fifteen feet in length.

It does seem to be the case, however, that crocodiles of, say, a century ago, grew to a much larger size than those of to-day, probably because few present-day crocodiles are ever allowed to live long enough to attain their maximum growth.

'GATORS

The alligators of the United States of America only rarely

A female alligator lays her eggs ashore among rotting vegetation. Whether or not she looks after them is a debatable point.

attempt to attack a human being, although there are records of such attacks. The really dangerous types are the crocodiles of the Nile. Many of these, for one reason or another, become confirmed man-eaters, and it has even been suggested that they kill almost as many people as cobras do.

CONFIRMED KILLER

The African crocodile is greatly feared by the inhabitants of the country in which it is found. The danger, apparently, is not confined to people in or close to water. On many occasions crocodiles have seized their prey ashore and carried it into the water to be drowned. This crocodile, therefore, is one of the few animals that can be considered a real danger to human life—that is by making deliberate unprovoked attacks and being powerful enough to kill them.

The crocodile itself is able to remain underwater for long enough to drown a prey, but not long enough to drown itself. It is enabled to do so because of a special adaptation of the tongue. The tongue of the crocodile, which is well developed, cannot be protruded like that of a serpent because it is attached to the bottom of the mouth along its entire length. It can, however, be raised to block off the throat, so preventing the entry of water into the windpipe. At the same time, valves in the ears and nostrils are closed, so that water cannot enter any of the passages when the beast is submerged.

ADAPTED FOR THE WATER

In addition, because its nostrils are situated on the top of its nose, the crocodile can submerge with a prey, while keeping its nostrils just clear of the water, and so breathe while the prey is drowning. In other words, though not an amphibian, the crocodile is perfectly adapted for life in the water.

EGGS

Crocodiles do not lay their eggs in water; they would not hatch there and, even if they did, the young crocodiles would drown at once when they hatched.

The eggs are laid ashore, in mounds, or nests, of vegetation and dirt. There has been considerable argument as to whether crocodiles show any interest in their eggs after they are laid, as a hen does, for instance. It is assumed that the female stays somewhere in the vicinity, waiting for the eggs to hatch, and there is evidence that the American alligator does so. It is possible that she also keeps the eggs moist.

PARENTAL INSTINCTS

Nevertheless, many people have opened the nests of crocodiles, without apparently outraging or being challenged by a watching female. But on the other hand, other observers insist that the female stands guard, and that she opens the nest when she hears the squeaks of the young, and escorts them safely to the water, like a duck with ducklings. In the case of the American alligator this does seem to be true, and adult females have been seen helping young from the nest and later swimming with them.

There is, apparently, one substantiated fact—that male crocodiles do not seem to have any parental instinct, and are more likely to kill the young ones than to guard them. The South American Cayman is alleged to eat its own offspring as opportunity offers, which has given rise to the joke that if it weren't for the male alligators the world would be up to the neck in alligators!

Squirrels

The red squirrel is the native species of Britain; the grey is an alien and comes from America.

Most Scottish red squirrels to-day are probably of English origin. It is now thought that the felling of the Scottish forests in the nineteenth-century virtually exterminated the red squirrel except in a few areas, and it is a matter of history that Scandinavian squirrels were brought into the country in 1790. But other parts of Scotland were stocked with squirrels from England. This was quite different from introducing exotic species, as in the case of the grey squirrel from America. English red squirrels which were turned down in Scotland were being released in a country of which their kind was a native, and actually came from another part of the same island.

The red squirrel is common in most parts of Europe and has been divided into several races—the red squirrels of Scandinavia; those of Central France and Holland; the Pyrenean race; the Spanish race; and the Eastern European race. At different times several of these races may have been introduced into Britain.

AMERICAN GREY SQUIRREL

In this country, the red squirrel has decreased in most areas, and disappeared from some, and because the American grey squirrel frequently established itself in these areas, it was once thought that the greys killed off the reds. It is true that the grey squirrel is hardy and adaptable and a hustling coloniser. He will travel over miles of open country to invade new woods. He did build up his numbers in the very places where red squirrels were dwindling and it seems to be true that the red finds difficulty in recovering ground which is held in strength by greys. But one has to be careful about

The red squirrel is a vegetarian which eats mainly nuts, cones and berries. It lays by a store of food for the winter and though it sleeps much, it does not hibernate.

drawing conclusions. Squirrels, like other animals, have their ups and downs, and the red squirrel is notable in this respect.

Monica Shorten, in her book on squirrels, has indicated that the red squirrel was in a decline anyway when the grey squirrel invasion took place. Thus the grey was merely taking over ground from which the red was already disappearing and probably completed the process by sheer weight of numbers.

ALIEN AND NATIVE

From time to time there are reports of grey and red squirrels interbreeding, just as there are of rabbits and rats, but there has never been any proof of squirrels cross-breeding. Grey squirrels with ruddy necks and shoulders are pure-bred Americans.

We have the grey squirrel so much with us now, and he has been so much publicised, that we tend to forget that our native red squirrel could be a pest too, and was quite a serious one in some forests. Both species bark trees, the greys concentrating on hard woods, and the reds on conifers. But the greys have recently been damaging conifers, and both species attack the leading shoots of larch, pine and spruce, thus causing distortion and flat tops.

The red squirrel will take fruit of all kinds as well as cones, beech-mast and acorns. He will also eat a variety of green stuff, hips, and other berries, twigs, buds, birds' eggs and, in some cases, nestlings. The squirrel can trim down a larch cone until it looks like a cigar with a small tuft at the end.

The time of great bustle for the red squirrel is early autumn. Then you will see him gathering and burying his harvest. In this way he plants hazel-nuts, acorns and beech-mast. Not all of these are recovered and so the squirrel plants trees. Whether the squirrel recovers his buried treasures by memory, scent or mere re-discovery, is a debatable point. Probably all three play a part. Where squirrels are provided with boxes, and have food put out for them, they will store surplus food in their box and visit the store regularly.

NEST OF SQUIRREL

The nest of the squirrel is called a drey. It is made of twigs and built in a tree, leaves and moss making up the structure, which is a ball with hardly any visible entrance. Bits of bark or moss, or twigs, lying at the bottom of the tree, show that a squirrel has been working, just as woodchips betray the woodpecker.

Squirrels do not hibernate in Britain, but they will lie up during storms or when the temperature falls below freezing point. They can be seen feeding in the trees in the early morning even when there is deep snow on the ground so long as there is some sun and the wind is not strong. Early morning is, in fact, the best time to see squirrels at any time of the year.

Nowadays, man is the squirrel's most serious enemy in this country, because he can organise destruction. Some terriers can catch squirrels. The wild cat is also a good squirrel hunter and some domestic cats become quite expert. The marten is, of course, a confirmed squirrel hunter fit to pursue its prey in the trees. In North America this animal is an important predator on squirrels. It is difficult to discover if many foxes kill squirrels; some certainly do.

VERY WATCHFUL

When feeding, the red squirrel is very watchful and likes

Chipmunks are small squirrels about six inches long and are found in America and Eastern Asia.

a prominent place to sit on, so it is not readily taken by surprise even on the ground.

Squirrels are rodents, but are easily distinguished from the other groups because of their bushy tails. They are found all over the world, except in Australia and Madagascar, and range in size from the pygmy squirrels of West Africa, which are about the size of mice, to the cat-size squirrels of India.

The tribe of squirrels can be roughly divided into three groups, according to habitat and behaviour. Thus we have those called ground squirrels, flying squirrels, and ordinary squirrels. In Britain, the native red squirrel is thus an ordinary squirrel, arboreal in habits, extremely active and agile when it comes to earth. It is a tree squirrel which comes to ground at certain times.

GROUND SQUIRRELS

Ground squirrels, on the other hand, live mainly on the ground, but some take to the trees at the threat of danger while others go to ground like rabbits. The ground squirrels are found mainly in North and South America and Central Asia, and a typical example is the chipmunk. Ground squirrels usually have longer bodies, shorter tails, and sometimes longer snouts than the typical arboreal squirrels with which Europeans are familiar.

FLYING SQUIRRELS

Britain's native squirrels are expert climbers and jumpers and can often make great leaps from branch to branch or tree to tree. But the flying squirrels are the real space travellers. They are well adapted for gliding because of the extension of skin between their legs and sometimes from the forelegs to neck. This enables them to glide from branch to branch or from the top of one tree into the lower branches of another. They cannot parachute down vertically. The adaptation for gliding does not hinder these squirrels when going about their ordinary business in the trees, where their behaviour is much like that of other squirrels. They tend, however, to be more strictly nocturnal than most squirrels, and to build their nests in dark places such as holes in trees. Flying squirrels are found mainly in Asia, but there is a species in North America.

BATS

There are species of mammals which have achieved the power to glide or parachute just as the flying-fish is able to leave the water and make short flights through the air. The bat is the only mammal which has achieved true flight and which is specially adapted for an aerial existence. It is the only mammal which can propel itself through the air as a bird does. Its wings are real wings, and are composed of a double fold of skin stretched over the bones of the arm and hand.

Though their distribution is world wide, and the number of species is second only to that of the rodents, bats are mainly animals of tropical and temperate zones. In the British Isles and North Europe, hibernation takes place, but this habit becomes less and less characteristic as one travels south. All British bats are insect-eaters, the fruit-eaters being tropical species. In one case, the insect diet has become modified: this is the vampire, which will attack other mammals to drink their blood.

For many years there was much discussion about how the bats managed to navigate accurately in the dark, and various theories were put forward to account for this, the nose-leaf in certain species being considered directional. It is a fact that bats confined to a room are able to fly with great precision avoiding every obstacle strung out in front of them. It was not until after the Second World War that the real explanation of the bat's ability was discovered, and this discovery was a direct result of the discovery of radar. The bat, in fact, navigates by echo sounding, being guided by the echoes of its own voice thrown back during flight. A bat with its ears plugged with wax cannot navigate because it can no longer hear. Muzzling similarly destroys its ability to navigate.

BORN IN SPRING

The phenomenon of delayed implantation, where development of the young does not begin immediately, occurs in bats in a modified form. While it is true that the young are born in the spring from an autumn mating, there is no immediate fertilisation followed by delayed implantation. The male sperms are, in fact, stored in the female's uterus throughout the winter and in some cases never fulfil their function at all, fertilisation following on a second mating in the spring. In certain other species, however, the stored sperms do eventually fulfil their function without any second mating being necessary. This has been established by the fact that in these species pregnancy has been observed while the vaginal plug was still intact.

Young bats are born in summer and are completely naked. By clinging to her fur during this helpless period, they are carried about by the mother. When they are too big to be carried about, they are left at the roost while the mother is hunting. By then their fur has grown and their teeth have appeared. Being mammals, bats suckle their young from nipples on the chest. In the horse-shoe bats there are additional nipples in the groin.

Generally speaking, bats give birth to only one young each season, which is all the more surprising considering the great volume of male sperm stored by the female during hiberna-

This bat, Pteropus calaeno, *has a wing span of more than four-and-a-half feet.*

tion. In Europe, however, twins have been regularly recorded. This difference in the productive rate between British and Continental bats has given rise to much speculation concerning its significance. It is thought that the tendency towards twins is a step backward, for bat evolution seems to have tended towards producing only a single young.

LIFE SPAN

In recent years, considerable work has been done on the life span of bats. This has been achieved by marking, which is now common practice with birds and certain mammals. On this basis, ages of the order of seven years have been

One of the best-known bats is the common pipistrelle.

The barbastel is found in Europe, Asia and Africa.

lobe lying in front of the ear called the tragus. In this group of bats the tragus is very large, almost a second ear, and each species has a tragus of characteristic shape. The horse-shoe bats on the other hand do not have any ear tragus but they do have the so-called nose-leaf which is an extension of the skin surrounding the nostrils. The function of these two appendages is not yet clearly understood. In the case of the tragus it may be concerned with the reception of ultra-sonic sound waves; while in the case of the nose-leaf it has been suggested that it may give the bat an extra sense of touch. While neither of these is certain and both assumptions may be false, it is a fact that some bats are extremely sensitive, even in a torpid state, to the approach of any object such as a human hand.

In Central and South America live the notorious vampire bats, whose taste for blood has been played upon by authors until it has become an animal of fearful reputation. The British native species, while so many people hold them in horror or fear, are inoffensive creatures, entirely insectivorous and therefore, if anything, useful to man. Let us look first of all at these European bats in which a tragus is present.

established. It has frequently been said that bats have poor sight because their eyes are small, but not all bats' eyes are small, and there is no reason to suppose that where eyes appear normal they do not function normally. There is no question about their sense of hearing, which is acute for sounds of high frequency. Just as a dog can hear a "silent" whistle which is inaudible to the ears of a man, the bat can hear clearly its own voice echoes. Many people, however, are completely deaf to the sounds uttered by bats.

Though hibernation is characteristic of bats, it is not brought about as was formerly thought by a drop in tempera-ture or a reduction in food supply. More likely the onset of hibernation is associated with the accumulation of fat on the animal's body. And it is a fact that bats which have gorged tend to become torpid at any time, while hungry bats may be seen hawking for flies in bright sunshine in mid-winter even where there is deep, frozen snow on the ground.

TRAGUS AND NOSE-LEAF

In the group of bats called Vespertilionid there is a small

BRITISH BATS

First of all there is the Noctule, or Great Bat, which is found all over temperate Europe and Asia. In the British Isles, it is scarce in the Midlands and almost entirely absent from Scotland. The wing span of the noctule is thirteen inches to fifteen inches. It has big feet and mouth glands, which give it a strong, musky smell. The noctule is gre-garious, hibernating in old trees, eaves and roofs, though less frequently in trees. Where roosts are composed entirely of one sex, hibernation lasts from October until March or later. This species feeds mainly on beetles, but also on moths and gnats, and is usually active shortly before sunset.

Leisler's bat is much smaller than the noctule and lacks its smell. It is similarly coloured and is found in Central Europe, westward to Ireland.

The Serotine bat, which is found in Central and Southern Europe, and from England to the Mediterranean and east into Asia, is found in Britain only south of the Thames. Its wing span measures from twelve to fourteen inches. The serotine is a sociable bat which lives in small colonies in churches, hollow trees, or cottage roofs. Its food is mainly cockchafers at one season, and certain moths at another.

The common British bat is the Pipistrelle which is found over most of the country. It is also found in Europe and into Asia. The pipistrelle's wing span is from eight to eight-and-a-half inches, and it is reddish-brown in colour. Though one young in the season is the rule in Britain, two are commonly recorded from the Continent. The young pipistrelle is born in July.

The pipistrelle hibernates from mid-October to mid-March, but may be seen out on fine days any time in-between. It roosts in large colonies in houses, trees, rocks and churches, but its winter sleep is light and it is easily disturbed. Some-times it roosts in association with other species of bat. The pipistrelle takes wing early in the evening and may, in fact, be seen in flight during the day in winter. Like some moths, pipistrelle bats are attracted by bright lights.

THE WATER BAT

Daubenton's bat, sometimes called the Water Bat because it frequents lakes and rivers, has a wing span of ten inches. It is found in most parts of Britain except the extreme north

Pteropus policephalus, *a grey-headed bat, found in Australia*

of Scotland. In Europe, it ranges from Norway to the Mediterranean, and into Asia and North Africa. It hibernates from September to April. The flight of Daubenton's bat over water is swallow-like, and it will sometimes hover. It drinks from the surface of the water and will take insects in this way, including fishermen's flies.

Natterer's bat is found in Central and Southern Europe, and north as far as Sweden. In Britain, it is fairly common in England and Wales, but an extreme rarity in Scotland.

The Whiskered bat, which has a wing span of eight-and-a-half inches, is common in most parts of England, but rare in Wales, and rarer still in Scotland. It is found all over Europe, Asia and North Africa.

RAREST BRITISH SPECIES

Bechstein's bat is the rarest of the British species. But it is found in Central and Southern Europe. Little is known of its habits. The Long-eared bat, on the other hand, is found all over the United Kingdom, but is rare in the Highlands of Scotland, common in temperate Europe, Asia and North Africa. It is mainly nocturnal, and roosts in trees, beginning to hunt about half an hour or more after sunset.

The Barbastel is a native of Central and Southern Europe, common in England and absent from Scotland. This species usually hunts in full daylight. It is solitary, and silent in flight.

HORSE-SHOES

Of the nose-leaf bats, in which there is no tragus, there is the Greater Horse-shoe which is found in England, Scotland and Wales. Abroad, it occurs in temperate Europe, Asia and North Africa. The greater horse-shoe has a wing span of thirteen inches, and has pointed ears. In this species the sexes hibernate separately, in great flocks, usually in caves. They do not associate with other species when roosting. They hunt late and probably stay on the wing all night, their main food being moths and flying beetles, usually of the bigger species.

The Lesser Horse-shoe bat, which spans only eight-and-a-half inches, is found in England, Wales and Ireland. In other areas it occurs in Central Europe, Asia and India. In Britain, the young lesser horse-shoes are born at the end of June. The lesser horse-shoe rarely hunts on windy nights.

PREDATORY BATS

Besides the common insect-eating bats and the fruit-eaters, there are the predatory species of the tropics. First of all there are the fish-eating bats which occur in India, Burma, and tropical America. In the Caribbean there is the species which flies out to sea at night where it swoops on small fish near the surface of the water, catching them in the claws of its feet, as a hawk would do. Then, of course, there are the legendary vampire bats of tropical America. Curiously enough, the real vampires are very small bats and the most bloodthirsty-looking big bats are not blood drinkers at all. There are three species of vampire. The vampire makes its attack lightly so that its weight is not felt. After carefully selecting the spot for its bite, it cuts the skin and laps up the blood with its tongue; it does not suck. It can, however, lap blood almost as quickly as a cat can lap milk. In actual fact, the amount of blood taken by vampires from man and domestic stock is completely negligible, the real danger from the vampire's bite being infection of the puncture. It has been established in the West Indies that this bat, like a rabid dog, can transmit rabies.

The fishing bat (Noctilio leporinus) *catches and eats fish.*

The long-eared bat, easily distinguishable from other species.

One of the so-called " false vampires " from Southern Asia.

The Wild Boar

Unlike the sleek, hairless, barrel-shaped pigs which man breeds for bacon and pork, their wild ancestor is a shaggy, muscular beast, sometimes reaching a height of thirty-two inches at the shoulder and weighing up to four hundred pounds. The bristles on his spine will sometimes stand nine inches high. Such a beast, with his weight well forward, his speed, his formidable tusks, and his undoubted courage, is a tough quarry for any hunter when he charges.

It is said that the wild boar is the only hoofed animal which will, flanked by tigers, drink at a water-hole.

In Europe and India, hunting the wild pigs was once a popular sport. It was known as pig-sticking because mounted men hunted the pigs with lances, and there are many stories of the indomitable savagery of these animals when they felt the point enter their body. Some have been known, when the lance pierced their bodies, to bite the shaft clean through and, before dying, to attack horse and rider.

To-day, the European wild pig is still found in Spain, France, Germany, and Poland. The European type is similar to the Indian pig, and is the best-known of a family represented in Europe, Asia, and North Africa. These animals dis-

Unlike the adult wild pig, which is dark and shiny-coated, the piglets are striped at birth. The striping disappears as the piglets grow, and they become like the adults with their first change of coat.

appeared from Britain a few centuries ago. They were ruthlessly hunted down and exterminated because of their depredations on crops. The wild pigs of Europe are still crop-destroyers and will raid arable fields at every opportunity. A field which has been raided by wild swine during the night looks as though a herd of cattle had stampeded through it.

DEFENCE OF YOUNG

A wild sow is very bold in defence of her young. The piglets, which may number up to half a dozen, are striped at birth, but the striping disappears as the young pigs grow older.

At the time of the nut-fall, parties of wild pigs root about in the forests for chestnuts. They are very fond of the Spanish or sweet chestnut, as they are of acorns and, in the mountains of Spain, they gorge themselves on the harvest of sweet chestnuts.

Nowadays, the wild boar is hunted mainly with the rifle, and pig-stalking, as distinct from pig-sticking, is a favourite sport. Boars' heads hang on the walls of many houses in Spain as trophies of the chase.

Besides being well distributed in Europe, the European wild pig is also found in the hills of Morocco and the Atlas

The wild boar, which normally minds its own business and is more concerned with feeding than fighting, is a savage fighter when roused, or cornered. It will face hounds or mounted men with indomitable courage and savagery.

The Bornean wild boar (Sus barbatus) is a large species which occurs in Borneo, Sumatra and the Philippines. It has a long, narrow head with naked snout and bunches of long reddish bristles on its cheeks. It wanders about in great herds.

The European wild pig (Sus scrofa) *is a destroyer of crops and will raid arable fields at every opportunity. The wild pig was exterminated in Britain several centuries ago.*

In Europe and India, hunting the wild pig was once a favourite sport. It was known as pig-sticking, because mounted men hunted the pigs with lances.

Mountains. Farther south, it is replaced by other species—for example the Wart-hog, Bush-pig and the Forest-hog.

AFRICAN PIGS

The forest-hog is confined to Equatorial Africa, but the wart-hog and the bush-pig are well distributed south of the Sahara. Both forest-hogs and bush-pigs are destructive to agricultural interests, raiding potato fields and maize fields in the night and doing great damage. Wart-hogs stand much the same height as the European wild pig but are much lighter in weight. The forest-hog is considerably taller, and half as heavy again. A wart-hog spends most of the day lying up in holes, which it enlarges for its own use much as a fox enlarges a rabbit burrow.

In America we find the Peccaries, which are forest and marshland pigs. They travel about in great herds, do a great deal of damage to crops, and can be extremely dangerous. Peccaries have been recorded killing and eating man.

There is in Bengal a tiny species of pig called the Pygmy hog. It frequents very dense cover and, being under a foot in height, often escapes notice. In the Babirussa, which is found in the Celebes and Buru islands of Indonesia, the upper canine teeth grow through the skin of the face and curve back at the top.

Though pigs are cloven-hoofed animals, they do not chew the cud. They have simple stomachs like the horse, and have four toes on each foot, although they walk on only two of these. Pigskin is still widely used for making gloves, handbags, and shoes, while the bristles are still in demand for shaving brushes.

DINOSAURS

To-day, the reptiles of the world are relatively unimportant in that they do not rule or threaten it. Most are harmless or non-poisonous, a few are highly dangerous; but nowhere do reptiles threaten the existence of man or make any part of the world impossible for him to live in.

Reptiles, however, have had their golden age, and it was a long one; so long indeed that the imagination cannot grasp the time span. The giant dinosaurs ruled the earth for a 100 million years. Before the dawn of the Cambrian period, about 500 million years ago, there were only soft-bodied creatures which have left no durable remains. From the early Cambrian period the story is told by fossils and skeletal remains, and to-day one can see in museums reconstructions of the giant lizards of the past.

Amphibians were in being for millions of years before the first reptiles. They lived in marshes and ponds and laid their eggs in the water as the frogs do now. They had a tadpole stage, but the adults could live on land.

For 50 million years the amphibians (some of them 50 feet in length), lived in a moist, green, warm world which suited them admirably. Then came a dramatic change in climate, the swamps dried, the waters shrank and the glaciers marched. Some amphibians went back to the water, others stayed on land to become the forerunners of the reptiles of the Permian period. The great days of the reptile's rule began in the Triassic period, which lasted for 30 million years; then, and right through the 25 million years of the Jurassic, they took over the earth. It was in this latter period, and for millions of years afterwards, that the great dinosaurs held sway in the truly golden age of reptiles.

The warm seas which flooded much of Europe and America, made the world of the times a paradise for these giant reptiles. Tropical plants grew where there is to-day almost permanent ice and the gigantic vegetarian dinosaurs waxed bigger and fatter with much eating. There were carnivorous dinosaurs as well, which were the terror of the vegetarians. Reptile types multiplied; some became flyers like the Pteranodons which had a wing span of over 25 feet.

The greatest of the plant-eating dinosaurs was Brontosaurus; the biggest animal ever to trundle over the face of the earth. He was 70 feet long and weighed 40 tons, yet his brain weighed only a few ounces.

BISON AND BUFFALO

To-day, the name buffalo still means, for all those people nourished on American films and canned American television programmes, the bison of America—the great, woolly-maned ungulate of the plains; important food animal of the red man, the vast herds, once millions strong, took days to pass a given point.

The history of the American bison, also called buffalo, is a salutory indication of what can happen to an animal population subjected to ruthless exploitation by man. So long as the bison was hunted by the Indians to supply their own needs its numbers remained at a spectacularly high level. The Indians used every part of the carcass—the meat, the bones and the hides, and treated the great herds as a continuing asset or, so to speak, the goose that laid the golden egg.

With the coming of the white man this relationship was completely changed. The bison was ruthlessly slaughtered and wastefully used. Frequently only small parts of the carcasses were taken, and vast numbers of bodies were left to rot in the sun and to feed the coyotes. The Indians saw a major food resource being destroyed before their eyes. It seemed at one time that both bison and Indian must disappear altogether from the surface of the earth.

In no field of colonisation does the white man's record appear more black than in his wanton destruction of these two native North American species.

DESTRUCTION OF THE HERDS

If the white man destroyed the Indians as a deliberate policy, he almost exterminated the bison because of unbridled exploitation of a seemingly-inexhaustible source.

The systematic and uncontrolled destruction of bison began at the end of the eighteenth-century. Here was an apparently endless supply of meat and hides. The colonisation of the West and the development of railroads meant increasing numbers of people to be fed, and the bison became everybody's source of meat. Helpless, the Indians stood by while

In the great cave of Altamira in Northern Spain are many pictures of bison painted by Palaeolithic artists.

The American bison, once almost extinct, has been saved by Government intervention. The European bison is smaller than the American.

the destruction took place. The railroad companies hired special hunters, recruited from hardy pioneers, to provide meat for thousands of workers and soldiers and to clear routes frequently passed by the great herds of the plains. Buffalo " stations " became more notorious than the pheasant " battues " so much talked about in England. The plains became a shambles and a vast graveyard.

Among the mighty hunters was the famous Colonel William Cody, better known as Buffalo Bill, who became notorious as the greatest bison-killer of them all. It has been said that more than four thousand animals fell to his rifle alone. As a result of the accomplishments of men like Cody, the vast herds of bison, totalling at one time sixty million animals, dwindled to a few hundred. The massacres were a great attraction to many people, and special trains were sometimes run so that tourists could view the prowess of Buffalo Bill and others at work.

It is a chastening reflection on our sense of values that a man like Cody should have become something of an international hero. Despite unprecedented killing the bison was saved at the last minute. When the Americans realised that extinction was within sight for this great animal, they collected the remaining stragglers and herded them in their great national parks. To-day, the bison herds of North America number about 20,000 animals.

In the pioneering days, the bison was a barrier to development in several ways, and there is no question that the great herds had to be reduced. It is the manner of their reduction and the complete disregard for the point of view of the Indian

The yak from Tibet exhibits the characteristics of both bison and buffalo and is a valuable working animal.

that stand condemned. The herds frequently barred the path of the pioneers for days at a time when the animals were migrating. In addition, the bison was there, physically occupying vast amounts of territory which was heavily punished and then evacuated for a period. These two factors made it difficult for colonists to establish any kind of arable farming or rear livestock of their own. What the bison did do was to provide a constant source of meat while farming and livestock rearing were developed and its own extermination as a species was being carried out.

The American bison is a heavier and more powerful animal than its relative of Europe and Asia. It has shorter horns and a denser mane. The European species used to be common, and at one time the herds of Eastern Europe and Asia were very large. Long ago they were certainly familiar enough animals, and they were a favourite subject with prehistoric artists. The famous cave of Altamira, near Torrelavega in Northern Spain, has perhaps the finest collection of Paleolithic paintings known. In Altamira, as in the case of Font de Gaume in France, the bison was a favourite subject, and the standard of the drawing is astonishing, considering the conditions under which the prehistoric artists had to work.

In Central Germany and in Poland, the European bison slowly passed from the stage until, at the beginning of the twentieth-century, there were only a few dozen animals left, and these were notably smaller than their ancestors. Among these ancestors the most notable was certainly the great auroch, the gigantic progenitor of the bovines, the wild bull (*Bos primigenius*). It was an immense animal more than six feet high at the withers, and certainly the largest survival from the Quaternary era.

Julius Cæsar affirmed that he had seen some of them in the German forests.

Apart from the bison the most notable bovines to-day are, perhaps, the great fighting bulls of Spain.

Close relatives of the bison, to which in America they have given their name, are the buffaloes found in many parts of the Old World. In Central Italy, there are enormous herds of buffalo living in a state of semi-domestication. While they find their own food, they are herded by men on horseback who round them up like cattle and use their milk. These buffalo inhabit marshy zones wherever they can find suitable pasture and water in which to immerse themselves during the hot hours of the day. Throughout the Balkan Peninsula and in Asia Minor, one can see buffaloes similar to those of the Tuscan marshes and of the country around Rome.

In Africa there are several kinds of buffalo—some semi-domesticated, others completely wild and potentially dangerous. The big African buffalo has a frontal shield where its large, sweeping horns unite in front of its head. Hunting this buffalo is considered more dangerous than hunting lions. Even people who have never seen a buffalo know what the phrase " charging like a wounded buffalo " means. The animal does not always retreat before the threat of danger; it is just as likely to turn towards the hunter and charge with the irresistible power of a locomotive. The structure of the horns, which protect the beast's forehead, makes him a difficult target from in front, because there is no vulnerable spot.

The Indian buffalo is similar to the African, and just as impressive, if it is not as dangerous. All these buffaloes, including those which are found in Europe, have long, curved, flattened horns, strong, broad bodies and smooth, dark coats.

In Tibet and the high plateau of the Himalayas, lives the Yak, which resembles the bison in physical characteristics. Like the bison, it has fourteen pairs of ribs instead of thirteen as in oxen, and it grunts instead of lowing. Patient, and resistant to cold, hunger and fatigue as no other bovine is, the yak represents one of the few assets of the Tibetan farmers, who have to call upon its strength and endurance every day of their lives in their fight for survival in their dour, rocky country.

Bison, buffalo, yak, belong to the same great family, yet each animal differs greatly from the other. Over long periods of time, and due to environment, each member of the family developed its own special characteristics into the animals we know to-day. The skin of the bison is used in various ways. From it are made jackets, caps, coats, leggings, moccasins, bags, tents, matting, and even cradles. The excellent flesh, which has been always highly prized by man, can be dried successfully and is then known as pemmican.

There is a widespread misconception that owls cannot see in daylight, but of course they can, and better than you or I can see in the dark. The fact is that they are specially adapted for hunting at night, which is something else entirely. While they appear to dislike strong sun, they can fly and manœuvre perfectly well in sunlight.

Owls have big eyes, extraordinarily large for the size of the bird, and as light fades, the pupils become larger to compensate for the reduced intensity. In exactly the same way, a photographer opens the lens of his camera wider and wider as the light becomes poorer. The owl's eyes are designed to catch all the light available and there is always some available even on very dark nights. In a state of total darkness no owl could see anything. On the other hand, owls are perfectly able to hunt in good light and, experimentally, a tawny owl has been known to catch a mouse in illumination of 500 watts. Owls, like other birds, have colour vision.

Although owls are specially equipped for hunting at night, it would be a mistake to think that none is active by day. There is one British species in particular—the Short-Eared Owl—which makes a habit of hunting in daylight and on the edge of dusk.

The short-eared owl nests on the ground among heather or deep grass, and its chicks start running about, or rather scrambling about, long before they can fly. At this time the owlets often fall prey to hunting foxes, especially when there are many owlets on the ground during a vole plague. This was shown particularly clearly by Dr. J. D. Lockie of the Nature Conservancy who studied a vole plague in Scotland recently. The connection between short-eared owls and voles is a striking one, for the birds flock in wherever these small mammals happen to be plentiful. Voles are subject to spectacular increases in numbers in certain years and whenever there is a plague, the short-eared owls appear on the scene. At such times you will find large numbers nesting close together and feeding their young almost entirely on voles.

OWLS WITH " EAR " TUFTS

The description " short-eared " for this owl should be clearly understood. The bird has no visible ears; what it has are short, feathered tufts on its head. When these are raised they look like ears and, because they are short, the bird has become known as the short-eared owl.

There are other " eared " species of owl. A familiar breeding species in Britain is the Long-Eared Owl. As the name implies, this bird has ear tufts very much longer than those of the species just described. As a matter of fact, when the long-eared owl is at rest with its tufts erect they look more like horns. The ear tufts are never erect when the bird is in flight.

The long-eared owl is a woodland species and is especially fond of dark pine woods or thick, dusty larch woods. It is almost entirely nocturnal in habits. By day, it prefers to rest, roosting in some dark tree. Hunting usually begins some time after the sun has set, and you will seldom see a

The long-eared owl, strictly nocturnal, likes dark, coniferous woodland.

long-eared owl flying by day unless it has been disturbed at its roost.

Observation has shown that the long-eared owl can hunt on the darkest nights—on nights when, literally, you couldn't see your finger in front of your face—but even on the darkest night the darkness is not total and the owl makes use of the little amount of light available. This species has orange eyes with black pupils, but when the night is really dark the pupils dilate so much that the orange can hardly be seen at all. As the light improves the pupils shrink steadily until they have contracted to their normal daylight size.

Long-eared owls take a great variety of prey, but the bulk is made up of voles, mice, shrews, young rats, and songbirds. During many nights of watching at nests of this species, the author noted that about one kill in ten was a small bird. Rats, mice, voles, and shrews made up the remainder. This doesn't take account of items like earthworms and beetles which are also caught by this species. The best night's hunting the author recorded for a cock long-eared owl was eight rats, one vole and one skylark, between 10 p.m. and 2.30 a.m. in the month of April.

Long-eared owls nest in March and April, but in most years the eggs are laid before the end of March. The bird builds no nest, but uses the old one of carrion crow or magpie. Some long-eared owls lay their eggs on the ground or in rabbit burrows. In such places, as in the case of the short-eared owl, the chicks sometimes fall prey to prowling foxes. The voice of the long-eared owl is a short, almost breathless hoot, more like a sigh than anything else, though on still nights it can be heard at some distance.

GREATEST AND LEAST

By far the biggest of the " eared " owls is the Eagle Owl, sometimes called in France the Grand Duc, and known in

North America as the Great Horned Owl. This is a huge, powerful species fit to kill prey like roe deer fawns, hares and capercaillie. It has been known to take turkeys. It does most of its hunting at dusk and dawn, roosting by day on branches of dark trees close to the main stem, or in hollow trees or rock clefts. The eagle owl does not nest in the British Isles, to which it is a very rare straggler. Nor does it nest in Northern France or the Low Countries. It is, however, found in Southern France, Spain, Italy, the Balkans, Poland, and Scandinavia, where it haunts forests and mountains or open steppe land.

In the winter of 1946-7, which was very severe and prolonged, an eagle owl appeared and spent several days on a Stirlingshire moor. On one occasion in daylight, it was harried by crows who forced it from its roost in a small tree right down into the heather. It is remarkable that British crows meeting an eagle owl for the first time should have behaved in a way which is normal in Scandinavia where the eagle owl is regularly mobbed by hoodie crows.

The smallest of the " eared " owls is the Scops Owl, which is found in Spain and along the Mediterranean coast. This species is not averse to living near human habitations, and will nest in gardens, using holes in walls, old buildings, or the old nests of other birds. The Scops owl feeds chiefly on insects.

TAWNY OWL

The Tawny Owl, which in flight always looks big-headed, is a common woodland species in the British Isles. It does not require big woods, and may be found where the tree cover is thin. This is the bird with the familiar hoot, which Shakespeare rendered as " tu-whit, tu-whoo ". In fact this rendering of Shakespeare's appears to be made up of two things—the bird's call of " kee-wick " and its hoot, which is a long drawn-out, bubbling " hoo-hoo-oo-oo ".

Tawny owls usually hunt from sunset until sunrise, but after a night of constant rain, during which no hunting is done, the bird will often fly by day when the weather clears. Tawny owls have been observed carrying prey to their chicks at two o'clock on a May afternoon following such a wet night. The tawny owl has a definite territory and the way to find the extent of this is to put the bird on the wing during the

The barn owl is closely associated with man, nesting in towers, in church belfries and in farm buildings. There are two phases: the light-breasted and the dark-breasted.

The tawny owl is the species with the well-known hoot.

day, disturbing it each time it pitches until, instead of flying onward, it turns back over your head. The point of return is the perimeter of its territory. If you pushed it out in other directions it will behave in the same way and thus you will get some idea of its home range. This technique was first used by H. N. Southern of Oxford. It must not be thought, however, that the bird confines itself to these areas during hunting. Birds which will not allow themselves to be pushed out of a wood by day will hunt far beyond it during the night.

Like the long-eared owl, the tawny is an early nester. In most years it has eggs in March. Again, no nest is built, the owl preferring to use a hollow tree or the old nest of crow, magpie, or sparrow-hawk. The tawny is bold in defence of her nest, and will attack, after dusk, even human beings if they intrude too closely. In such circumstances the tawny owl can be really dangerous and any person visiting, after dusk, a nest containing chicks should wear eye-shields. One British bird photographer lost an eye through failing to take this precaution.

In this species cannibalism has been recorded. If an owlet dies in the nest as a result of hunger and no other food is immediately forthcoming, the parents will tear up the body of the dead chick and feed it to the living ones.

Tawny owlets have dark eyes quite unlike the orange-and-black of the long-eared or the yellow-and-black of the short-eared owl. They are very noisy after they leave the nest and in this way advertise their presence.

The food of this species is much the same as that of the long-eared owl, but in the experience of some observers it takes even more mammals and fewer birds. Prey items noted at a nest include young rats, mice, voles, shrews, baby rabbits, and an occasional weasel. In addition, the tawny owl takes a great many earthworms, as has been shown by H. N. Southern of Oxford. Unusual prey found in a nest was a snipe.

TERRIFYING SCREECH

The Barn Owl is the species most closely associated with human dwellings in Britain. It is the owl of the church belfry and the farm loft, and has a terrifying screech which gives it one of its other names—screech owl.

This bird likes to nest between rafters in a loft and often the " nest " is composed of nothing but the bones and fur of rodents. It lays more eggs than the woodland owls and sometimes nests twice in one season. The chicks hatch at all times and you will find a great variety of ages in the nest.

Like all owls and certain other birds, the barn owl regurgitates indigestible matter in the form of pellets or castings. These are composed of bones, fur, teeth, feathers and other indigestible matter, and vary in size from species to species. In lofts where the barn owl nests, the accumulation of such pellets over the years can cover an area of thirty-six square feet to a depth of ten inches or more.

The food of this species is mainly mice, voles, and young rats. At certain times the parent owl can be seen hunting during the late part of the day or just before dusk, and you can see it hunting wherever there are rats and mice for killing. There are two colour phases of this species, the light-breasted and the dark-breasted.

AN IMPORT

The Little Owl is a bantam among British species. It is not a true British subject, but an import. It has bred widely in England since its introduction to Britain and has now been recorded in Southern Scotland. On the Continent it is widely distributed throughout Europe, except Scandinavia.

Much has been said and written about the little owl's depredations on songbirds and game chicks, but as a matter of fact all investigations into its food have shown that it kills mainly worms, beetles, moths, mice and voles.

This species nests in holes in trees and walls, and under the tiles of old roofs. Many people would have liked to see the little owl black-listed by law, but like all other owls in Britain it is completely protected.

The little owl has a flat head and face and yellow eyes, and has always a rather fierce expression. By daylight, it can be seen perching on fences, walls, and such places.

HUNTS BY DAY

The smallest European owl is the Pygmy which has a much more restricted range, being found in Central and Eastern Europe, and in Scandinavia. This species is smaller than the common starling; it has small yellow eyes and appears

The little owl (Athene noctua) *is an alien which has settled down successfully in England and is now colonising Scotland.*

The snowy owl is an Arctic species, and hunts by day.

to have bristly white eyebrows. The pygmy hunts freely and regularly by day, when it can be seen pursuing and killing small birds in flight. In the main, it frequents coniferous forests and mountainous areas, nesting in hollow trees and woodpecker holes.

Tengmalm's owl is very like the little owl but has a bigger and rounder head and deeper facial discs. It is found over much the same area as the pygmy owl. This species is strictly nocturnal outside the Arctic region, where it will hunt in good light. It spends the day roosting in coniferous trees. Its favourite habitat is coniferous forests and mountain areas, but it shifts ground in the winter, going down into the valleys. The usual nesting site is a hole in a tree, either natural or drilled out by woodpeckers.

PREYS ON HARES

With the Snowy Owl we return to the giants. The snowy is a powerful Arctic species, white in colour, barred with brown, although some birds appear almost entirely white. The snowy owl is almost entirely a day hunter, flying down birds on the wing and taking prey up to the size of a hare. Lemmings are a frequent prey of this species. Every four years or so the snowy owls erupt from the Arctic so that the birds turn up well outside their usual range, some making their landfall in north-east Scotland.

The Great Grey Owl, sometimes called the Lapland Owl, frequents the dense, coniferous forests of the north in Arctic Norway, Sweden and Finland. Like the snowy owl, it erupts in certain years, reaching East Prussia and Estonia. For breeding, it uses the old nests of large birds of prey.

The Ural Owl, as its name suggests, is found in Eastern Europe and parts of Scandinavia. It is a smaller bird than the great grey owl, and its behaviour is described as being much like that of the tawny owl, although the Ural is a much larger bird and has yellow eyes. This species frequents mixed woodlands, nesting in hollow trees and the old nests of birds of prey.

The Hawk Owl, a Scandinavian species, occurs in Britain, Switzerland, and Southern Europe as a vagrant. Its normal range is Scandinavia where it frequents coniferous forests and birch thickets, nesting in the old nests of hawks or in hollow trees.

GAME BIRDS

The group of birds which we refer to as Game *is one which man has long preserved for his sport, and there is a considerable literature regarding their preservation, management and*

shooting. But the real study of their natural history has taken place in very recent times, and goes on at greater tempo to-day. An example is the red grouse survey.

The largest European game bird is the Capercaillie, the hen of which is often mistaken for a turkey, while the cock might well be mistaken for a golden eagle. The species is widely distributed in Europe, from Norway and Sweden to the Cantabrian Mountains of Spain, North Italy, and the Balkans. Closely related types are found in Finland, Siberia and Mongolia. Capercaillies prefer coniferous forest at all times and are closely tied to them. They also prefer woods on hillsides and it is notable that the nesting hens choose sloping ground wherever possible. The nest is almost always sited within a few feet of the base of a tree or tree-stump, often with some kind of surrounding cover but sometimes with none at all. Occasionally nests are found *in* trees, or in heather far from tree cover. The entire work of incubating the eggs and rearing the chicks is undertaken by the hen.

The cock capercaillie is black and grey and bottle-green and brown, with bright crimson wattles. The hen is noticeably smaller; the plumage is mottled brown with a chestnut patch on the breast, with a voice quite like that of the hen pheasant's, but the cock's cry is raucous and rattling, and sounds like the popping of a cork.

DISLIKED BY FORESTERS

The birds feed largely on the leading shoots of spruce and pine trees so they are never short of food even in the wildest weather. Because of the nature of their food many foresters dislike them, but in Great Britain the Forestry Commission has shown a commendable willingness to tolerate capercaillies. Indeed the Forestry Commission has helped the bird to colonise new territory in recent years.

Although the capercaillie is a grouse, and therefore specifically a game bird, it is not included in the game laws of Britain because it was extinct when the Game Act was passed in 1831. In the British Isles the bird is still confined to Scotland, to which country it was reintroduced from Sweden in 1837. The capercaillie now has protection in Britain under the 1954 Protection of Birds Act.

BLACK GROUSE

In the Black Grouse the sexes are quite distinctive. The cock, referred to as the blackcock, has a lyre tail and plumage of ebony with brilliant crimson wattles. The hen, called the greyhen, is like a small edition of the hen capercaillie, but the greyhen has a slightly-forked tail which the other has not.

In spring, the black grouse has a wonderful display ritual which is referred to in Britain as lekking. The ground on which this display is held is called a lek and is usually hillocky; it may be close by a wood or on the open hill. Here the blackcocks gather in the early morning (and in the afternoon) to posture and challenge and fight.

Black grouse are birds of the tree fringe, usually found on moorland among scattered birches and pines. The greyhen, however, is just as likely to nest far out on the hillside as under the cover of trees. This species is subject to erratic population fluctuation, and at one time it was feared that the species would disappear altogether from Britain. In recent years, however, it has re-established itself and recolonised many areas from which it had disappeared. During periods of colonisation, black grouse and capercaillies sometimes interbreed, producing hybrid offspring.

The male black grouse is called the blackcock. In the breeding season the blackcocks have a specialised display called lekking, and the ground on which it takes place is called a lek. Here the birds gather early in the morning, and sometimes in the afternoon, to posture and challenge and fight.

The red grouse, the game bird of the heather moors, is subject to great fluctuation in numbers, the reasons for which are still not properly understood. It has been discovered that red grouse regulate their own population density.

This species is mainly vegetarian, but it does take insects, including heather beetles and the pupæ of ants, familiarly called ant-eggs. In winter, the buds of birch are a favourite food; so are the catkins of the alder. The bird also takes the leading shoots of larch and Scots Pine, and for this it often incurs the enmity of foresters. In summer, the food range is much wider and includes heather, grass, sedges, a variety of weed seeds, and many types of wild berry.

RED GROUSE

The Red Grouse of the British Isles was originally confined to them. But it has been introduced into western Europe from time to time and has been acclimatised in Belgium and West Germany.

In the past, the red grouse was an extremely important game bird in Great Britain, and sportsmen came from many parts of the world to shoot it. In the period between the two world wars, great numbers of Americans came to Scotland and paid fantastic sums of money for the privilege of shooting red grouse in the Highlands of Scotland and in northern England. So, in many ways, this species is the élite among game birds.

This species is the true bird of the heather. It lives on and among heather, and nests there. Because heather was the bird's main food it was for a long time thought that it could not live without it. Some grouse do, however, manage to survive on ground where heather is scant, and it is a well-ascertained fact that " grouse that have never set eyes on a sprig of heather will live and flourish for years." Nevertheless, grouse numbers are influenced profoundly by the quantity and quality of heather on their territory.

Cock and hen grouse are very strongly attached to each other and feed and guard the chicks together. The cock is, in fact, extremely bold in defence of his nest or young. The eggs are laid in deep heather, usually, and may number from five to nine.

When red grouse become overcrowded in an area they are periodically thinned down by disease (a disease called strongylosis which is caused by a parasitic worm), but there is evidence that the disease can break out to some extent under other conditions. Recent work has shown that grouse, in fact, tend to distribute themselves after the breeding season, relating their numbers to the acreage available. This means

that the number of grouse on a moor at the beginning of the shooting season may be very much lower than the population of adults and young living on it until then. Predation by birds of prey and ground predators such as the fox, does not appear to make any significant impact on grouse populations. Tentative conclusions along these lines have been arrived at by Doctor David Jenkins, who is in charge of the red grouse enquiry in Glen Esk in the County of Angus.

PTARMIGAN

The Ptarmigan is the grouse of the high tops, living mostly above the three-thousand feet contour. The race found in Scotland is confined to Scotland, but is replaced by closely-related types in Europe, Finland, Russia, Japan and North America.

The ptarmigan changes to white in the winter, although many birds retain a fleck or two of black here and there in their plumage. In summer, the plumage is brown and grey laced with white, with white belly and wing tips.

The birds are reluctant to leave their heights and during a period of blizzard they are the last to come down to lower ground.

The birds nest in the Alpine zone of the mountains from about two-and-a-half-thousand feet to four-thousand feet. The nest is a hollow scraped in stony ground by the female, among grass or heather or crow-berry. Sometimes a lining of grass is added during the laying period. Only the hen incubates, but the male remains nearby and helps to guard the chicks after they have hatched. Ptarmigan tend to pack later in the season, packs often being made up of males in areas where the species is numerous.

The food of this game bird is almost entirely vegetable, although it does occasionally take insects.

PHEASANTS

Pheasants are not natives of Europe, to which they were introduced by the Romans. The wild pheasants which inhabit Britain to-day came from the region of the River Colchis in China.

Pure types less commonly seen as wild game birds are the Ring-necked Pheasant, the Black-necked Pheasant, and the Melanistic Mutant. A great many species, however, have been reared privately in aviaries, and indeed it now seems that some of the rarest species will be saved in this way. Wild pheasants are, however, mainly mongrels, the cocks all showing a white ring, or part of a white ring, on their necks. This is the marking found in the pure ring-necked pheasant which, as soon as it is put down in any area, becomes the dominant type and leaves its mark.

In Britain it is doubtful if pheasants would survive for any length of time were it not for the practice of artificial rearing, which involves hatching large numbers of eggs under broody hens and putting the pheasants into coverts as poults. On the other hand, war-time experience has shown that pheasants breeding wild are better able to take care of themselves than we thought possible.

Hen pheasants have become notorious for nesting in stupid places and for being very poor mothers. It is true that many hens nest in places where discovery is easy, and lose a high proportion of their family in the early days. Probably this is the result of generations of hand-rearing and coddling.

One is liable to find a hen pheasant sitting on a nest almost anywhere; by a roadside, footpath or railway track, in the middle of a field, in crops, in hedge-bottoms or woods. As a matter of fact, many so-called stupid nests escape notice for that very reason, and there are plenty of records of birds successfully rearing families which were hatched two or three feet from the edge of a busy road.

The cock pheasant is polygamous, but, sometimes, where the birds are thin on the ground, he has to be satisfied with one hen. In such cases it is not unusual for him to take a turn on the eggs. This he does not do when he has several hens brooding. The cock draws attention to his presence by his crowing, a sound with which every countryman is familiar. Not so familiar, however, is his drumming, a display during which he stands on tiptoe with his chest puffed out, crowing and beating his wings rapidly. This drumming is heard most frequently towards or during dusk in the spring.

Pheasants eat a great variety of food, animal and vegetable. In some parts they eat a lot of grain, but there is no doubt that in others they consume large quantities of such agricultural pests as wire-worms and leather-jackets. The bird is probably best described as omnivorous.

PARTRIDGE

The Common Partridge is widely distributed in Europe.

The partridge is a bird of arable farms and the heather fringe, nesting in hedge bottoms and waste ground with plenty of dry cover.

It is replaced by closely-related types in certain parts of France, in the North of Spain, Italy, and Eastern Europe. The birds have been introduced to North America from Hungary and the British Isles.

It has been said that good farming and partridges go hand in hand and, in the main, this is true. Where you get arable cultivation you expect to find partridges.

Like the red grouse, the partridge is monogamous, and although the cock does not take any part in incubating the eggs, he does brood the first chicks to hatch until the rest of the brood is off, and thereafter takes his full share in rearing the family. If the hen is killed he will, in fact, attempt to brood all the chicks himself, but this is rarely possible considering his size, so that some of the brood is lost.

Partridges pair very early in the year although nesting does not begin until May. During the winter the birds fly in coveys. These break up at pairing time, but a spell of wintry weather with snow will drive the birds into temporary packs again.

The hen partridge makes her nest in a hedge-bottom (double hedges being preferred) in a bank or below a wall. The exposure is usually a southern one, not liable to flooding. When the eggs are being laid, the hen covers them during

On the high tops, above 3,000 feet, the ptarmigan lives and breeds. Only severe snowstorms will bring it down.

her absence. After she has begun to sit, she does the same when she is off feeding. At hatching time, the cock bird goes to the nest and sits close by waiting to take charge of the first chicks out. In the first few days of their lives partridge chicks live mainly on insects, after which an increasing amount of vegetable matter is taken. When adult, their insect food may be as low as ten per cent.

The call of the partridge is as well known in the countryside as the crow of the cock pheasant, and has been described aptly as a sound like a key being turned in a rusty lock.

RED-LEGGED PARTRIDGE

The Red-legged Partridge, frequently referred to as the French Partridge, is resident in France, Switzerland, parts of Italy, Corsica, and the Balearic Islands. He turns up in Belgium, Holland, and West Germany, where repeated attempts at introduction have been made. Related types are found in Spain and Portugal.

The species has been successfully introduced into certain parts of England and Wales, and is now plentiful in parts of Yorkshire and the Midlands down to Somerset and Wales.

The red-legged partridge nests in hedge-bottoms, fields and waste-ground and in plantations. Unlike the eggs of the common partridge, those of the red-legged variety are slightly spotted. There is evidence that the hen will lay two clutches, one of which she broods herself while the other is brooded by the male. This probably explains the fact that sometimes a brood of chicks is seen in charge of one adult instead of two.

The quail is a small bird, like a bantam partridge.

The Quail is like a bantam partridge, no bigger than a starling. In some years it will be found nesting in the South of England, more rarely in the South of Scotland. It is completely unpredictable in this respect, and can now be described as very scarce in Great Britain.

In Europe, however, it is well distributed from France to the Mediterranean. It is a shy bird, with a call which has been rendered as " Wet-my-lips ".

ANIMALS WHICH ATTACK MAN

Despite the great number of potentially dangerous animals in the world, man is more likely to be bitten by a dog in the street than a bear or a tiger in the forest, and many species have suffered at the hands of sensation writers, making them appear as though they were constantly seeking human blood.

None has suffered more in this respect than the wolf. We still have the legend of the great wolf pack with us, and the belief persists that human beings in certain parts of the world go in constant danger of attack by these animals. In fact, there is hardly a single authentic instance in North America or Russia of a wolf attacking man.

The real menaces to human beings such as man-eating tigers or leopards are, ironically enough, usually brought round to this habit as a result of injury; that is to say, as a result of their powers becoming impaired. The tiger or the leopard, maimed by gunshot or porcupine quills, turns to man because man is the easiest quarry of all, whereas formerly in the proud days of their strength, they hunted more difficult prey. Generally speaking, it is no more dangerous to walk in a jungle where there are tigers than it is to walk in a field among sheep.

Human beings have been killed from time to time by bears. In almost all known cases where bears have turned on man it is because they were pushed too far and too hard. The bear, admittedly, is unpredictable, but he is not given to attacking man; and the one with the worst reputation of all, the grizzly, is least likely to do so, under any circumstances.

It would be truer to say that with the exception of man-eating tigers and leopards, an animal which " attacks " man is really counter-attacking after an attack upon itself. We recognise this, in fact, when we speak about a cornered rat, or a cornered wild cat, or a cornered stoat. What we are saying is that the animal becomes dangerous only when it considers it has to fight back, or perish.

Let us see if we have any dangerous animals in Britain and let us look first at the hunters, or predators.

Is the fox dangerous, or the pine marten, or the wild cat? The answer to all of these questions is that they are not. The real problem with these creatures is, in most cases, being able to see them at all. It is perfectly true that a badger could take your finger off, if you insist on pestering him in his den; that a fox is liable to snap when picked up wounded; that a weasel or stoat will bite as soon as handled, and that a wild cat will rip and claw to free himself, but none of these is attacking. Each is an instance of self-defence.

There is one exception to all these and that is in the case of the stoat. Infrequently, where stoats are running in a party in winter, they may turn on man with little or no provocation. It has happened to a number of people and the experience is not a pleasant one, but one could live for a hundred years in the British countryside, walking about daily in all weathers, without having this kind of experience.

REPTILES AND AMPHIBIANS

The animal kingdom is divided into five distinct groups: mammals, birds, fish, reptiles and amphibians. The first two are warm-blooded creatures; the remaining three are cold-blooded.

Reptiles and amphibians have some things in common. As already mentioned, both are cold-blooded, which means that their temperatures are influenced by the temperature of their surroundings. They cannot tolerate great heat or great cold. In Britain, they hibernate, emerging in the spring. The habit is common to frogs, toads, snakes and lizards.

BLOOD CIRCULATION

Reptiles and amphibians have the same kind of circulation and a heart with three compartments: two auricles (receiving blood from the body and the lungs) and a common ventricle (sending blood to both body and lungs). Purified blood coming from the lungs to the heart becomes partly mixed with impure blood returned from the body. This is quite different from the circulation in birds and mammals. In these, pure blood from the lungs is sent out pure from the heart, and used blood is sent back to different compartments of the heart, from which it is pumped to the lungs for oxygenating. There is no mixing.

These are the main characteristics common to reptiles and amphibians. In other ways they are quite different.

MINIATURE VERSIONS

Reptiles lay eggs from which hatch out exact replicas of the adults. A snake is a snake from the moment it leaves the egg; so is an alligator; so is a turtle. In the amphibians, like frogs and toads, the eggs do not hatch into frogs or toads. They hatch into tadpoles and they hatch in water. There is no tadpole stage in the reptiles and reptiles cannot live under water.

The tadpoles of the frogs and toads spend the first part of their lives entirely in water. The development into the final stage is gradual, and it is some weeks before they become toads and frogs. The finished product, the perfect toad or frog, can still breathe under water. Young snakes or lizards cannot. Amphibians, at any stage, can breathe under water. Reptiles cannot do so at any stage.

REPTILES TO AVOID

There are a number of poisonous reptiles in the world: two lizards, called the gila monster and the beaded lizard; and about 250 species of snake. There are, however, no poisonous amphibians, not even among the much-dreaded salamanders. Some amphibians bite, but their bite is not poisonous. Several, like the toad, secrete fluids that make them distasteful to eaters of flesh. These fluids are toxic, and in some cases can cause convulsions if swallowed in quantity. But these are extremely rare occurrences.

The following are reptiles: snakes, lizards, crocodiles, alligators, turtles and tortoises. You will note that while crocodiles and alligators are adapted for living in water, they are reptiles and not amphibians. The amphibians are the frogs, toads, newts and salamanders, all of which can live in and under the water.

BRITISH SNAKES

There are three snakes in Britain: the adder or viper, the grass snake, and the smooth snake. There are three lizards:

Everywhere in the Mediterranean region lizards of the Lacerta family are to be seen darting in and out of crevices in old walls, in which places they pass the winter in a state of torpor. These are usually the well-known lizards (Lacerta podargis muralis).

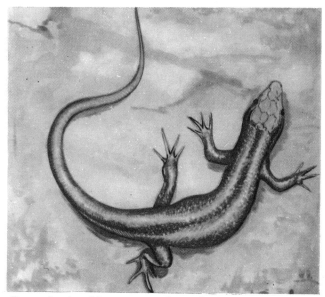

From the tip of its snout to the end of its tail, the green lizard (Lacerta lacerta viridis) measures close on sixteen inches. This species is found in Southern Europe where it lives among scrub and bushes. It feeds on flies and other insects. The green lizard is a hibernator.

the slow-worm (often mistaken for a snake because it is legless), the common lizard, and the sand lizard. There are no crocodiles or alligators, and no native turtles or tortoises. There is the common frog and the edible frog, the common toad and the natterjack, the crested newt, the palmate newt and the smooth newt. There are no salamanders.

ADDER

The adder is the only poisonous snake in Britain, and the only snake found in Scotland. There are no snakes in Ireland.

Male adders are usually slimmer and more active than females, and more boldly marked. Dull colours suggest females, bright ones males. The black zig-zag line down the spine is present in most specimens, but in a dark adder it may be lost, or broken up into spots. Adders aren't big snakes, usually about 22 or 23 inches, and seldom over 24 inches.

The adder has two large poison fangs in the upper jaw.

Bigger than the European green lizard is this species (Lacerta lacerta lepida) *which reaches a length of eighteen inches or more. It will be noted that it is green up to the neck and that it has eye-shaped markings on its head.*

They are immediately ready when the mouth opens. Only these two fangs inject poison. The other teeth in the mouth, back-curving, are for drawing the prey down the throat.

HIBERNATING AND " DANCING "

From some time in October until April the adder hibernates. In the spring, mating takes place, and the young are born in August or later. At birth they are from five to eight inches long, and their poison fangs are active. The adder is viviparous, which is to say it produces living young. The young escape from the egg sacs at, or just before, laying.

The so-called dance of the adders, when two snakes rear up and face each other, is really a territorial battle between rival males and not a form of courtship as was once thought. The snakes push and thrust, but do not bite, and eventually one gives up the struggle and glides away.

Adder bite is not a desperately serious thing in this country, and there are, fortunately, few deaths. A great deal depends on the health of the person bitten, but no one really knows why the bite is fatal in some cases and not in others. In

France, it is reckoned that about one person dies out of every twelve bitten by snakes.

GRASS SNAKE

The other two species of British snakes are harmless. The first of these, found over most of England but absent from Scotland, is the grass or ringed snake. This species grows much bigger than the adder, and adult males reach about 3 feet in length. Females are larger and reach a length of 4 feet. The grass snake varies a great deal in colour: it may be olive-green, grey, brown, dark green or olive-grey. There is usually a prominent yellow collar, which identifies the snake at once, but in some specimens this is absent altogether, while in others it may be white.

The grass snake pairs in May, and in July or early August the females lay their eggs in manure heaps, well-rotted mould or weeds. The eggs number from a dozen to fifty, depending on the age of the snake. The older females lay most eggs. Sometimes several snakes lay their eggs together, and as many as 1000 have been found in one place. The eggs hatch in about two months' time, shorter or longer depending on temperature and moisture. They are six to eight inches long, and at first live on worms and insects.

RELUCTANT CAPTIVE

Though quite harmless, a grass snake when captured behaves wildly, and will hiss loudly. Though it will sometimes strike again and again it rarely bites. The bite is more of a chew than anything else, and of no consequence. Some grass snakes will soil the hands of the captor with a stinking, excrement. This is the snake's only defence. Despite all the fuss it makes when caught, the grass snakes tames quickly and soon makes an excellent pet.

Frogs are the main food of grass snakes, and are swallowed alive. Young grass snakes, in turn, are eaten by frogs and toads. The grass snake eats toads, and some individuals prefer them to frogs.

SMOOTH SNAKE

The rare smooth snake, which is also harmless, is confined

The red salamander has coral-coloured skin studded with black spots. Like most members of its group the red salamander lives in America, preferring a wooded or grassy habitat, near water.

to the south of England (Hampshire, Dorset, Surrey and Berkshire). Like the adder it gives birth to living young, usually about half a dozen. They are born in August and September. The smooth snake hisses and bites when captured, but tames quickly. It feeds on lizards, small snakes, voles, shrews, beetles and other insects.

SLOW-WORM

One of the commonest reptiles is the slow-worm, or blind-worm, which is often called a snake but is, in fact, a legless lizard. It is quite harmless. It isn't slow, it isn't blind and it isn't a worm. And it certainly isn't a snake. Unlike snakes, the slow-worm can close its eyes when it goes to sleep. So can the other lizards.

A big slow-worm may be 12 inches long. One more than 12 inches long is a very big one. Females are bigger than males, and a female 17 inches long is a giantess.

The slow-worm lays eggs in the autumn. These usually burst open at laying so that the young are actually born alive. In some cases the eggs are produced intact, the young

This worm-like amphibian which belongs to the Pletho-dontid group of salamanders has a long tail and four stumpy legs, each with four toes. It is found in America.

breaking out a short time afterwards. The young are silvery when born, with black underparts and black lines down their backs. They live, at first, on spiders and insects, then turn to worms. As adults, their food is slugs, snails, earthworms and insects, so they are useful reptiles to have in the garden.

COMMON LIZARD

The common lizard produces living young, and is often referred to as the viviparous lizard. It is widely distributed in the British Isles and is the only reptile found in Ireland.

Males of this species are usually about six inches long, of which the tail accounts for nearly four. Females are an inch or so longer, with tails of more than four inches in length.

Young lizards are born in the autumn, and number usually from six to twelve. They are almost black, and measure under two inches in total length. Young and old hibernate from October, digging holes in the ground to sleep in, or burrowing into deep mould, well away from the bite of frost.

The sand lizard is rare. In Britain it is confined to a few parts of the south of England. It is found mainly on sandy soils, as its name suggests.

COMMON FROG

Everybody is familiar with the common frog, which awakens in early spring and spawns in ponds and ditches during March. Most people are also familiar with the common toad, which spawns a little later, but often in the same places. Frogs are smooth-skinned and great jumpers; toads have warty skins and are confirmed walkers. Neither is dangerous.

After laying, frog spawn absorbs water and becomes a jelly-like mass, with the eggs dotted all over it like currants in a pudding. Toad spawn is laid in long chains, usually anchored round the stems of water plants, and the eggs are paired like the dots on a domino. When toads and frogs spawn in the same pond they tend to stay apart and lay their spawn in different places.

YOUNG TADPOLES

The eggs hatch into larvæ, and then become tadpoles. The tadpole eventually grows legs, the hind legs being the first to appear. A tadpole can grow a new leg if it loses one. A fully-developed frog or toad cannot. Frogs and toads have backbones, but no ribs, no tails and no gills. They are, however, able to breathe through their skins and by their lungs.

The development of the common toad is typical of the *Salientia*, the group to which frogs and toads belong.

At first the larvæ begin to wriggle in the eggs. Then they break out and hang on to the spawn-jelly for a day or two. After that they wriggle away and attach themselves to water weeds. Presently they develop a mouth and gills, and begin to eat and grow. The gills change after about a month, becoming covered in a case. The larva is now a tadpole, breathing like a fish, and eating mainly vegetable matter. The hind legs begin to appear after some seven weeks. The tadpole can be seen coming to the surface to breathe air, because it now has proper lungs. In something over two months many changes take place at once. The gills disappear, and the blood circulation changes its route.

The small salamanders of the Triturus group are commonly referred to as newts. They live in lakes and ponds and are found in Europe up to a height of 8,000 feet. The species illustrated here is Triturus alpestris, *which is about 4 inches long.*

The forelegs break out, and the tail is absorbed. At this time the almost-toad fasts, its life being maintained by the absorption of its tail. In just under three months the young toad is ready to leave the water. It chooses a warm, wet day to do so. It is then you may see them in thousands.

Toads reach maturity slowly, and are long-livers.

LEAVING THE WATER

Young frogs also leave the water on a warm, wet day, and this has given rise to the notion of " raining frogs." At this time houses are often invaded by the small creatures during their first travels.

Both toads and frogs hibernate, the former in holes far from water, the latter usually in or near water. Most adult frogs hibernate in water, but some do not. It appears that most immature frogs hibernate away from water. On good days in winter the frog will come out of his hibernaculum for a look around, and in a mild winter all the frogs in an area may be out by February, and spawning. In other parts of the country they may be a month later.

Frogs feed on insects, snails and worms. Toads eat almost anything that moves if they can catch it and swallow it. A big toad can eat a small mouse. More usually the food comprises slugs, snails, worms, caterpillars and beetles. Only moving food is taken, so it would seem that the toad doesn't recognise a prey until the prey moves.

Frogs and toads have many enemies. Frogs are eaten by foxes, stoats, hedgehogs, otters, birds and man. Great numbers are killed by man each year for scientific experiments. Toads are eaten by grass snakes and some birds. Rats will kill them. But, so far as is known, no mammal will eat one.

The toad, when handled, will often " sweat " a milky fluid on to the hands of the captor. This is a secretion of the warts on the skin and is toxic. It makes the toad distasteful to eaters of flesh.

NEWTS

There are three newts in Britain: the crested, the smooth

According to ancient legend, the fire salamander was gifted with mysterious powers. Superstitious people still fear it. It is, indeed, a notable creature because if it loses a foot, or a tail, it can regenerate either quickly.

and the palmate. Newts are tailed amphibians, with lizard-like bodies. They swim by sideways movements of the tail. They can re-grow a lost limb. Newts have no claws, a soft, moist skin, a fleshy tongue, and a finned tail, so their resemblance to lizards is very superficial.

The crested newt is the biggest of the trio, the females reaching a length of six-and-a-half inches and the males five-and-a-half inches. They do not live in the water outside the breeding season. Most of them live on land, but some stay in the water until late in the year, and a few are always to be found there. The breeding season is in April. Early in the month the newts leave their hibernation quarters and make their way to the water.

LAYING EGGS

The female crested newt lays her eggs one at a time, and rolls each one in the leaf of a water plant. Some eggs are simply stuck to stones.

Newts hunt equally well in water or ashore. On land they are mainly nocturnal, and hunt worms, snails and centipedes. In the water they take many types of animal food, but are very fond of frog tadpoles and even small newts. Unlike the toads and frogs they do not catch food with the tongue. Prey is snatched by mouth.

HIBERNATION

Crested newts hibernate away from water, and usually underground. Sometimes they hibernate socially, and large numbers have been found bunched together.

The smooth newt is smaller than the crested. It is not so particular about wrapping its eggs in properly folded leaves. It does not remain in the water after the breeding season is over.

The palmate newt is the smallest of the British species, being no more than two-and-a-half to three inches in length. The tail of this species ends in a thread. The skin is smooth. In breeding attire the male has black webbing, a smooth crest, and a fold in the skin along the back. This species can tolerate considerable saltiness in the water.

The crested newt seen here is under 6 inches in length, a puny creature compared with the giant reptiles of the past. It is common in Europe, North America and Asia.

INDEX